# The SEARCH for AL QAEDA

# *The* SEARCH
## *for* AL QAEDA

### Its Leadership, Ideology, and Future

BRUCE RIEDEL

BROOKINGS INSTITUTION PRESS
*Washington, D.C.*

*Library of Congress Cataloging-in-Publication data*
Riedel, Bruce O.
  The search for al Qaeda : its leadership, ideology, and future / Bruce Riedel.
      p.      cm.
  Includes bibliographical references and index.
  Summary: "Profiles the most important figures in the al Qaeda move-
ment—Osama bin Laden, Ayman Zawahiri, Abu Musaib al Zarqawi, and
Mullah Omar, giving a comprehensive analysis of its origins, leadership,
ideology, and strategy. Focuses more closely on what has happened to
al Qaeda since 9/11 and outlines its ultimate goals"—Provided by publisher.
  ISBN 978-0-8157-7414-3 (cloth : alk. paper)
  1. Qaida (Organization) 2. Terrorism. 3. Ideology. 4. Leadership. 5.
Zawahiri, Ayman. 6. Bin Laden, Osama, 1957– 7. Muhammad Omar,
Mullah, 1960– 8. Zarqawi, Abu Mus'ab, 1966-2006. I. Title.
  HV6432.5.Q2R54 2008
  363.325—dc22                                    2008027655

3 5 7 9 8 6 4 2

Typeset in Sabon

Composition by Peter Lindeman, OSP Inc.
Arlington, VA

Printed by R. R. Donnelley
Harrisonburg, Virginia

*To my father*

MILTON A. RIEDEL

# Contents

# Preface

Al Qaeda is the first truly global terrorist organization in history. Over the past ten years it has carried out acts of catastrophic terror around the world. From New York to New Delhi, al Qaeda and its allies have killed thousands of innocents. Using the Internet and cell phones, it has created franchises throughout the Islamic world and clandestine cells in the Muslim diaspora in Europe and elsewhere to build and deploy a global weapon.

This book attempts to search for al Qaeda and explain the danger it poses. It relies heavily on al Qaeda's own words and statements. These are available on many websites and in various collections of statements. I have relied primarily on the translations provided by the former Foreign Broadcast Information Service, now known as the Open Source Center. I have also benefited from the insights and comments of many colleagues from my career in the Central Intelligence Agency (CIA), both Americans and others in Europe, the Middle East, and South Asia.

When I joined the CIA in 1977, one of my first mentors was Robert C. Ames, an officer who had served for years in the Middle East and South Asia. He taught me many skills but especially a belief in the urgency of bringing peace to the Levant. Tragically, he was killed in the terrorist attack on the American Embassy in Beirut on April 18, 1983. Like many other colleagues in the intelligence community and elsewhere in the U.S. government over these twenty-nine years, Bob Ames helped to shape this book.

I wrote this book at the Saban Center for Middle East Policy at the Brookings Institution. Strobe Talbott, Carlos Pascual, and Martin Indyk gave me the opportunity and the encouragement to think creatively and rigorously about al Qaeda and the contemporary Middle East and South Asia, and I am very grateful for their support and assistance. My research assistant, Bilal Saab, and the editors and staff of Brookings Institution Press were invaluable to my work.

My precious wife, Elizabeth, helped with every aspect of the research, the thinking, and the writing. She listened to every idea, good and bad, and encouraged the best. My father first took me to the Middle East as a very young boy and instilled in me his love for Jerusalem and Beirut. I am happy to say my son has the same affection for Tel Aviv and Jerusalem. Both share thoughts on the region with me often.

Of course, the judgments and arguments in this book are my own responsibility. All statements of fact, opinion, or analysis are those of the author and do not reflect the official positions or views of the CIA or any other U.S. government agency. Nothing in the contents should be construed as asserting or implying U.S. government authentication of information or agency endorsement of the author's views. This material has been reviewed by the CIA to prevent the disclosure of classified information.

## CHAPTER ONE

# The
# Manhattan
# Raid

The coordinated suicide attacks of September 11, 2001, were the first major foreign assaults on American soil since 1814, when the British Army and Royal Navy bombarded the city of Baltimore. The attacks of 9/11, as all have come to know those events, also marked the second most violent day in U.S. history, with 2,793 deaths.[1] Only the battle of Antietam on September 17, 1862, surpassed this figure. Even the casualties on D-Day and at Pearl Harbor were lower.

September 11 was a costly day not just in lives lost or families broken apart. The property damage and lost productivity alone probably exceeded $100 billion. The economic implications of the attack on Wall Street in terms of lower profits and economic volatility pushed the price tag up even further, as high as $2 trillion according to some estimates.[2]

Americans should now know a great deal more about the origins of and planning for what al Qaeda calls the Manhattan Raid. They know when the plot was hatched, when key members of the conspiracy were informed of it, what its role model was (an earlier hijacking in Algiers), what arguments arose over the timing of the attack, who trained the plotters and where, and, most important, what their objective was. And yet many in America fail to comprehend the realities surrounding the assault. That ignorance leaves the United States vulnerable to committing the same policy errors that helped lead to 9/11 and to the quagmires in Iraq and Afghanistan that flowed from it.

In large part the public's ignorance and vulnerability are a result of a decision by the George W. Bush administration not to clearly explain to the American people the nature of the enemy, namely al Qaeda. The president chose to declare war not on al Qaeda, but on "terrorism," a concept that he and Vice President Dick Cheney arrived at by confusing 9/11 with Saddam Hussein's Iraq. They have also argued that the attacks were motivated by a hate for America's "freedom." As former governor of Arkansas Michael Huckabee has written, "The Bush administration has never adequately explained the theology and ideology behind Islamic terrorism or convinced us of its ruthless fanaticism. The first rule of war is 'know your enemy' and most Americans do not know theirs."[3]

One has only to look at the opinion polls on Saddam Hussein's role in the 9/11 attacks. Even two years after the attacks, seven out of ten Americans—a clear majority—believed that Saddam was personally involved.[4] Yet by that time experts who had studied the evidence agreed almost unanimously that there was no link between Iraq and the 9/11 atrocities. The Bush-Cheney administration did nothing to disabuse Americans of these erroneous impressions.

What is more remarkable is that this misperception lingered several more years. A Zogby poll in September 2006 found 46 percent of Americans still believed Saddam was connected to the attacks, and among Republican voters the figure jumped to 65 percent.[5] By that time the only significant evidence even remotely connecting Iraq to the attacks—an alleged meeting in Prague in mid-2001 between one of the hijackers, Mohammed Atta, and an Iraqi intelligence officer—had not only been generally discounted but also formally recalled by the Czech intelligence service, which had originally produced the report and subsequently admitted to a case of mistaken identity.

Indeed, even as the events were unfolding, intelligence experts like myself had no doubt that the responsibility lay with Osama bin Laden and his al Qaeda organization. The attacks had all the hallmarks of al Qaeda and were preceded by months of warning that an assault on America was coming. Gary Schroen, one of my colleagues who led the first CIA team into Afghanistan after 9/11 to hunt for bin Laden, remembers the day at CIA headquarters in Langley this way: "As soon as the second aircraft smashed into the second tower, everyone said, 'Bin Laden. It was bin Laden. This isn't an accident; this isn't some tragedy that, you know,

that's some tragic accident. This is the attack that bin Laden's been promising.'"[6] I came to exactly the same conclusion at the White House at the
same time and told National Security Adviser Condoleezza Rice.

Al Qaeda has not been bashful about the raid. It has put out extensive
commentaries on the purpose and planning of the attack on each subsequent anniversary of the crashes, often including the martyrdom testi-
monies of the terrorists taped before September 11 in video format.
Several of 9/11's key planners, most notably Khalid Sheikh Mohammed,
have been captured and debriefed and their stories made public by the
9/11 Commission. Journalists and scholars have tracked the planning and
the movements of the perpetrators in detail. Key players like then CIA
director George Tenet have published their memoirs of what they knew
and what they learned after the fact.

What, then, are the actual facts? First, the operation was inspired by
a terrorist attack that took place six years earlier. On December 24,
1994, four Algerian terrorists dressed as policemen took control of Air
France's flight 8969 as it prepared for takeoff at Houari Boumediene
International Airport in Algiers. On board were 220 passengers and 12
crew members bound for Charles de Gaulle Airport in Paris. The Algerian authorities surrounded the plane and refused to let it depart. The terrorists then began executing hostages until the plane was allowed to
leave late on December 25.

French counterterrorism authorities learned that the terrorists were
planning to crash the aircraft into the Eiffel Tower to cause a mass-
casualty disaster in Paris. They persuaded the terrorists to let the plane
land in Marseilles on the pretext that it was running short of fuel. Once
in Marseilles, the terrorists demanded that the plane be fueled to its maximum capacity: 27 tons of jet fuel, far more than needed to get to Paris and
a clear indication of their intention to crash into the tower. Elite French
commandos then stormed the aircraft and in an intense firefight killed all
four terrorists and saved the hostages. Eleven commandos, thirteen passengers, and three crew members were injured. Although filled with explosives, the aircraft did not blow up because the detonators were not
properly wired together.

At the time, I was serving as the CIA's national intelligence officer for
the Near East and South Asia, with a special concern for Algeria because
of the growing strength of the Islamist jihadist movement there. As I fol-

lowed the events in Algeria and France, it was clear to me and other observers that the idea of using an aircraft as a guided missile to attack a target on the ground meant a new and horrific threshold had been crossed in international terrorism. Save for the French commandos and their counterterrorism expertise, 9/11 would have happened on Christmas 1994.

The counterterrorism community was not the only one keeping an eye on this incident. Terrorists were watching too—including Osama bin Laden and a young Pakistani, Khalid Sheikh Mohammed, or KSM, as he is known in the intelligence world—and were inspired by it. In 1994 KSM was already planning terrorist operations involving aircraft. He and the mastermind of the first attack on the World Trade Center, Ramzi Yusuf, were working on a plot to blow up several American aircraft flying over the Pacific.

The plot to attack the United States began in earnest in 1999, after al Qaeda carried out its first major operations against American targets, the simultaneous bombings of the American embassies in Kenya and Tanzania. Bin Laden and KSM began hatching their plan after meeting at bin Laden's headquarters in Kandahar, in Taliban-controlled Afghanistan.[7] The original idea was of even greater proportions than what transpired on 9/11: it was to have a West Coast component to match the attacks on the East Coast, with a total of ten aircraft smashing into targets in the District of Columbia, Virginia, New York, California, and Washington State. KSM was eager to use his connections with jihadists in Southeast Asia, particularly the Indonesian terrorist group Jemaah Islamiyah, with which he had developed a close personal connection while in Afghanistan and the Philippines.

Bin Laden decided this was too ambitious and ordered the plotters to focus on the East Coast but to keep open the option to follow it up with a second wave in California. The first two operatives entered the United States from Malaysia on January 15, 2000, at Los Angeles International Airport, ironically the target of an earlier foiled al Qaeda plot, in December 1999.

In early 2000 bin Laden personally recruited the plot's tactical leader, Mohammed Atta, in Afghanistan. Atta was an Egyptian architect studying in Hamburg, Germany, who came to Kandahar with several colleagues to join al Qaeda. He immediately impressed bin Laden as a smart and ruthless individual, eager to achieve martyrdom. Bin Laden made him the emir of the Manhattan Raid and dispatched him back to Germany to learn to fly an aircraft. Atta chose to take his flight training in Venice, Florida, instead and arrived in the United States in June 2000.

Bin Laden also personally recruited all the so-called muscle terrorists—the fifteen operatives who would control the passengers during the hijackings—from the large pool of Saudi al Qaeda volunteers in Afghanistan. Fourteen were Saudis and one was from the United Arab Emirates. They entered the United States in late 2000. KSM arranged the logistics and the funding for their travels and those of the pilots, while Atta commanded the team on the ground in the United States. KSM also supervised the training of the muscle in a safe house in Karachi, Pakistan, and in camps in Afghanistan.

The prerecorded wills and final statements of the terrorists reveal a great deal about their motivation. Over the years, al Qaeda has gradually released some of these details on the anniversaries of the attacks. Other such information comes from the testimony of KSM himself after his capture and from bin Laden's own remarks on the attack in several messages since 9/11. In addition, al Qaeda has commented on the attacks extensively in audio and video messages on every anniversary since 2001.

Taken together, these statements clearly indicate that the Arab conflict with Israel, especially the perceived grievances of the Palestinian people, is the all-consuming issue for the terrorists. The Palestinian intifada, the fierce uprising in the fall of 2000 on the West Bank and in Gaza, was a particularly powerful motivating event for the terrorists, KSM, and bin Laden. It had been sparked by the visit of Israeli Likud Party leader Ariel Sharon to the holy mosque in Jerusalem in September 2000. The wills of the terrorists reflect their outrage at the thought of Israelis, especially females, violating the sanctity of Islamic shrines and holy mosques. As terrorist Walid al Shihri put it in his will, released in 2007, "The condition of Islam at present makes one cry. . . . The daughter of Zion plays in the mosques. Dance with pride, daughter of Zion, over our scattered limbs, for we are slaves."[8] Other grievances mentioned include the U.S. military presence in Saudi Arabia and Saudi support for the repression of jihad in Syria in 1982.

These several issues form the backdrop of the narrative and ideology of al Qaeda explored in this book. The intifada's power over bin Laden's thinking about the 9/11 raid is underscored by his repeated attempts to push KSM to advance the timing of the crashes. In September of 2000 he urged KSM to tell Atta to attack immediately to respond to the Sharon visit to the holy sites in Jerusalem; Atta told bin Laden he was not ready yet.

When bin Laden learned that Sharon, who had become Israel's prime minister in March 2001, was going to visit the White House early that summer, he again pressed Atta to attack immediately. And again Atta demurred, arguing he needed more time to get the plan and the team ready to go. Bin Laden agreed to give his emir more time, probably because another key aspect of the plan—the assassination of al Qaeda's main enemy in Afghanistan, the strongest leader in the Northern Alliance, Ahmad Shah Massoud—was not fully ripe for action either.

Bin Laden was also intimately involved in the selection of targets for the Manhattan Raid. He pushed repeatedly to include the White House (where I happened to be sitting the morning of the attacks), despite the difficulty posed by its small size, in contrast to the Twin Towers, the Pentagon, and the Capitol Building. Bin Laden personally handled other essential elements of the plot as well, bringing on board the Taliban—the Afghan militia that hosts al Qaeda in the badlands of Afghanistan and Pakistan—and its leader, Mullah Omar. In his interrogation, KSM suggests the Taliban were uninformed about the Manhattan Raid until the last moment and even pressed bin Laden not to attack American targets. However, other evidence strongly suggests Mullah Omar was well inside the loop much earlier and a partner in the overall plan, if not the details.

For the Taliban leadership, the critical prerequisite to an attack on the United States was another al Qaeda plot in which they had a vital interest, the murder of Massoud, their principal enemy in Afghanistan (see chapter 4). Bin Laden was also in direct command of this plan, which began in 2000 with his recruitment of the Belgian operatives who would carry out the assassination. In her memoirs, the widow of the team leader has given an extensive account of the family's visit to Kandahar, where they stayed at the bin Laden home to prepare and train for the attack on Massoud.[9]

The timing was critical because it had to coincide with the U.S. strike, which in the end it did. Bin Laden and Omar wanted Massoud killed on the eve of 9/11 to decapitate Afghanistan's Northern Alliance and thus render it impotent when America would need it to retaliate. The two operations were interdependent. This, too, was clear to many experts by midmorning on September 11. Gary Schroen connected those two things as soon as the second aircraft hit: "I was standing in the parking lot at the CIA, saying, 'Ah, that's what Massoud's death was about. It made Mullah Omar indebted to bin Laden for removing his only major enemy.'"[10]

The connection is also hinted at in the memoirs of Pakistan's military dictator, Pervez Musharraf, who says Mullah Omar was aware of the plot against America in 2000 and was initially not pleased with the idea of taking on the United States so directly. In time, however, probably after being briefed on the plot to kill his rival in the north, Omar apparently came around. In any case, as Musharraf notes, he did nothing to stop bin Laden once he learned of the plan.[11]

Osama was in Kandahar on September 11 and gathered some of his closest lieutenants together to watch the plot unfold on television. Apparently he alone anticipated the magnitude of the destruction, perhaps because of his work in construction for his father, although he was surprised at the total collapse of the two towers. Meanwhile Khalid Sheikh Mohammed watched events unfold in an Internet café in Karachi.[12] He returned to Kandahar later in the month and immediately began working on another plot, this time to repeat 9/11 in London, targeting Heathrow and Canary Wharf and using aircraft hijacked in Eastern Europe. The al Qaeda infrastructure in Saudi Arabia was tasked to find the pilots, but KSM's capture in Pakistan upset the plot.

From all that bin Laden and other al Qaeda spokesmen have said since 9/11 and the testimony of captured lieutenants like KSM, their objective was to provoke the United States and it allies to retaliate: specifically, to invade Afghanistan and enter into a long and bloody war of occupation in a repeat of the Soviet struggle there in the 1980s. Al Qaeda believed that the United States would bleed to death in the mountains of Afghanistan just as the Soviet Union had bled into collapse at the hands of Afghanistan's Muslim guerrilla warriors, the mujahedin.

The jihad against the Soviet Union in Afghanistan was a defining event in the lives of the al Qaeda leadership—bin Laden, Ayman al-Zawahiri, and KSM—and their Taliban host, Mullah Omar. The experience shaped their perception of history and politics. To them, the defeat of the Soviet Fortieth Army was an act of God, and they were the instruments used to accomplish this holy duty, a successful jihad against a superpower. They were (and are) convinced that it would happen again, that the Manhattan

Raid was the opening sortie in a long war that will destroy the United States and compel it to leave the Muslim world and abandon its allies, especially Israel, to their fate.

But bin Laden and Mullah Omar miscalculated. Instead of entering with a heavy footprint that would produce another guerrilla war, the United States made a light counterattack, spearheaded by CIA teams working with the Northern Alliance, which had survived Massoud's death. Backed by American airpower, they defeated the Taliban on the battlefield in a matter of weeks.

Moreover, bin Laden and Omar did not anticipate that their Pakistani friends—who had helped create the Taliban and with whom both had worked for years—would change sides and desert them. The reasons for this betrayal and its temporary character are examined in chapter 4. For now, suffice it to say that Musharraf's change of heart, from being de facto defender of al Qaeda and the Taliban to colluding with the invasion, was quite unexpected.

The invasion in the winter of 2001–02 should have destroyed al Qaeda and the Taliban. The leadership was rapidly cornered along the border between Pakistan and Afghanistan. Bin Laden was caught between what was supposed to be an American hammer and a Pakistani anvil.

Two events saved him and his organization: the U.S. decision to go to war with Iraq and the Pakistani decision to provoke a crisis with India. Invading Iraq diverted key resources from the job of finding the al Qaeda leadership. As Max Cleland, former U.S. senator from Georgia, noted: "Attacking Iraq after 9/11 was like attacking Mexico after Pearl Harbor."[13] Key intelligence and military forces were withdrawn from the Afghan-Pakistani borderlands as early as March 2002 to prepare for the war in Iraq. Gary Schroen points out that "the U.S. military did this in order to allow them to regroup and train in preparation for the coming war with Iraq." The best Arabic-speaking CIA collection officers were removed as well.[14] According to Pakistan's ambassador to the United States, Mahmud Durrani, "We had almost licked al-Qa'ida after 9/11 because of the U.S. invasion of Afghanistan. . . . But what happened? The focus shifted to Iraq big time. This was a rebirth of al-Qa'ida."[15] The hammer was gone.

So was the Pakistani anvil, which had been forced to shift its attention to India. On December 13, 2001, five Kashmiri terrorists from groups long associated with bin Laden attacked Lok Sabha, the lower house of India's parliament in New Delhi. India blamed Pakistan for harboring the terrorist leadership that ordered this assault and dozens of earlier ones. India mobilized along the border, causing Pakistan to mobilize in turn and divert to the east troops that were needed in the west. For the next year, almost a million soldiers faced each other in a nervous showdown.

It is not clear that diverting forces from the hunt for bin Laden was one of the intentions of the Lok Sabha planners, nor that the real mastermind behind the attack was the Kashmiris on their own, Pakistan's Inter-Services Intelligence (which had allegedly trained them), Musharraf and his generals, or al Qaeda. Some believe it was orchestrated by al Qaeda deliberately to allow bin Laden to escape but this remains unproven. Yet the impact was critical. At its moment of greatest peril, the diversion of resources enabled al Qaeda to recover and slip away from the hunt. Although some important al Qaeda figures—Musharraf claims more than 600—were captured in Pakistan, including KSM and Abu Zubayda, the top leadership remained at large.[16]

Dozens of works about al Qaeda have appeared since 9/11, but the finest analysis and an outstanding example of its kind is the report of the 9/11 Commission. It covers the events of that day, the operational background of the al Qaeda plot, and the efforts by the Clinton and Bush administrations to foil it. The report relies heavily on the interrogations of KSM and other captured terrorists but also had access to material on the development of al Qaeda compiled by the CIA and other intelligence agencies.

One excellent book about the path to September 11 is the Pulitzer Prize–winning *The Looming Tower*, by Lawrence Wright, a seasoned journalist. It will probably remain the definitive work on this aspect of 9/11 for some time. Steve Coll, another renowned journalist, has written the definitive account of the bin Laden family.

This book aims to do something different. Although it reviews al Qaeda's origins and development before 9/11, the bulk of the work is devoted to what happened to the terrorist network afterward. My hope is to explain why the terrorists did what they did and how they justified the largest mass murder in American history. This, then, is a book about the development of al Qaeda's ideology as reflected in the statements of its senior leadership since 9/11. In aggregate, those commentaries constitute a complex narrative about why al Qaeda went to war with America.

Of course, an important aspect of the story is the immediate objective of the Manhattan Raid, which was to lure the United States into an invasion first of Afghanistan and then of Iraq, so as to replicate the quagmire that brought down the Soviet Union in the 1980s. Part of the discussion is therefore about the leadership's efforts to survive the American counterattack in the winter of 2001–02, its patient reconstruction of a safe haven in Pakistan, its well-planned work to build a trap for the United States in Iraq, and its efforts to overthrow U.S. allies in the Muslim world such as Saudi Arabia.

Since 9/11, al Qaeda or its sympathizers have struck targets the world over: in London, Casablanca, Madrid, Algiers, Istanbul, Mombasa, Bali, Mumbai, New Delhi, Islamabad, Riyadh, Doha, Amman, Sharm al-Shaykh, Taba, Mogadishu, and a host of other places. Almost daily they attack targets in Iraq and Afghanistan. They probably murdered Benazir Bhutto, after a decade of failed attempts. The breadth and audacity of al Qaeda's operations since 9/11 are astounding given the small size of the organization's membership and its extreme notoriety: it is the most wanted organization on the planet with multimillion-dollar rewards posted for all its senior leaders. This is the story that I want to unravel and reveal.

For many of the telling details, I turn to biographical narratives, beginning with the life of Ayman al-Zawahiri, the Egyptian co-leader of al Qaeda and its principal spokesman. Although his life is not as well documented as that of Osama bin Laden, it provides a mine of information on the origins of the jihad. Even more important, since 9/11 Zawahiri has produced dozens of taped messages commenting on the group, its actions, and current events. He has also published several books on the ideology and narrative of al Qaeda. Zawahiri is a central figure in the creation of the terrorist organization and almost certainly would succeed bin Laden upon the latter's death.

Next, I look at the life of al Qaeda's undisputed leader and creator, Osama bin Laden. He is now a larger-than-life, almost mystical figure, known as the man who engineered 9/11 and has escaped justice. Although much has been written about his life, key aspects of it have received insufficient attention, especially his own writings, which clearly explain the reasons behind his campaign of jihadist violence, the 9/11 attacks, and alienation from his native land, Saudi Arabia. An evil figure, he is without doubt one of the most important men of the current age.

The life of Mullah Omar, the leader of the Taliban, provides further insight into al Qaeda. Omar is a very secretive man; only a handful of non-Muslims have ever met him. He avoids the press and interviews. He is probably only semiliterate and writes very little. But he created the first and only jihadist state in the Muslim world and was a partner in the attacks of 9/11. Today he has regrouped his Taliban forces and threatens the North Atlantic Treaty Organization's hold on Afghanistan.

The last portrait is of Abu Musaib al-Zarqawi, the leader of al Qaeda's franchise in Iraq and until his death in 2006 a fierce and unrelenting opponent of the American and British occupation. Zarqawi is now a legendary figure among jihadists and the al Qaeda international organization. Rockets fired at Israel are named for him. He brilliantly set an evil trap for George W. Bush and the United States in Iraq and executed it with a ferocity that is remarkable even by al Qaeda's standards.

These four portraits provide a clear indication of al Qaeda's current strategy, laid out in chapter 6. Its three key objectives are to create and nurture "bleeding wars" that will defeat the United States just as the mujahedin defeated the Soviet Union, to build a safe haven in Pakistan for the operational headquarters of the al Qaeda leadership and establish franchises throughout the Islamic world to overthrow pro-American regimes, and to conduct more "raids" on the West like 9/11 and the Madrid and London atrocities, someday perhaps with a nuclear weapon. The ultimate goal is to drive the United States from the Muslim world (the *ummah*), destroy Israel, and create a jihadist caliphate along the lines of the Ottoman Empire at its height.

Perhaps the most important conclusion to emerge from this exploration of al Qaeda's leadership is that the Israeli-Palestinian conflict is the central all-consuming issue for al Qaeda. Many observers have argued otherwise, claiming that al Qaeda is only a latecomer to the issue, that Arab and Muslim perceptions of injustice arising from the creation of Israel are only tangential to the story of al Qaeda and its appeal, and that al Qaeda has not directly targeted the state of Israel in its history.

On the contrary, Muslims feel a profound sense of wrong about the creation of Israel that infuses every aspect of al Qaeda's thinking and activities and has become the rallying cry used to convince the ummah of the righteousness of al Qaeda's cause. The organization's two key leaders, Zawahiri and bin Laden, decided to become terrorists because of efforts to negotiate a peaceful solution to the Arab-Israeli conflict that would leave Israel in the heart of the Muslim world. Zawahiri opposed the Egyptian-Israeli peace agreement and was a minor player in the assassination of Anwar Sadat, the man who more than any other opened the door to such a solution. And as bin Laden's writings underscore, the Oslo peace process of the 1990s turned him into a violent enemy of Saudi Arabia and the United States.

For al Qaeda, the only way to undo the wrong perpetrated against the Arab world is not to negotiate a peace agreement or a bargain between the Israelis and Palestinians, but to destroy Israel. However, its end will come only when its protectors and creators, the United States and Great Britain, are routed and driven from the region, the parties that have made peace with Israel are swept from power, and a united ummah can defeat Israel in battle.

A second major conclusion is that Pakistan is the country most critical to the development and survival of al Qaeda. It is the eye of the storm. Ironically, Pakistan itself has been a prominent victim of jihadist terrorism (recently in the murder of former prime minister Benazir Bhutto) while offering it considerable sponsorship (including a long and intimate relationship with Osama bin Laden). The global jihadist movement was born in Pakistan, in the war to drive the Soviet Union from Afghanistan. The Taliban, too, emerged in Pakistan, in its Islamic schools, the *madrassas*, and was nurtured by the country's intelligence service (interestingly, under the aegis of Bhutto at first). It was in Pakistan that al Qaeda found refuge after the United States intervened in Afghanistan in late 2001. And al Qaeda continues to make Pakistan its home, even as it wages jihad against the state. As Benazir Bhutto wrote just before her death, "My homeland of Pakistan has become the epicenter—the ground zero if you will—of either reconciliation or disaster."[17]

Clearly, Pakistan has played a complex but crucial role in the growth of al Qaeda—and will continue to do so. No country is more important for the United States to work with to defeat al Qaeda and jihadism, yet none is a more difficult partner in this venture. Pakistan is the most dangerous country in the world today, where every nightmare of the twenty-first century—terrorism, nuclear proliferation, the danger of nuclear war, dictatorship, poverty, and drugs—come together in one place. As Mike Huckabee rightly states, "If al Qaeda strikes us tomorrow, the attack will be postmarked 'Pakistan.'"[18]

A final critical point is this: the Sunni-Shia divide that has become a hallmark of Islamic politics in the past decade reverberates in al Qaeda, which since its birth in Afghanistan has been an advocate of extreme Sunnism. The anti-Shia violence promoted by al Qaeda's leader in Iraq, Abu Musaib al-Zarqawi, was not an aberration but a reflection of fundamental jihadist and al Qaeda thinking. For the Sunni jihadist, Shiism may well be the worst enemy of all because it rejects the principle that the laity can define jihad for itself and instead insists on the primacy of clerical leadership. On a deeper level, al Qaeda's rejection of Shiism is rooted in centuries of extreme Sunni prejudice against the Shia minority in the ummah.

The clash between Sunni jihadist and Shia thus forces al Qaeda into an antagonistic posture toward the one prominent Shia power on earth today, the Islamic Republic of Iran. That is not to say the two are always in conflict—there have been periods of tacit cooperation, but they are the exception. On the whole, al Qaeda and its sympathizers are more often than not fighting the Shia even as they are battling the West. That has certainly been the case in Afghanistan and in Iraq.

To help elucidate the nature of the struggle against jihadism today, I include a few vignettes from a lifetime spent in the American national security apparatus, especially in the intelligence community. They are provided as glimpses into some of the harsh realities of modern intelligence's battle against extremism. Many of my colleagues have endured far more costly encounters. Some have made the ultimate sacrifice for defending their country. It is to their memory that I dedicate this account.

## CHAPTER TWO

# The Thinker:
# Zawahiri

$B$ill Casey's mumbling made him difficult to understand, but when he was eating it was much worse. It was midday on October 6, 1981, and the director of central intelligence (DCI) was in a hurry to finish his lunch before leaving Central Intelligence Agency (CIA) headquarters in Langley, Virginia, for an emergency meeting at the White House on the developing situation in Cairo, Egypt. A few hours earlier, Egypt's president, Anwar Sadat, had been assassinated during a military parade celebrating the eighth anniversary of the start of the 1973 Arab-Israeli war. As the CIA's senior analyst on Egypt, I was asked for an update on the outlook for Egypt after Sadat.

Before I could start, however, Casey pointed to a copy of a memo on his desk that I had written less than a month earlier on the succession issue in Egypt and asked if it were still accurate. In it I had argued that the political situation in Egypt was becoming increasingly tense, that the risk of an attack on Sadat's life by Islamic extremists was increasing, and that should Sadat die, his vice president, Hosni Mubarak, would no doubt succeed him and continue his policies of peace with Israel and alliance with the United States. The memo had been widely circulated in Washington's policy community in the past couple of weeks and that very morning was being reprinted by the CIA to get more copies to anxious parties downtown. I told the DCI the memo was still very much on the mark, in my judgment. He asked a few questions about Mubarak and then hurried off to the White House.

A few days later, Casey leaked the essence of the memo to the media because it made the CIA look good in the aftermath of Sadat's death. After all, it correctly predicted both the attack on Sadat and Mubarak's smooth succession. The CIA needed the good press since it had also come out that the agency had trained the bodyguards who had failed to protect Sadat on October 6.

In the next few weeks, I spent endless hours reviewing video footage of that day's events with colleagues from the CIA, Federal Bureau of Investigation (FBI), Secret Service, and U.S. military, searching for clues to the identity of the assassins and any possible help they received from traitors inside the Egyptian army or security forces, or from a foreign power. Casey was particularly interested in whether a Libyan had a hand in the assassination. No evidence of a Libyan role ever surfaced. What is clear now, however, more than a quarter century later, is that Sadat's death marked the beginning of the modern jihadist challenge to U.S. interests in the Islamic world and the birth of the ideology that would generate al Qaeda.

Sadat's assassination was the work of Egyptians violently opposed to his peace treaty with Israel. The leader of the assassins' team was a young lieutenant in the Egyptian army, Khalid Ahmed Shawki al Islambouli, who had begun plotting the murder only a couple of weeks before, when he was told he would be leading a detachment from his 333rd Artillery Brigade in the annual parade to commemorate the start of the Arab-Israeli war of October 1973. Every October thereafter, Sadat held a massive military parade in Cairo with the country's latest army and air force equipment on display to remind Egyptians that he had retrieved Egyptian honor and dignity by ordering the assault across the Suez Canal, which surprised Israeli and American intelligence and demonstrated that Egypt was not to be ignored.

Islambouli and his colleagues halted their truck directly in front of the presidential reviewing stand, leaped out, and began firing at Sadat. As Islambouli opened his Kalashnikov, he cried out, "Death to Pharaoh"—a highly symbolic way of marking Sadat as a corrupt and fallen despot in the tradition of pre-Islamic Egypt. At his trial, Islambouli explained that the peace treaty with Israel had made Sadat an enemy of Islam and necessitated his execution. More personally, Khalid had been enraged by the arrest of his brother a month before the assassination in a massive crackdown on dissidents.

Among those arrested in the even more massive crackdown that followed the assassination was an English-speaking physician, Ayman al-Zawahiri. By virtue of his language skills and his education, Zawahiri became the spokesman for those tried for Sadat's death. The Egyptian courts were unable to link Zawahiri directly to the murder plot, however, and after several years of incarceration and brutal torture, he was released in 1984. Ayman al-Zawahiri would go on to become the intellectual leader of the al Qaeda movement, second in command only to Osama bin Laden and a prominent figure in the 9/11 plot. Subsequently, Ayman would emerge as al Qaeda's leading spokesman and perhaps most important individual in its resurgence after the fall of Afghanistan.

## WHO IS AYMAN AL-ZAWAHIRI?

Zawahiri is the ideological brains behind the war launched against America on September 11, 2001. He was born on June 19, 1951, in Cairo to a respectable upper-middle-class family that had emigrated to Egypt from the Arabian peninsula some generations earlier. His father, Mohammed Rabie al-Zawahiri, a professor of pharmacology, was also a trained physician, as were many of Ayman's relatives. His family was more famous for its religious credentials, however. A great uncle had been the rector of Al-Azhar University, the thousand-year-old center of Islamic learning in Cairo and most prestigious Islamic school in the Sunni Muslim world. Ayman's grandfather and great-grandfather had also been scholars at Al-Azhar. The family name thus bore the cachet of Islamic learning.

His mother, Umayma, came from an equally distinguished family. Her father, Abdul Wahhab Azzam, was the founder of King Saud University in Riyadh, Saudi Arabia, and president of Cairo University. He had also served as Egypt's ambassador to Pakistan, Yemen, and Saudi Arabia. Meanwhile his uncle Abdul Razzaq Azzam had been the founder and first secretary general of the Arab League. From his mother's side of the family, Ayman was naturally drawn to politics. The mélange of Islam and politics would produce a dangerous brew that went right to heart of the contemporary Egyptian political debate, then and now.[1]

In the early and middle 1960s Egyptian politics was dominated by the clash between the ruling secular Arab nationalists, headed by President Gamal Abdel Nasser, and the opposition, led by the Muslim Brotherhood and its rising star, Sayyid Qutb. The Muslim Brotherhood was the oldest Islamist political organ in Egypt, founded in 1928 by Hassan al-Banna to promote traditional Islamic law and social mores after decades of de facto British imperial rule. It quickly expanded and developed links throughout the Muslim world. The organization sent volunteers to fight Israel in the 1948 war alongside the Egyptian army and supported Nasser's military coup in 1952. It then fell out with the Arab nationalists when they refused to share power. For its troublemaking and an alleged attempt to assassinate Nasser, the Brotherhood was violently repressed by the secular regime.

Sayyid Qutb came from Asyut, a city in Upper Egypt renowned as a hotbed of extremism. It has a large Coptic Christian minority, and sectarian violence is common. Rarely visited by the thousands of tourists who flock to the rest of the country to see its fabulous antiquities, Asyut is instead a place of many converts to radical ideas, Qutb being one of the most prominent.[2]

Between 1948 and 1950, Qutb lived in the United States, first in Greeley, Colorado, where he arrived on a scholarship to study at the state teacher's college, and subsequently in New York. What he found in American life repelled him: especially its racism, sexual promiscuity, and pornography. Qutb was, above all, dismayed by America's hostility to the Palestinian cause. Upon his return to Egypt, he began criticizing the Nasser regime for its secularism and its attempt to modernize Egypt along Western lines.

To Qutb, Nasser's Egypt marked a return to the pre-Islamic corruption of pagan society, with a false Muslim at its head. The true believer, argued Qutb, owed such a government no loyalty or allegiance and should seek its overthrow. In response, the regime imprisoned Qutb in 1954, subjecting him and his followers to severe torture. Conditions eventually improved, and he was allowed to write and study in prison. He produced his most important works there, which hailed Islam as the solution to his country's problems and called for a government run strictly under Islamic law. He was released briefly in 1964 at the request of the Iraqi government, which was flirting with Qutb's Islamist policies at the time, then rearrested in 1965, and executed in August 1966.

After the execution, his brother, Mohammed Qutb, moved to Saudi Arabia, where he had many of Sayyid's books published and circulated throughout the Islamic world, often clandestinely. With the crushing defeat of Nasser's Egypt in the June 1967 war against Israel, the image of Arab nationalism and Nasser's socialist regime became badly tarnished. Many Egyptians and Arabs saw in Qutb's works an inviting alternative that would bring a new dignity to the struggle against Israel and the West: a return to their Islamic roots and values.

One of Qutb's earliest supporters was Zawahiri's uncle, Mahfouz Azzam, who became his defense attorney after his arrest in 1965 and was given power of attorney to dispose of his property after the death sentence came down. Mahfouz passed on his admiration for Qutb and his philosophy to his nephew, Ayman—who eventually came to see Qutb as "the most prominent theoretician of the jihadist movement."[3]

Qutb's execution made such a searing impression on fifteen-year-old Ayman that it led to his first political act: he organized a small cell of students at his high school to study Qutb's writings and prepare to overthrow Nasser and create an Islamic state. Like many other cells in the underground Islamist movements in Egypt in the late 1960s and 1970s, Ayman's was loosely organized, more a talk shop than a real militant organization. Gradually, however, it reached out to other cells, developed more serious capabilities, and attracted followers, with him as their emir.[4] At the same time, he continued his education and graduated from medical school in 1974 (missing the October war), then served three years in the Egyptian army as a surgeon. In 1978 he was married and began practicing medicine in clinics associated with the Muslim Brotherhood, also known by its Arabic name, the Ikhwan. In 1980 his Ikhwani clinic sent him to Pakistan on a humanitarian mission: to assist the tens of thousands of Afghan refugees fleeing the Soviet occupation of their country and the war against the communist satellite regime installed in 1978. Ayman spent four months in Peshawar, on the Afghan border, tending to the refugees' needs and working for the Kuwaiti Red Crescent Society, the Islamic arm of the International Red Cross Society. Zawahiri thus became one of the first Arabs to see the Afghan war up close and to meet with the mujahedin, the Afghan resistance fighters challenging the Soviet invaders and their Afghan communist allies. He apparently made a few visits across the border for a firsthand view of the war.

Upon his return to Cairo in late 1980, Zawahiri told his cell of his experiences and began recruiting others to help the refugees and the mujahedin. He made another, shorter visit to Pakistan in early 1981 to do more work for the Red Crescent Society. Again he returned to Cairo with accounts of the heroism and courage of the Afghan mujahedin. This early exposure to the Afghan cause would be very important in building Zawahiri's credentials as a supporter of the jihad against the Soviet Union and communism. That the CIA was also backing the mujahedin did not bother the jihadis at the time.

The defining moment in Ayman al-Zawahiri's life occurred on October 6, 1981, with the assassination of Anwar Sadat. In one stroke, his life took a dramatic turn, one he had not planned but welcomed. It transformed him from an agitator and critic of the Egyptian government to a spokesman for revolutionary violence, even if it meant the murder of a head of state.

Zawahiri had only a marginal role in the plot to kill Sadat and probably learned of the details only a day or even a few hours beforehand. Zawahiri's cell was one of several trying to find a way to overthrow Egypt's secular regime, but it was Sadat's decision to make peace with Israel in 1979 that motivated the Islamists to seek his death. As Zawahiri wrote in his book *Allegiance and Disavowal*, the peace treaty recognized "the state of Israel, acknowledged its capture of Palestine, prevented Egypt from assisting any country being subjected to Israeli aggression and disarmed Sinai to guarantee Israel's security."[5]

The plotters who did kill Sadat, though under the command of Khalid Islambouli, found their ideological inspiration in a pamphlet written by an obscure electrician named Abd al-Salam Faraj. All of the cell members involved in the assassination had apparently read and commented on the pamphlet in their conspiratorial sessions beforehand, and many referred to it in their trials. Titled variously *The Hidden Imperative* or *The Absent Precept*, it refers to jihad as the missing element in modern Islam and thereby takes Qutb's arguments further than had yet been done. It is the duty of all Muslims, says Faraj, to wage jihad to purify Islam of Western corruption, and this may entail killing the corrupt rulers who make peace with the West and Israel: "Jihad is the only way to reestablish and reenhance the power and the glory of Islam. . . . [E]ach and every Muslim should do his utmost to accomplish this precept, having recourse to force if necessary."[6]

Faraj found justification for the extreme step of killing a Muslim ruler, especially a corrupt one, in the works of a radical thirteenth-century Islamic scholar, Taqi al-Din Ibn Taymiyya, who lived from 1263 to 1328.[7] This was the period of the Mongol invasion of the Middle East, highlighted by the sacking and destruction of Baghdad, the capital of the caliphate. Leading the resistance in Damascus, Syria, Ibn Taymiyya denounced the invaders for converting to Islam and then being unfaithful to its core beliefs. Far from true Muslims, they were actually closer to pagan nomads who were corrupting the faith. In response, he urged a return to the fundamentals of Islam as practiced by the Prophet Muhammad and a strict interpretation of the Koran. Though imprisoned for these extreme views, he would lay the groundwork for today's most fundamentalist Islamic current, the puritanical faith of Saudi Arabia, Wahhabism.

Faraj devotes much of his critical analysis to comparing Sadat to the Mongols, arguing that both were only superficial Muslims. By making peace with Israel and abandoning Islamic lands, Sadat qualified for the same treatment as the Mongols, namely, elimination.

Following Sadat's assassination, the Zawahiri cell briefly considered attacking his funeral procession to kill Mubarak and the many foreign leaders who would be in Cairo for the memorial. But they never got the chance. The Egyptian government arrested thousands of Islamists who might have had even a remote connection to the assassination. Zawahiri was picked up in the manhunt and thrown in prison, where he became a spokesman for the Islamist movement because of his command of English, his education, and his political and professional background. He was also severely tortured and probably compelled to give testimony against other members of the movement. His books contain guarded references to this possibility, and other Islamists have accused him of selling out under the pressure of the regime's torture.

In prison, Zawahiri met many other prominent Egyptian jihadists of the underground, including its most famous cleric, the so-called blind sheikh, Omar Abd al Rahman, who had been a leader of the Islamic opposition to Nasser and Sadat in the 1960s. Rahman had also been an early advocate of the radical notion that Muslim rulers who made peace with the infidels should be wiped out, but he had skillfully avoided calling explicitly for Sadat's death. Thus Rahman was released from prison after but a few months, only to resume preaching a very radical brand of Islam. Whatever time he and Zawahiri shared in jail, they and their respective followers seem to have spent it in heated argument about the best way to advance the jihad. These differences would eventually split the Egyptian jihadist movement into two groups: Zawahiri's Islamic Jihad and Rahman's al Gamaa al Islamiyya, or Islamic Grouping.

Convicted of arms dealing but not of direct participation in the plot to kill Sadat, Ayman was released three years after his capture. He testified that he learned of the plot only a few hours before it was carried out and was not responsible for it, even though he supported its cause. Upon his release, Zawahiri fled to Saudi Arabia on a false Tunisian passport.

Zawahiri found a home in Jiddah, the largest city in the Hijaz—the Saudi province that is home to Mecca and Medina (the holy cities of the Prophet Muhammad and the scene of the annual Islamic pilgrimage, the Hajj). There he returned to the practice of medicine. At some point he met Osama bin Laden, who would become his partner in the creation of al Qaeda a decade later. The two found each other easily as both had worked in Pakistan's refugee camps and had a common bond in their support for the mujahedin and the Afghan cause. In addition, notes one Arabic commentator, both had an aristocratic background and a common goal: "fighting the enemies of Islam."[8] Bin Laden probably saw in Zawahiri a man who had already proven his devotion to the jihad against Israel by his role in the Sadat assassination and trials. Looking back years later, Zawahiri would remark:

> With the killing of Anwar Sadat the issue of jihad in Egypt and the Arab world exploded and became a daily practice. Confrontation with the corrupt regime which was against the shariah and allied with America and Israel, became a battle of continuous chapters that did not stop until today. On the contrary, jihad is increasing day after day, gathering more supporters and increasingly threatening its enemies in Washington and Tel Aviv. The killing of Sadat at the hands of Islambouli and his honorable comrades was a strong blow to the U.S.-Israeli plan for the region.[9]

In the decade following Sadat's assassination, Zawahiri wandered through the Islamic world seeking to support the jihad in Egypt from exile. The details of his travels are unclear and some of his reputed adventures may be deliberately exaggerated to enhance his mystique. His followers named their movement Islamic Jihad. He spent a considerable time in Pakistan and Afghanistan, sometimes with bin Laden, but apparently worked with émigré groups in Europe as well to support the jihad at home. In 1993 he traveled to the United States, raising funds for the jihad in the mosques of California.[10] In the mid-1990s he spent time in Sudan, now a haven for bin Laden and the closest base for conducting operations in Egypt. And in 1996 Zawahiri was arrested and released in Russia for allegedly supporting Chechen rebels fighting for independence in the Caucasus.

While Zawahiri was in Sudan, his Islamic Jihad supporters in Egypt engaged in an intense campaign to overthrow the government of Hosni Mubarak, Sadat's successor. In August 1993 they targeted prominent members of the government for assassination, including the minister of interior. This attack featured the use of a suicide bomber, a new first for Islamic Jihad. They also tried to kill the prime minister in a bomb attack in Cairo, but the only victim was an innocent young girl, whose death turned many Egyptians against the jihad group. A foiled attempt on Mubarak's life during a visit to Ethiopia in June 1995 was not the work of Islamic Jihad but that of its rivals, al Gamaa al Islamiyya.

However, the group had begun expanding its attacks beyond Egypt, targeting Egyptian diplomats and embassies abroad. In November 1995 Islamic Jihad bombed the Egyptian embassy in Islamabad, accusing it of spying on Egyptians supporting the Afghan refugees. In his book *Knights under the Prophet's Banner,* Ayman took full credit for the attack, noting that his first choice for a target was the U.S. embassy there, but it was so strongly fortified that he judged it too hard to hit. The Egyptian embassy would serve the jihadists' purpose just as well: namely, to harm the "vile alliance" of corrupt Egyptians, the United States, and India, which were using the embassy not only to spy on them but also to conduct intelligence work against Pakistan.[11] In short, the attack in Islamabad represented the perfect mixture of targets in jihad ideology.

After the attack on Mubarak and the embassy bombing in Islamabad, Khartoum succumbed to Western and Arab pressure to clamp down on terrorists, and they gradually fled. By 1996 the heat on the Sudanese government was too intense for Zawahiri. Where he went is a mystery. For a time he may have been in Copenhagen, hiding behind the cover of an Islamic newspaper and nongovernmental organization.

By May 1997 he had reunited with Osama bin Laden in Afghanistan. The two would be inseparable for the next four years. Meanwhile Zawahiri's Islamic Jihad continued to attack Egyptian targets, but since the regime had grown increasingly impervious to assault, it now aimed at softer targets that would weaken the Egyptian economy, including Western and Israeli tourists visiting Egypt's antiquities. In the eyes of many Egyptians, Zawahiri's movement shared responsibility for the worst of these atrocities: on November 17, 1997, al Gamaa followers killed sixty-two tourists and policemen at Luxor's Temple of Hatshepsut, beheading some of the victims. The terrorists apparently committed suicide after the operation to avoid capture and torture.

The attack backfired. Egyptians were outraged by the slaughter and horrified at the cost to their economy. Both Gamaa and Islamic Jihad, largely fringe movements, lost whatever support they had outside of radical circles. The Luxor attack would be their last significant operation inside Egypt. Mubarak orchestrated a massive crackdown and vastly increased the police force on the streets and the informant networks spying on everyone in the country. Egyptian intelligence also attacked Zawahiri's support structure in Europe. An Islamic Jihad cell in Albania was wrapped up in 1997 and the captured cell members brought to Egypt to stand trial. Zawahiri was indicted and tried in abstentia and sentenced to death.

As mentioned earlier, Zawahiri's group often clashed with al Gamaa al Islamiyya, not to mention other jihadist groups, which Ayman found too soft and unwilling to wage relentless jihad. He even criticized the blind sheikh for being too accommodating because he refused to endorse attacks on tourists. When other radical groups agreed to a truce with Mubarak's government, Zawahiri refused to be part of it and called for more attacks. In response, the Mubarak regime mounted a relentless campaign to hunt down Zawahiri's supporters at home and abroad, with considerable success: the movement found it more and more difficult to raise funds, and soon Zawahiri was very much on the run.

On February 23, 1998, however, Zawahiri resurfaced, blazing a new path: he and bin Laden merged their organizations with groups from Pakistan and Bangladesh to form the World Islamic Front for Jihad against

Jews and Crusaders, creating the organization now known as al Qaeda. The new front promised to wage jihad against all Americans—civilians and military alike—until the holy cities of Jerusalem and Mecca were liberated from Israel and the corrupt Saudi regime and all American military forces were expelled from the Islamic world. By 1998 Zawahiri had become bin Laden's éminence grise, with considerable influence on the latter's thinking and worldview. But theirs was a symbiotic relationship in which they influenced each other's thinking deeply, so it is impossible to say who had the greater impact. What is clear is that together they forged a single worldview and approach to the jihad.

Understanding al Qaeda's ideology is the first key to defeating the group. In World War II the Allies understood the need to counter the Nazi ideology and studied it carefully to find ways to defeat it in the battle for hearts and minds. The same was true in the cold war. Indeed, dozens of institutions of higher learning devoted considerable effort to studying the Soviet system and understanding Marxism. A similar effort is needed to defeat jihadism.

With a few notable exceptions, little has been done along these lines to date. The 9/11 Commission's report, for example, provided only a cursory explanation of Qaeda's ideology, focusing on its desire to expel American forces from Saudi Arabia and ignoring the centrality of the Israeli-Palestinian issue in its worldview. And the Bush administration's emphasis on al Qaeda's hatred for America's democratic and free way of life seems off the mark. As bin Laden has said, if al Qaeda hated the West for its sexual promiscuity or its democratic institutions, it would have attacked Sweden, not America. What, then, is the driving force here?

## ZAWAHIRI'S IDEOLOGY OF TERROR

In his writings and interviews both before and after 1998, especially in his audio and video statements since September 11, 2001, Zawahiri has laid out an extensive ideology justifying extreme violence and its use against Americans. This ideology of terror is not rooted in a hatred for Western culture or values, nor the status of women there, nor the alleged decadence of the West. It is not a critique of democracy or freedom as practiced in America or England. Like Qutb, Zawahiri may find American civilization racist and corrupt, but that is not at the center of his thinking.

Rather, his ideology focuses entirely on what he believes the West has done to the Islamic world, to the ummah. It is about policy, not values. It is a very specific charge sheet about very specific Western political actions of the past century that have pushed Islam into decline, dividing it into weak states ruled by corrupt false leaders who cooperate secretly with the West and give its wealth to the West.

For Zawahiri, this decline began with the fall of the Ottoman Caliphate. He sees the empire established by the Ottomans in the fifteenth century as the last legitimate Islamic government in the world until the creation of the Taliban state in Afghanistan in the 1990s. The Ottomans' greatest leader and perhaps one of the outstanding Muslims of all times, says Zawahiri, is Sultan Mohammed the Conqueror, who laid siege to Constantinople in 1453 and brought down the Byzantine Empire. Though not a perfect Islamic state because it did not defend all Muslim territory effectively, the Ottoman Caliphate was the last, best political successor to the caliphates of the time of Muhammad and early Islam. The fall of the Ottoman Empire ushered in disaster for the ummah.

In Zawahiri's version of history, the fall of the Ottomans was the result of a conspiracy between the Christian powers of the West, especially Great Britain and France, and the Zionist movement, which was aimed at the creation of a Jewish state in Palestine. The Ottomans, he claims, had managed to block earlier attempts to set up a Jewish state, led by Napoleon in the late 1790s. Zawahiri makes a great deal of Napoleon's reputed correspondence with Jewish leaders in Palestine and Syria when he invaded Palestine in 1799. This, he says, is but one sign of Western imperialism's centuries-old effort to control Palestine through the Jewish movement. In fact, however, there is little in the historical record to suggest Napoleon was a closet Zionist.[12]

Zawahiri's emphasis on the Ottoman Caliphate is important not only in itself but also because it distinguishes him from other radical Islamists, who look back to the time of Muhammad for a political model. Why do that, says Zawahiri, when the ummah was still a world power in just the past century. At the dawn of the twentieth century, the Ottoman Empire controlled all of Islam's most holy cities—including Mecca, Medina, Jerusalem, Najaf, and Karbala—and most of the ummah's traditional heartland in the Arab world, the birthplace of Islam. All the states of the Levant, Iraq, and most of the Arabian Peninsula were more or less under its control. It still had claim to Egypt and Libya. Although led by Turks, it was home to Arabs, Kurds, Persians, and other Muslim peoples, all living in an Islamic system. The Ottomans grew weak, however, and failed to protect the ummah from the West.

To restore its former power, says Zawahiri, the ummah need not look back thirteen centuries to the time of the Prophet for a worthy political model. After all, it was a world player and capable of defending itself not that long ago. Zawahiri is not interested in an ideal world dating back to medieval times but in the power politics of today. He envisions not a fundamentalist revival (although he surely would welcome that), but rather a political resurgence of the ummah, deliberately weakened by the West a century ago and now ready to fight back. He holds up the Ottomans' defeat of Napoleon in Egypt and Palestine as an example of how the ummah can successfully resist Western invasion and the Zionist menace.

The defeat of the Ottoman Turkish Empire in World War I is the pivotal moment in modern Islamic history for Zawahiri and one that he laments in his books and speeches. He blames the British Empire for this collapse and for the resulting weakening of Islam's position in the world. One of its galling repercussions, says Zawahiri, is that the ummah was exposed to the depredations of the West, especially its political designs for enfeebling the community and stealing its land.

Zawahiri's fervor for the Ottomans is unusual in modern Arab history. Most Arabs see the Ottoman Empire as a historic relic whose demise actually opened the door to Arab nationalism. The traditional narrative of modern history for Arab nationalists sees the Arab revolt against the Ottomans in World War I as the beginning of modern Arab history. In Zawahiri's view, however, the new Arab states built on the ashes of that empire were illegitimate creations of Western imperialism that merely weakened the ummah further and spread false un-Islamic doctrines such as Nasserism and Baathism.

Worst of all, the demise of the caliphate in 1919 made possible the British Mandate that would make Palestine a national homeland for the Jewish people and thereby fulfill the Zionist dream of creating the state of Israel. No tragedy is as powerful in Zawahiri's history of Islam as the loss of Palestine to the Zionists. The Balfour Declaration of 1917, with its promise of British support for Zionism, was, lamented Zawahiri, the crime of "someone who didn't own the Holy Land of Palestine giving it to someone who didn't deserve it."[13] Not only was Palestine given to the Zionist enemy, but the rest of the Arab world was carved up between the British and French empires under the terms of the Sykes-Picot Agreement, thereby weakening the ummah and facilitating the capture of Jerusalem and Palestine.

"Sykes-Picot" is a term of ultimate derision appearing often in Zawahiri's writings. It is a reference to the secret agreement between British diplomat Mark Sykes and his French counterpart François George Picot on May 16, 1916, at the height of the First World War, concerning how their governments would divide the Ottoman Empire between the allies at the end of the war. For Zawahiri this agreement not only violated the ummah's right to control its own destiny but also confirmed the West's intent to divide the Muslim world into small states and thus perpetuate its domination of Islam indefinitely.

Zawahiri's outrage over the Balfour Declaration and the Sykes-Picot Treaty is, of course, consistent with most Arab and Muslim sentiment, although he goes a step further, accusing Arab leaders of the time of treason in supporting the British against the Ottomans. The leaders he has in mind are the Hashemite Sharif of the Hijaz and the Saudi leader Abd al Aziz al Saud, who led a campaign against the Turks in the Nejd, the vast central plateau of the Arabian peninsula, where the Ottomans were "stabbed in the back." Though his invective is directed primarily at the Hashemite and Saudi rulers, Zawahiri considers the British liaison officers—the famous Colonel T. E. Lawrence of Arabia, who worked with the Hashemite Prince Faysal, and the less well-known Captain W. H. I. Shakespear, who assisted with the Saudi revolt—to be the agents of Islam's undoing.

The Ottomans had "repelled the Crusaders from our countries for five centuries," says Zawahiri, and "revived the jihad. It defeated Constantinople. It defended Palestine."[14] But the Hashemites and Saudis betrayed it and set the stage for the creation of Israel and the division of the ummah into the bastard states ordained by Sykes-Picot.

Zawahiri would see the same hands of the 1916 betrayal in our times as well. To compound the earlier treason, the Mecca agreement of 2007 negotiated by the Saudis called for a national unity government between Fatah, the major faction of the Palestine Liberation Organization, and

Hamas, its Islamist rival, so as to rein in the jihadists. King Abdullah of
Saudi Arabia

> whose father fought the Ottoman state and worked for its fragmen-
> tation on behalf of the English has today brought together the lead-
> ership of Fatah and Hamas to agree to surrender four-fifths of
> Palestine to the Jews in Mecca. And King Abdullah of Jordan is
> equally guilty as his grandfather declared a rebellion against the
> Ottoman state from Mecca in the first war on behalf of the English
> [and] is today weaving conspiracies and plots against the Islamic
> state of Iraq from Amman on behalf of the Americans.[15]

By linking the Ottoman downfall to the actions of the Hashemite and
Saudi royal families in the First World War, Zawahiri attacks the legitimacy
of the two most important monarchies in the modern Arab world and
thus prepares the ground for attacks against their successors. In his historical narrative, the corrupt Saudi and Hashemite regimes are the very perpetrators of the conspiracy against the ummah in 1916 because they
betrayed the community at the moment of its greatest vulnerability. Over
the next century they were handsomely repaid for this betrayal as the local
henchmen of the West. More galling still, they have given the West control
of the ummah's energy resources and thus its unique national wealth.

The defeat of the Ottomans and the creation of the British Mandate in
Palestine set in motion the events that would lead to the creation of Israel
in 1948. For Zawahiri, this is the West's most evil act: the "Zionist entity
is a foothold for the Crusader invasion of the Islamic world. The Zionist
entity is the vanguard of the U.S. campaign to dominate the Islamic Levant. It is a part of an enormous campaign against the Islamic world in
which the West, under the leadership of America, has allied with global
Zionism."[16] As Zawahiri argues, "after the fall of the Ottoman Caliphate
a wave of psychological defeatism and ideological collapse spread"
throughout the Islamic world.[17] This defeatism made possible the Zionist victory in the 1948 war, which Palestinians consider to be the great
catastrophe, the *naqba,* of their history.

In Zawahiri's view, the goal of the West today is virtually identical to
that of the original Crusades a thousand years ago, which is to dominate
the Islamic world and control its holy places. The corrupt regimes of Jor-

dan, Saudi Arabia, Egypt, the Gulf states, and Turkey are the witting agents of this betrayal and are rewarded with control of their small states, which their ruling elites plunder for their own profit. Another such agent is today's Pope Benedict XVI, in imitation of Pope Urban II, who preached the First Crusade in 1095.

Israel plays the central role in this plot. The West wants a Greater Israel with which to control and dominate the heartland of the Muslim world and support the corrupt Sykes-Picot regimes that make peace with it, like those of Sadat or the late King Hussein. Israel serves as the West's enforcer in the region, weakening and dividing these corrupt states.

Critical to this strategy is Israel's nuclear capability, which gives it military superiority and supreme reign over the region without fear of Muslim response. Despite the West's support for nuclear nonproliferation, Israel was allowed to acquire a nuclear weapon with the particular help of the French, who built its first nuclear reactor at Dimona in the late 1950s. This double standard toward Israeli nuclear weapons, says Zawahiri, indicates what the West really wants: a weak ummah dominated by the Crusaders and Jews. As Zawahiri explained to a television audience in October 2002, five months before the American and British invasion of Iraq, such an invasion would "confirm Israel's uncontested monopoly over weapons of mass destruction in the region, so as to ensure the submission of Arab and Islamic states to its wishes and ambitions."[18]

Zawahiri sees the plot against Islam on every front, fomented by the United States and Europe in the west, Israel nearby, and India in the east. Never having accepted the partition of the subcontinent in 1948 at the end of the British Raj, India's Hindu governments want to dominate South Asia so as to restore the old borders and recover control of Pakistan and Bangladesh. Hence they actively plot with America and Israel against Pakistan to subvert and ultimately subjugate it.

Like Mubarak, the Saudi and Jordanian royals, and other corrupt Arab leaders serving as henchmen of the American and Israeli plot on the western front, the Pakistani military dictator, President Pervez Musharraf, fills this role in South Asia. Indeed, Zawahiri gives Musharraf more attention than any other world leader, portraying him as the one who betrayed the Islamic Emirate of Afghanistan to the Americans in 2002 by withdrawing Pakistani support for the Taliban at a critical moment: during the U.S. attack in the aftermath of 9/11.

Pakistan's defection was an unexpected blow. Al Qaeda and Taliban leaders had assumed Pakistan would continue to be a covert supporter of the Afghan Emirate. After all, it had ignored repeated American requests in the 1990s to halt aid to the Taliban and had rejected several United Nations Security Council resolutions that called on Islamabad to press the Taliban to surrender bin Laden and Zawahiri to face trial for their support of terrorist attacks such as the 1998 bombings of two American embassies in East Africa. Pakistan had rebuffed all these requests before 9/11 but subsequently broke relations with the Taliban and allowed its territory to be used to support Operation Enduring Freedom, the U.S. campaign joined by anti-Taliban Afghan forces that helped topple the Taliban regime.

As early as September 2003 Zawahiri called on the Pakistani army to overthrow Musharraf, whom he accused of betraying not just the Afghan Taliban movement but also the Kashmiri cause. Musharraf, he warned the army, has "brought the Hindus to your backs in Afghanistan," aiding the downfall of the Taliban state and replacing it with a government supported by the United States and India. "This U.S.-Jewish-Indian alliance is against Muslims. Musharraf is stripping you of nuclear weapons to implement U.S. policy."[19]

Nuclear issues again factor into his analysis: since the United States and Israel will not allow any Muslim country to acquire or keep nuclear weapons, they have allegedly persuaded Musharraf to secretly disclose Pakistan's nuclear secrets and thereby weaken the ummah. In March 2004 Zawahiri accused Musharraf of a "plan to paralyze the Pakistani nuclear program to enable the Americans to get acquainted with all its secrets, which will go to Israeli and Indian intelligence . . . to deprive the Pakistani army of its nuclear weapons."[20]

Zawahiri has repeatedly claimed that the West's goal is to weaken Pakistan and divide it into entities that India can control. By way of evidence, he cites the 1971 war that led to the creation of Bangladesh and the breakup of the original Pakistani state created in 1947. If the Pakistani army does not kill Musharraf, he warns, it will suffer the same humiliation as it did in 1971 when 100,000 Pakistani soldiers surrendered to the Indian army in Dhaka, Bangladesh, the darkest day in Pakistan's history.

In the eyes of the jihadists, Musharraf and his supporters are the twenty-first century's equivalents of Sadat: corrupt traitors who have aligned themselves with the United States and Israel. The Islambouli Brigades, in reference to Sadat's killers, have even taken responsibility for the attempt on the life of Musharraf's prime minister, Shaukat Aziz, in 2004.[21]

The Western threat also blows from the south. Zawahiri is a strong critic of the American-brokered peace deal in Sudan that ended the decades-old civil war between the Arab north and the African south. To Zawahiri, the peace deal is another attempt to divide the ummah, a replay of Sykes-Picot, because it promises the south a referendum in a few years that would allow the south to secede. Yet another Muslim state would be divided into smaller states and more easily manipulated by the West to gain control of their oil and weaken the Islamic community.

Darfur figures in the conspiracy as well, according to Zawahiri. The revolt there is another aspect of the Sykes-Picot plot to carve up the ummah in the Sudan and Africa. Efforts by the United Nations and the North Atlantic Treaty Organization to stop genocide in Darfur must be resisted to prevent the West from weakening Islam further.

The picture Zawahiri paints is one of an unprecedented assault on the Islamic world by its enemies: Crusaders, Zionists, and Hindus. But Zawahiri has devised a plan for repelling the attack, defending the ummah, and recreating the caliphate. Its key element is jihad, just as Ibn Taymiyya foresaw. Thus every Muslim is duty-bound to fight the enemies of Islam, including the unbeliever and the corrupt followers who ally themselves with the enemy.

As Zawahiri recognizes, however, the jihadist movement has not yet garnered the support of the Muslim masses because they are still under the sway of their corrupt leaders. He is fully aware that the movement has not found a way to overthrow the Nasser, Sadat, or Mubarak sympathizers in Egypt and create an Islamic state there. Nor has it defeated the Saudi or Hashemite rulers or Musharraf's military regime. Only the Muslims of Iran have been able to develop a mass movement powerful enough to depose a corrupt leader, the Pahlavi Shah, but then they are not Sunni but Shia, Zawahiri adds, who have deviated from the path of true Islam.

That leaves the struggle for victory in the hands of a small cadre of brave Islamic warriors, "knights" who will by their courage and heroism inspire the masses to follow their lead in jihad. The first such knights appeared on the ummah stage in 1981: the assassins of Sadat. "Khalid al-

Islambouli and his righteous comrades, killed Sadat amid his soldiers in the most courageous operation in contemporary history," says Zawahiri, and thus set a pattern for martyrdom operations that strike at the enemies of Islam and its corrupt henchmen.[22] Though it failed to remove the corrupt regime in Egypt, this operation provided an excellent example for others to follow.

The knights achieved their greatest success, of course, with the September 11, 2001, attack on the World Trade Center and the Pentagon by nineteen al Qaeda terrorists. Zawahiri has also claimed credit for other "raids" into the West since then, the most important being the July 7, 2005, attack on London's underground, in which fifty-two innocent people and four terrorists were killed. In a message videotaped only a month later, Zawahiri called this the "blessed London raid . . . like previous raids in New York City, Washington, and Madrid" (the last a reference to the much more deadly attack on the metro system in Spain's capital on March 11, 2004, in which 191 died and more than 2,000 were wounded). To validate his claim of responsibility, Zawahiri included footage of the last will and testament of one of the bombers, Mohammed Siddiq. Zawahiri called the attack a "slap in the face of the arrogant British Crusader hegemony [and] a raid that moved the battle to the land of the enemy after it kept moving the battle for many ages to our land."[23]

Within another few weeks Zawahiri provided further justification for the attack in London, after first praising the "knights of monotheism who carried out the London raid," noting they were sons of Pakistani immigrants to the United Kingdom and thus hero brothers to the people of Pakistan. The purpose of the raid was "to wage war against the Crusader-British haughtiness and against the Crusader-British aggression against the Islamic nation for more than 100 years; against Britain's historical crime in establishing Israel; and against Britain's continued crimes against Muslims in Afghanistan and Iraq."[24] Still later, al Qaeda would broadcast a second will and testament videorecorded by another one of the four terrorists to prove the group's role in the London operation and thus underscore that it was still deadly and active.

These foreign attacks were an essential component of al Qaeda's theory that the key to success in the jihad against the corrupt West and its traitorous allies in the Muslim world was to take the struggle to the West directly. By 2001 Zawahiri had come to see that the regimes of these allies were too strong to be brought down by the jihadist knights alone and in their homeland. Even in Egypt, where they had succeeded in killing Sadat, the regime did not change. Only the ruler was punished and replaced, while the same policies remained in force. The only place where jihad met with success in the Islamic world was Afghanistan, owing to the unique political situation there: the mujahedin's defeat of the Soviet Union had created the opportunity for the Taliban to triumph.

Thus al Qaeda needed to revise its strategy and take the battle to the *far enemy*, the United States and the West, in order to weaken their support for the *near enemy*, the corrupt leaders of the Sykes-Picot states. In that event, its stooges would be weaker and thus more vulnerable to jihad at home. For Zawahiri, defeat of the far enemy was the key to defeat of the near enemy.

At the same time, Zawahiri and bin Laden knew that no operation they could mount in the United States or Europe would be capable of robbing the West of its power. They did not have weapons of mass destruction, although they wanted them, to cause catastrophic damage to the United States and United Kingdom. It would certainly take more than one such weapon to destroy America's power in the Muslim world and its support of al Qaeda's near enemy.

Consequently, the real purpose in striking the far enemy at home was not just to create mass casualties but also to provoke the United States to strike back and invade Muslim lands. The jihad could then rally popular opposition to the invaders and inflict a decisive defeat on U.S. and other Western forces that would so undermine morale that America would withdraw from the Islamic world and retreat to an isolationist posture, leaving its corrupt allies in the Muslim world without a protector and at the mercy of the armies of jihad. They, in turn, would have swollen in strength and power during the battle against the occupation.

As his case study and exemplar for this strategy, Zawahiri used the war he had personally observed since 1980 in Afghanistan. In his analysis, the mujahedin's war against the Red Army was what first bled the Soviet Union of its best soldiers and bankrupted its economy, then broke the morale of the Russian leadership and people and persuaded them to give up the struggle to impose communism on Afghanistan.

Zawahiri laid this approach out in an audio statement in March 2006. The first front in the jihad struggle, he said, is to "inflict losses on the Crusader West" through raids on Western cities, the "best examples" being the strikes in New York, Washington, Madrid, and London. The second front develops when the Crusaders respond and invade Muslim countries, inciting the masses to expel the Crusader and Zionist army from the lands of Islam: "They should leave our lands defeated after the collapse of their economies. This way we can set up the Muslim caliphate state on our land."[25]

For al Qaeda and Zawahiri, the wars in Iraq and Afghanistan represent the hoped-for turning point in Islamic history. Once the Crusader armies in these two countries are conquered, the era of Muslim defeatism begun in 1916 will end. In fact, the al Qaeda leadership in Iraq believes the veil is already lifting: "For the first time since the fall of the Ottoman Caliphate in the last century, the region is witnessing the revival of the Islamic Caliphate through the mujahedins' persistence to establish a state where Muslim people can go to enjoy the rule of God's law."[26] This message of triumph is appearing with increasing frequency in Zawahiri's statements as the wars in Iraq and Afghanistan grow more difficult for the United States to wage.

Zawahiri's messages also warn the ummah not to be tricked by the West's offers of a political settlement. The electoral process in Afghanistan and Iraq merely produced new governments sympathetic to the West, he complains, especially in Afghanistan. He sees these democratic elections as a conspiracy designed to create puppets that will do the West's bidding.

The West's political trickery poses its greatest danger in Palestine, says Zawahiri. The Palestinian Islamic movement, Hamas, must not give in to Western pressure to recognize Israel or to resume the peace process with Israel that was begun by Yasser Arafat. Hamas must stay committed to jihad, urges Zawahiri, because the only solution to the Palestinian issue is the liberation of every inch of the region, not just the West Bank and Gaza. He singles out Palestinian leaders like Mahmoud Abbas and Mohammed Dahlan who negotiate with Israel as the worst traitors in the entire ummah and who should therefore be killed: "Mahmoud Abbas and Muhammad Dahlan aren't merely two corrupt individuals but rather they represent a class of corrupt secularists who cooperate with America, sell Palestine, surrender to Israel and make war on Islam."[27]

Because Hamas plays a crucial role in the struggle against Israel, its commitment to the cause must not falter. But Hamas is an outgrowth of the Muslim Brotherhood, which Zawahiri rejected years ago as being too soft and too weak in the jihad in Egypt, and thus must be kept in check whenever it appears to be going soft on the war, as seemed to be the case when it acceded to the Mecca agreement with Fatah in 2007. Zawahiri promptly issued a mournful statement attacking Hamas for agreeing to the unity government: it was abandoning the path of true jihad in accepting the bargain. Such a move was fraught with danger, Zawahiri warned, that would lead to accepting Israel as a legitimate partner for negotiations and accepting the Oslo agreements as the basis for a peace agreement. The end result would be a betrayal of the Palestinian movement. Rather than succumb to Saudi pressure, Hamas should stay in the jihadist movement and make no accommodation. Zawahiri's rhetoric makes clear that even the slightest movement by Palestinian Islamists, especially Hamas, toward peace with Israel is a great disappointment for the al Qaeda leadership. He enthusiastically welcomed its collapse several months later but remains extremely wary of Hamas's intentions.

Zawahiri must also find great disappointment in al Qaeda's poor progress in his home country and in his unfulfilled dreams of regime change there. After twenty six-years in office, the Mubarak government is firmly in control. Egypt has emerged from the turbulent 1990s, with their frequent and deadly terrorist attacks, to enjoy a period of relative peace and quiet—despite al Qaeda's frequent calls for violence against the government. Indeed, Mubarak's name remains on the group's hit list of corrupt Muslim leaders.

The violence aimed at Egypt did not subside completely, however. In October 2004 the Hilton Hotel in Taba, just across the border in Sinai from the Israeli city of Eilat, was attacked and several campsites used by Israeli tourists in the Sinai were bombed. Thirty-four people died and more than 100 were wounded.

On July 23, 2005, three explosions rocked tourist sites further south in Sinai, at the Sharm al-Shaykh tourist center. Some eighty-eight people were killed and several hundred injured, making this the worst incident of terror in recent Egyptian history and exceeding the Luxor massacre of 1997 linked to Zawahiri. Responsibility for this attack was unclear. Zawahiri did not take credit for it in any statement. Recent evidence suggests that Hamas, or at least elements of it, had a role in the attack, but this is far from established.

All the same, the violence never spread to Egypt proper. The Egyptian security apparatus successfully confined the threat to the Sinai and away from the center of Egyptian political life. A cadre of terrorists and sympathizers almost certainly still exists in the peninsula, but it does not threaten the regime.

To defeat Zawahiri, the authorities have turned Egypt into an armed camp. By 2006 the internal security police force had almost one and a half million men under its command, four times the size of the Egyptian army and operating with a budget of $1.5 billion. More than 80,000 political prisoners are in jail—the vast majority jihadists and a quarter being held without any charge. While the country's population doubled after Sadat's death, the number of prisons quadrupled.[28]

So Zawahiri is a failure at home. The only bright spot for him there in recent years was the news that Mohammed Islambouli, the brother of Sadat assassin Khalid Islambouli, formally joined al Qaeda. For Zawahiri, this meant a new "knight" was added to the "line of jihad against the enemies of Islam: the Crusaders, the Jews, and their treacherous agents" and marked another step in the campaign begun in Cairo so many years before.[29]

In late 1994 I traveled to the Middle East with DCI Jim Woolsey, stopping first in Egypt. Our hosts in the Egyptian security establishment were eager to demonstrate their effectiveness in the war against Zawahiri and other radicals. The visit began with a private evening showing of the treasures of the Egyptian Museum, with its splendors of Egyptian antiquity under the pharaohs. But the highlight of the visit came the next day.

At dusk we were taken to the Nile to watch a special event: a team of Egyptian commandos from the Egyptian intelligence service, the Mukhabarat, showed us how they could "take down" a tourist floating hotel captured by Zawahiri terrorists. Using stun grenades and machine pistols, the commandos stormed the boat after first reaching it by stealth in frogmen outfits and fast zodiac boats. The "terrorists" were quickly killed or captured and the tourist hostages freed.

It was an impressive demonstration of the Mukhabarat's power, even more so as it was done in public—in the middle of Cairo on a normal workday—where everyone could see their skills on display. It was also a pointed reminder that Mubarak's Egypt was not to be defeated by the likes of Ayman al-Zawahiri.

## CHAPTER THREE

# The Knight: Osama

It was a beautiful autumn morning. I had walked from my office in the Old Executive Office Building to the White House Situation Room for the National Security Council senior staff meeting. Just before I left, reports were coming in that an airplane had crashed into the World Trade Center, but they were sketchy and confused.

The Situation Room was paneled with dark wood and held a long table that comfortably seated about a dozen. Another twenty or so chairs were arranged along the walls. By chance, I sat next to the head of the table where my boss, National Security Adviser Condoleezza Rice, was about to open the meeting. The chatter was about the World Trade Center, but no accurate information was yet available.

Condi began with a brief rundown on the president's day. The door suddenly opened, and a watch officer summoned Deputy National Security Adviser Steve Hadley to step out for a moment. He came back in and whispered in her ear. I could not help overhearing the message: a second plane had just crashed into the other tower of the World Trade Center.

In that instant, the world was transformed. The staff meeting was canceled and within minutes the building evacuated. As news of the disaster spread, Washington came to a standstill. I had to walk to my home in Old Town, Alexandria, because my car was parked within the White House perimeter, now closed off. It took but a few hours to learn that the operation had been planned and carried out by al Qaeda, and that the mastermind of this event—one of the bloodiest in American history—was Osama bin Laden.

## WHO IS OSAMA BIN LADEN?

Since 9/11 Osama bin Laden has become one of the most famous people of the modern age. Millions of words have been written about him; thousands of young boys have been named after him. For some, he is a hero; for many, he is the devil incarnate. His image can be seen everywhere—even in Russian doll sets for sale in Eastern Europe or in carpets woven in South Asia. And yet his story is shrouded in mystery, and his motives for creating al Qaeda are often misunderstood.

Osama's exact birth date is in dispute. Some say he was born on March 10, 1957; others say it was in early January 1958, or sometime that summer. This was not unusual in the Saudi Arabia of the 1950s. No one kept these kinds of records. They were unimportant.

What is certain is that he was born into one of the richest families in the world. However, it happened to live in a monarchy that only permitted royal blood to have access to the political decisionmaking circles of the kingdom. The bin Laden family originated in a remote corner of a remote country, the Hadhramaut region of southeastern Yemen. It is a harsh and wild country that was only loosely under the control of the British when Osama was born. Tribal customs and tribal law governed the area. To this day, no central government has exercised real authority there. The British ruled it through tribal sheikhs with no serious English presence on the ground.

Osama's father, Mohammed bin Awad bin Laden, left the Hadhramaut to make his fortune in the construction business in Saudi Arabia. Until the 1930s Saudi Arabia was almost completely undeveloped. The Saudi royal family had seized control of the Arabian Peninsula only a couple of decades earlier, at the end of World War I. Just before the war, it had driven the Ottoman Turks and their Bedouin tribal allies out of the center of the peninsula, then expanded to the east during the war. Immediately afterward, in the early 1920s, the family took control of the remaining western province, the Hijaz, from its rivals, the Hashemites. This was actually the second Saudi kingdom. An earlier kingdom built by the Saudi family dominated the peninsula for several decades at the start of the nineteenth century, only to be harshly repressed by the Ottomans in the 1820s, again in the 1860s, and finally in the 1890s, when the family was driven into exile in Kuwait for the rest of the century.

The conquest of the Hijaz gave the Saudis control of the two holy cities of Islam—Mecca and Medina—and made the royal family the custodians of the holy mosques. This brought new income in the form of fees pilgrims paid to visit the holy sites. The annual pilgrimage of tens of thousands of Muslims to the Hijaz was the kingdom's principal source of income before the discovery of oil in the late 1930s.

Osama's father was illiterate when he arrived in the kingdom, but he was a business genius with a natural talent for the construction industry. First he built roads linking the holy cities together and to the port of Jidda, the main entryway to the Hijaz. Then he was granted a royal commission to help expand the holy mosques to accommodate more pilgrims. Next, he built the Saudi family palaces and the highways that connected the regions of the huge kingdom. The construction work on the two holy mosques was a huge and ongoing project, which continues even to this day in order to improve access and safety for the millions who now visit them during the Hajj, the annual Muslim pilgrimage to Mecca. Renovations of the past half-century have cost more than $20 billion. Between 1956 and 1979 the size of the Grand Mosque in Mecca increased sixfold and now occupies 45 acres. It can accommodate a million worshippers at one time.

Osama's father also won the contract to refurbish the third holiest site in Islam, the Haram al-Sharif, or Noble Sanctuary, a vast sanctuary in the heart of Jerusalem (known in Arabic as al-Quds), with the celebrated Dome of the Rock at one end. According to Islamic belief, the Prophet Muhammad ascended into heaven in a dream from the rock. For almost a decade, Osama's father and his family were frequent visitors to the city as the work was being done, even owning a home in east Jerusalem. In time the family became very close to the king and the Hashemite family. The company completed the sanctuary project at a loss as an act of piety. Only when the Israelis took over Jerusalem in the June 1967 war did the bin Ladens stop coming to the city.[1]

Through these projects Mohammed bin Laden gained entry to the very center of political and religious power in the kingdom. His business grew and diversified into many fields of construction throughout the kingdom, Jordan, and their Gulf neighbors. The bin Ladens and Osama found themselves not only at the very center of the world of Islam, but also on the front line in the Arab-Israeli and Palestinian conflict.

As part of his effort to promote business, Mohammed courted the kingdom's religious leadership, the Wahhabi *ulema* (clerics), who had been aligned with the Saudi family since the eighteenth century. In the early 1700s, a cleric, Mohammed ibn al-Wahhab, preached a return to fundamental Islam that had developed in the peninsula since the Prophet's time, denouncing the worship of saints and local deities, especially the worship of shrines and holy sites. For Wahhab, Islam had to be simple and pure: an expression of complete devotion to one God. Today Wahhabism provides the religious and ideological legitimacy for the Saudi state.

Mohammed bin Laden often hosted dinners and other events for the kingdom's prominent clerics, especially those associated with the two holy mosques. His sons would have been present and involved in these events. In 1967, at the age of fifty-nine, Mohammed was killed in an airplane crash, leaving a fortune of $11 billion to his almost five dozen (variously reported as fifty-four to fifty-seven) children.

Osama was the product of one of his father's briefer marriages, his tenth, to a fifteen-year-old Syrian woman later remarried to another Yemeni. As a child, Osama often visited Syria with his mother, placing him in another of the states at war with Israel early in his life. His mother may have been an Alawi, a member of a small Islamic sect that most Sunnis regard as heretics but that has dominated the Syrian regime under the Asad family since 1968. If she was an Alawi, it had no impact on Osama's faith, which would have been strictly in the Sunni tradition of his father. Another story claims she was a Palestinian but the evidence for this is unclear.

Osama's formative years in the world of Saudi princes and establishment clerics had an enormous impact on his life. For him, the Islam of Wahhab is the correct Islam. His quarrel with the Saudi leadership is about living up to the principles of the faith they both claim to share. Osama would come to believe that the Saudi family, or at least the senior members who ruled the country, had betrayed the true path, a path that he was exposed to at the side of his father in Mecca, Jerusalem, and Medina.

Like many members of his family, Osama obtained his early education in Lebanon, another front-line state in the struggle with Israel.[2] Later he attended the business management school at King Abdul Aziz University in Jidda, the commercial and political capital of the Hijaz. There he took courses in Islam taught by Mohammed Qutb, the younger brother of Sayyid Qutb, who had such great influence on Ayman al-Zawahiri. He also was influenced by another teacher, Abdullah Azzam, a Palestinian member of the Muslim Brotherhood and a scholar. Azzam introduced Osama to the Palestinian "narrative" and influenced his view of the conflict with Israel profoundly. He also recruited Osama to the Brotherhood.

Azzam, like Qutb, began his ideological journey in the Muslim Brotherhood. Convinced that Palestine could only be liberated through a unifying Islamic revolution across the Muslim world, he was frustrated by the Arab states' unwillingness to fight Israel in concert and free his homeland. To remedy the situation, argued Azzam, a vanguard of committed leaders had to come forth to show by their actions and words the steps needed to defeat the West and Israel: "Every principle needs a vanguard to carry it forward. . . . [T]here is no ideology that does not require a vanguard to achieve victory. This vanguard constitutes the strong foundation (*al Qaeda al-sulbah*) for the expected society."[3]

The young bin Laden never completed his studies. Instead, he went to work in his father's company and learned to master the construction craft. He traveled throughout the kingdom to oversee construction projects and may also have accompanied his father on journeys of a more spiritual nature. Mohammed was fond of saying that with the company jet he could pray in Islam's three holiest mosques—Mecca, Medina, and Jerusalem (then still in Jordanian hands)—all in one day. Like many Saudis of his generation, Osama was caught between the fading traditions of tribal life in Arabia and the new and modern world fast emerging there.[4]

Much has been written about Osama's youth in Beirut and Jidda, both by his friends and his enemies. Stories have been told of wild parties in Beirut or even in London. These almost certainly are inventions. There are no reliable accounts to verify them.

Some stories tell of an early involvement in Islamic politics. One alleges that in the late 1970s and early 1980s Osama helped smuggle money into Syria to support the Muslim Brotherhood's battle with the country's Baathist ruler, Hafez al-Asad. By another account, Osama was actually in the Syrian city of Hama during its siege and destruction by Asad's army. This, too, is probably an invention of later admirers—although the siege of Hama marks an important milestone in Islamist Sunni politics. It was the first effort by a Sunni group to seize power in the aftermath of the successful revolution in Iran. The brutal repression in Hama, which left perhaps 20,000 people dead, was an early sign that the Arab "police regimes" would fight back hard and effectively.

I happened to be in Syria during the Hama revolt and watched the regime's elite forces, commanded by Hafez's brother Rifaat al-Asad, move into the city from their barracks south of Damascus. As they approached their destination, the message of their mission was unmistakable: "We will destroy you if you revolt." A few years later, on a return visit, I saw the center of Hama still bulldozed and destroyed, the message to the jihadists now sealed in stone and cement. The defeat in Hama merely hardened the jihadists' resolve, however: they still want to take revenge on the Alawi masters of Syria.

## A MUJAHEDIN AGAINST COMMUNISM

One story about Osama is certainly known to be true: like Zawahiri, he made his way to Afghanistan to join in the struggle against the Soviet invaders. He became a major financier of the mujahedin, providing cash to the relatives of wounded or martyred fighters, building hospitals, and helping the millions of Afghan refugees fleeing to the border region of Pakistan. A unique figure—wealthy, charismatic, and clearly devout—he quickly became a celebrity. Arab newspapers and magazines began to write about him, advancing his notoriety.

Though said in some quarters to be on the payroll of the CIA, there is no basis to this charge, as the 9/11 Commission noted.[5] Indeed, this suggestion hardly tallies with the CIA's support of the insurrection in Afghanistan. All CIA money was channeled to the Pakistani Inter-Services Intelligence Directorate (ISI). Every dollar from the CIA was matched by an equal amount from the Saudis. The agency's director, Bill Casey, met regularly with the Pakistanis to coordinate strategy and tactics, but the business of providing the arms and training to the mujahedin was entirely in the hands of the ISI. Pakistan's dictator, Mohammed Zia ul-Haq, wanted it that way, and the CIA went along. After all, this gave the agency a measure of deniability.

But if Osama had no ties to the CIA, it is all but certain he did have a close connection with the ISI. It would otherwise have been impossible for bin Laden to function as he did in Peshawar in the 1980s. He would have been seeing the same people and providing aid to the same groups as the ISI did. Was he an agent of the ISI? How long did his contacts with Pakistani intelligence continue? How extensive were ISI contacts with al Qaeda after its founding in 1989—and more important, after 9/11? Only the files of the ISI can answer those questions.

According to prominent Pakistani politicians, Osama was working with the ISI on more than just the anti-Soviet project. Benazir Bhutto, who served twice as prime minister of Pakistan and was ousted both times by the army and ISI, reported in her updated memoirs that the ISI asked bin Laden to help bribe members of Bhutto's political majority in parliament to support a no-confidence vote against her. Bin Laden had a "long and close relation" with ISI, says Bhutto, as a result of which the "robust sum of $10 million" was donated to the ISI campaign against her in 1989.[6] She also claims that Ramzi bin Yusuf—the relative of Khalid Sheikh Mohammed, and the mastermind behind the first bombing of the World Trade Center in 1993—tried to assassinate her twice in 1993 on the orders of the ISI and bin Laden, and that Yusuf admitted to this when caught in Pakistan in 1995. He was extradited to the United States on her orders.[7] More recently, Benazir claimed that KSM was also a party to the plot to kill her in 1993, supplying the weapons for Yusuf.[8] Other Pakistani politicians have told me that ISI has had close ties with bin Laden from the beginning of his days in Pakistan.

Osama also worked with ISI in the creation of a key Kashmiri jihadist group in the late 1980s, the Lashkar-e-Tayyiba (LeT). This is one of the most violent and aggressive terrorist groups targeting India in the past two decades. Created in 1987 by several Islamic scholars in Pakistan (including the Palestinian Abdullah Azzam) to support the Afghan mujahedin with Kashmiri volunteers, the group shortly began to play a role in the Kashmiri insurgency but then went beyond Kashmir to target India itself. ISI played a key role in LeT's creation, supplemented by Osama's donation of $200,000, almost certainly with the ISI's encouragement.[9]

Another certainty is that bin Laden began his political career as a wealthy financier of the jihad, announcing that he would fund any Arab who wanted to travel to Afghanistan to fight, would pay for their ticket, find them a residence, and connect them with the mujahedin. Few came forth at first, but in time a growing number of Muslims from Arab and non-Arab nations would take Osama's money and join the war. Although never critical on the Afghan battlefield, this contingent grew politically important. Money the Saudi state was providing together with the private flow of funds and the backing of men like bin Laden gave the Arabs, especially the Saudis, a voice in the decisionmaking about the war among the mujahedin and the Pakistanis.

To add to his stature, Osama became a warrior in Afghanistan. He recruited his own band of fighters and led them into conflict against the Soviet invaders. By most accounts, he was a brave soldier on the battle-field, standing up to the hardships of the Afghan weather and the danger of war along with the others. Already something of an ascetic, he seemed to welcome the hardships of bad food, extreme temperatures, and violent death. Reports of Osama's exploits in battle naturally attracted great attention in the kingdom and throughout the Arabian Peninsula, quickly turning him into a celebrity back home, famous for his spirited jihad against communism.

At this time, bin Laden was working closely with Azzam in Afghanistan and Pakistan. Azzam had also moved to Pakistan to support the muja-hedin, arguing that the jihad in Afghanistan should take precedence over the struggle against Israel because the Soviet Union posed a much greater threat to the ummah as a whole. Azzam's book, *Defense of Muslim Lands,* urged every Muslim to come to Afghanistan and fight. The preface was written by the kingdom's leading Wahhabi cleric, or mufti, Sheikh Abdul Aziz bin Baz, who issued a *fatwa* (ruling) endorsing the Afghan jihad in the bin Laden family mosque in Jidda.[10] Bin Laden and Azzam set up an office in Peshawar to serve as a hostel for Arabs coming to fight and to produce propaganda for the war.

The "Services Bureau," or Makhtab al Khadamat, also received some money from the Saudi intelligence service. The head of Saudi intelligence, Prince Turki, met with bin Laden in Pakistan from time to time to coor-dinate their activities in support of the struggle against the Soviet forces. Much later, Turki would tell me that he found bin Laden to be a quiet, even shy, young man at this time, firmly dedicated to fighting communism but still unsure of himself. He was, remembers Turki, "very soft-spoken. He seldom spoke. He seemed to be extremely shy and retiring."[11]

Another wartime colleague was Zawahiri, who had brought some of his followers to join with bin Laden's Arab brigade, and bin Laden funded them. The Egyptians became an influential group around the Saudis and were instrumental in attracting some of Osama's first media attention in the Muslim world. The Egyptian core proved to be the military masterminds of bin Laden's band. Turki believes Zawahiri came to have more and more influence on Osama's thinking and helped transform him from a shy introvert to the leader of the jihad.

In time Azzam and Zawahiri became rivals for bin Laden's ear and his financial support. Azzam lost out and was assassinated in November 1989. Who was responsible is not clear—some even blame bin Laden or Zawahiri. Others point to Israel's Mossad or the CIA. There is no evidence of CIA involvement. Most likely Azzam was the victim of the internecine fighting within the mujahedin movement and among the Arabs congregated around it in Pakistan.

Some time before the death of Azzam in the summer of 1988, bin Laden began calling his cadre al Qaeda al Askariya ("the military base") and gave it somewhat greater organizational structure. Many more Arabs were now flocking to join the war as it became clear the mujahedin were winning, and the name al Qaeda took hold.[12]

U.S. intelligence noted the sharp increase in Arab fighters at this time, voicing some concern inside the CIA about the long-term implications of a large number of trained and radicalized Arabs returning from Afghanistan as heroes at the end of the war. Though made aware of this potential issue, the U.S. leadership paid it little attention, focusing instead on winning the cold war. A few Arab jihadis seemed unimportant, according to Robert Gates, deputy national security adviser in 1988–91:

We began to learn of a significant increase in the number of Arab nationals from other countries who had traveled to Afghanistan to fight in the Holy War against the Soviets. They came from Syria, Iraq, Algeria and elsewhere. Years later, these fundamentalist fighters would begin to show up around the world from the Middle East to New York City, still fighting their Holy War—only now including the U.S. among their enemies. Our mission was to push the Soviets out of Afghanistan. We expected post-Soviet Afghanistan to be ugly, but never considered that it would become a haven for terrorists operating worldwide.[13]

When the Soviet forces announced in 1988 that they had had enough and were leaving, the mujahedin prepared for the kill. While all agreed they wanted to oust the communist puppet regime installed by Moscow and led by Mohammed Najibullah, they failed to reach a consensus on what or who should replace him. The Soviet Fortieth Army departed in 1989 amid widespread expectations that the Najibullah government would collapse immediately. It did not, partly because it continued to receive some Soviet arms but also because it received a measure of support from the urban educated population of Kabul and other cities, who were not eager for Islamic rule by a group of warring warlords.

And the warlords did battle each other—as much as they did the communists. The world quickly lost interest, including the United States. I served on President George H. W. Bush's National Security Council in 1991 and 1992 and cannot recall a single senior-level meeting on the subject. The greatest problem Washington thought it still had in Afghanistan at that point was that the CIA had sent more Stinger surface-to-air missiles to the mujahedin than needed to defeat the Soviet forces, and these highly accurate weapons were starting to get out to the world black arms market where they could be picked up for devious purposes, such as shooting down a commercial airliner. So the CIA was authorized to buy them back at the taxpayers' expense and did so over the next decade. Meetings in the White House Situation Room frequently monitored the progress of these transactions (called Operation MIAS, missing-in-action Stingers). Many of these weapons came from Pakistan's ISI, which bought them from the mujahedin on America's behalf.[14]

Bin Laden and Zawahiri participated in the struggle against the Najibullah regime for some time. Both were present at the siege of Jalalabad, the critical city on the road to Kabul that the mujahedin needed to take to advance on the capital. The Arabs were now becoming more numerous as more came to participate in what they thought would be an easy march to triumph. Al Qaeda grew increasingly structured and larger, with a new cadre. The Egyptians remained at its core, and Zawahiri continued to exercise considerable influence on his Saudi friend, whom he also cared for as his physician.

But the Najibullah regime did not fall apart. The siege of Jalalabad failed, and the mujahedin civil war deepened. Osama himself became disenchanted with the Afghans, communists, and mujahedin alike, not to mention their constant conflict. He returned to Jidda and resumed his role in the family's construction industry empire—except that now he was a famous man whose views were sought by the media and others.

Until 1990 Osama's attention had been focused exclusively on the communist threat to the ummah in South Asia. When he returned from Afghanistan, he proposed to the Saudi leadership that he lead a new jihad to undermine and overthrow the communist government in South Yemen. The People's Democratic Republic of Yemen had long been an enemy of the Saudis and a target of covert plotting by the Saudi intelligence service and others. The republic was the creation of an anti-British insurrection in the mid-1960s that was strongly supported by Egypt until its defeat in the 1967 war. With Cairo forced to abandon Yemeni politics after its defeat by Israel, the Soviet Union stepped in to back the communists, helping them to take over when the British left in 1968. It was the only communist regime in the Arab world and seemed a good target for jihadist efforts after the Soviet withdrawal from Afghanistan.

When Bin Laden approached Saudi intelligence offering to help organize a jihadist movement against the regime in Aden, Prince Turki turned him down. Although the Saudi leadership had long plotted the overthrow of the communists in the south, it did not want a private army doing its bidding and may have been already worried about bin Laden being difficult to control. Osama persisted, however, despite being warned to stay out, and began providing money to anticommunist tribes in the south. The Saudi minister of the interior, Prince Nayif bin Abdul Aziz, a full brother of the king, called Osama into his office in the ministry's ultramodern headquarters in Riyadh and told him to cease any plotting immediately. To underscore his point and to control the troublesome young man, Nayif confiscated bin Laden's passport.[15]

In fact, by late 1989 and early 1990 South Yemen was already heading toward collapse because it had lost its Soviet patron as well. Soviet advisers and experts were withdrawing everywhere around the world and cutting financial aid to all of their former clients. Turning to its bigger neighbor, the Yemen Arab Republic, South Yemen negotiated a merger, which took place in May 1990 and ended communism's brief interlude on the Arabian Peninsula. Osama's target was gone.[16]

With communism destroyed, Osama took up a more sedate project in early 1990: a boycott of American-made goods to protest U.S. support of

Israel. This was his first concrete anti-American action, but it was a far cry from his anti-Soviet activities.[17]

August 2, 1990, changed everything in Saudi Arabia. The Iraqi invasion of Kuwait was a staggering surprise to the kingdom. I became the deputy chief of the CIA's Persian Gulf Task Force that evening, when it was established in response to the invasion. At the CIA, we had correctly tracked the buildup of the Iraqi invasion force and warned that Saddam was not bluffing and would attack. Though we got it right, every Arab leader in the region assumed the opposite and told President Bush they were not alarmed.

King Fahd and his brothers in Riyadh had assumed Saddam Hussein was simply going to shake down Kuwait for some debt relief and some cash. They never imagined he would invade and rob the bank. Even more terrifying, they never imagined he might do the same to them. But by August 5 the Iraqi army was poised to do just that: 100,000 strong, the Republican Guard had finished digesting Kuwait and was preparing to invade the kingdom. We alerted the Saudis that an attack was imminent, and this time they believed us.

At the same time, Osama bin Laden stepped forward requesting an urgent audience with Saudi defense minister Prince Sultan, one of the richest men in the royal family. He has been defense minister since 1963 and has met every American secretary of defense since Robert McNamara. Sultan was well aware that the Saudi army and National Guard were no match for Saddam's Republican Guard. Despite spending billions on defense, the Saudi military was too small, too inexperienced, and too poorly led to defeat its Iraqi nemesis alone.

Osama had a proposal for Sultan: he would raise an Islamic army of Afghan veterans to defend the kingdom. All he wanted was the royal family's approval to do so and then assistance with the logistics and financing. To his credit, Osama had been a vocal critic of the Baathist government in Baghdad for months before the invasion. Saddam, he complained, was a secular socialist closely aligned with the former Soviet Union all his life and thus an enemy of Islam and now a threat to the kingdom. Baathism was a cancer in the Arab world to the jihadists, who had felt its brutal repression in Syria and Iraq.

After stalling Osama all of August, Sultan politely dismissed him in September. By then the family had accepted President Bush's offer to deploy a quarter of a million American soldiers to defend the kingdom. A few months later, the United States would double its deployment to prepare for the liberation of Kuwait. The Saudi royal family secured the approval of the senior Wahhabi clergy for the deployment, including that of chief mufti Sheikh Abdul Aziz bin Baz, as well as other senior Sunni ulema, including the Egyptian sheikh of Al-Azhar University in Cairo.

Bin Laden opposed the decision to bring in the Americans and their allies, but he did not call for the overthrow of the House of Saud at the time. The Saudi government had been good to his family, and he was probably reluctant to make a complete break. He and other critics of the American rescue—some arguing that America was an even greater enemy than Saddam—came under increasing suspicion by the internal security forces. The extent of bin Laden's role in mounting this opposition is unclear, but there is no doubt that he felt increasingly uncomfortable in the kingdom.

In 1991, after the liberation of Kuwait by the American-led multinational army, Bin Laden chose to go into exile in Sudan across the Red Sea. He asked Nayif to return his passport so that he could travel to Afghanistan again to help its war refugees, but his real destination was Sudan. In imitation of the Prophet Muhammad's flight from Mecca to Medina, Osama left his home because his political views were out of tune with those of the ruling government. At this point, bin Laden's criticism was still directed at the Saudi family, but it had not yet taken a violent and revolutionary turn. That was still to come.

The Sudan of the early 1990s was a safe haven for all kinds of radicals and dissidents. Seeking to make Sudan an exemplar of a true Islamic state, the government of Hassan Turabi and his National Islamic Front was eager to invite other Islamic figures in, especially one with a great war record in Afghanistan. To this end, Turabi hosted an Arab and Islamic conference in 1991 that attracted Islamic groups and figures from around the world. Bin Laden was just one of a potpourri of Islamic and Arab radicals on his list.

The cast of characters that arrived in Khartoum for the meeting ranged from Sunni jihadists like bin Laden and Zawahiri and members of the Palestinian Sunni Hamas movement to Shia jihadists from Lebanon's Hezbollah group, representatives of Iran's Revolutionary Guard and Intelligence Ministry (MOIS), secular Palestinian radicals like Abu Nidal, and even foreign revolutionaries like the infamous Carlos. By now extremely fundamentalist, Osama hated Shia as any Wahhabi would and detested secular revolutionaries, yet seemed willing to mix with all these elements while in the Sudan.

According to the 9/11 Commission's report, bin Laden had contact with several of the more unsavory groups in Sudan, including Hezbollah and the Iranian intelligence service. The report also suggests he had contact with Iraqi intelligence operatives from Saddam's regime. There is no compelling evidence to suggest that any of these contacts developed into operational connections or relationships of substance and importance. Khartoum was a place for rivals to meet, but they did not necessarily form partnerships.

There has been a great deal of speculation about whether bin Laden began terrorist activity and operations while in the Sudan. Some have claimed, for example, that he was involved in the anti-American insurgency in Somalia in 1992 and 1993. The 9/11 report suggests such a role in part because he frequently referred to the U.S. defeat there in later years. His fellow Arab Afghans allegedly taught the Somalis the techniques they used to shoot down American Blackhawk helicopters. Some also say he was involved in the bombing of a hotel in Aden, Yemen, where U.S. soldiers were staying to help support operations in Somalia and two tourists were killed.

Neither appears to be true. Though bin Laden was providing funds to various organizations opposed to the U.S. presence in the region and some of his coterie of followers may have engaged in violence, he seems not yet to have made the transition from critic to active terrorist. The Somalis, including their military experts on the ground in Mogadishu, have soundly rejected the idea that he helped them in 1993.[18] He may have had a larger role in Yemen, where the group that attacked the Movenpick Hotel had some connections to bin Laden from his previous plotting to undermine the communist state in the south. But again there is no smoking gun linking the operation to him or those around him in Khartoum.

Similarly, no compelling evidence is available to implicate bin Laden in the November 1995 bombing of a Saudi National Guard training facility in Riyadh used by American officers, five of whom were killed. The Saudis caught and hanged four of their own countrymen for the crime. On Saudi television the perpetrators confessed to having been influenced by bin Laden's writings and statements but did not indicate he was involved in the attack itself, nor did he take credit for the operation, although he later said he admired the attackers for their jihadist actions. At the time, I was the deputy assistant secretary of defense for the Near East and South Asia in the Pentagon with direct responsibility for reviewing the issue for the secretary of defense, and the Saudi security services told me that bin Laden was not involved.[19]

I was also working in the Pentagon in June 1996, when a second and more deadly bombing targeted the Khobar barracks at the Dhahran air base in the kingdom's Eastern Province. Nineteen Americans were killed in that attack, which struck at the most important military base used by the U.S. air force in the Gulf then. Bin Laden was certainly an early suspect. I was traveling with Secretary of State Warren Christopher on one of his many peace missions to broker Arab-Israeli agreements when the attack occurred. We flew immediately to Dhahran, arriving only hours after the attack.

It was a frightful site. Half the barracks had been blown apart. A huge crater appeared where the truck bomb had detonated. The dead were still being recovered from the ruins, and the wounded were everywhere. Even the young air force lieutenant assigned to be my liaison had slight wounds on her arm and face from the splinters of glass spread all over the base by the force of the explosion. She considered herself lucky to have been only moderately injured.

I stayed at Dhahran for the next week to investigate the attack with the air force and Saudi authorities, including the Saudi ambassador to the United States, Prince Bandar, who had arrived from leave in Jidda. Bandar was an old friend by then, someone I had worked with intensively in the days after the Iraqi invasion of Kuwait and its subsequent liberation. He was overseeing the Saudi intelligence investigation of the attack on Khobar. After a few days, Secretary of Defense William Perry, my boss, arrived to see the devastation for himself and to review the investigation.

From the start, the Saudis were skeptical of any involvement by bin Laden. They pointed a finger at the extreme elements in the Eastern Province's Shia community, which had ties to Iran. The investigation of Khobar would take months and never be entirely conclusive, but in time it was abundantly clear that the initial Saudi view was correct: Iran and its ally, the Hezbollah movement in Lebanon, had orchestrated the attack using local Shia to conduct the actual operation. Tehran ordered it, Lebanon's Hezbollah provided the bombmaker, and Saudi Hezbollah the terrorists. As with the Riyadh bombing, bin Laden would later express support for the attack but not claim responsibility. "I have great respect for the people who did these [Riyadh and Khobar] actions," he remarked in a March 1997 interview with CNN. "They are heroes. I also say that they did a great job; theirs was a big honor that I missed participating in."[20]

## THE BREAK WITH THE HOUSE OF SAUD

As bin Laden indicates through his own words, however, the shift from critic to terrorist occurred in late 1994, while he was in Sudan. In December Osama wrote an open letter to the chief mufti of Saudi Arabia—the same blind Wahhabi cleric named bin Baz who was still the senior religious figure in the kingdom—with a list of complaints against the House of Saud and its clerical supporters. He criticized the Saudis for alleged corruption, for inviting Americans to defend the kingdom against Saddam in 1990, for not being sufficiently anticommunist in Yemen, and for arresting clerical leaders who opposed the family on these issues. But the bulk of the letter spoke of another sin: Saud support for the peace process with Israel. Bin Baz had issued a statement endorsing the Oslo peace process between Israel and the Palestinians, which the Saudi royal family itself strongly supported, even sending Prince Bandar, its ambassador in Washington, to the signing ceremony on the White House lawn between Chairman Yasser Arafat and Prime Minister Yitzhak Rabin in September 1993.

Bin Laden refers to this as "your latest astonishing juridical decree justifying peace with the Jews, which is a disaster for Muslims."[21] He says the Saudi leadership and bin Baz are "not satisfied with abandoning Saudi Arabia, home of the two Holy Sanctuaries, to the Crusader-Jewish forces of occupation," but now they have "brought another disaster upon Jerusalem, the third of the Sanctuaries[,] by conferring legitimacy on the contracts of surrender to the Jews." Citing Ibn Taymiyya, bin Laden argues that every Muslim has an obligation to fight the occupation of any Muslim land like Palestine that has been taken from the ummah by foreign hands. The Oslo accords he calls "nothing but a massive betrayal . . . by the traitorous and cowardly Arab tyrants."

Osama urged the elderly bin Baz to keep his distance "from these tyrants and oppressors who have declared war on God" and thus save himself. Most significant, bin Laden called for a jihad against the Crusaders, Jews, and tyrants in order to recover "every stolen Islamic land from Palestine to al-Andalus and other Islamic lands that were lost because of the betrayals of rulers and the feebleness of Muslims." This letter marked bin Laden's transition from critic to avowed jihadist.

The letter was signed by bin Laden but addressed from the Advice and Reform Committee in London, which he had set up earlier in the year to serve as a political headquarters for the growing number of critics of the kingdom living in exile in the United Kingdom. The committee would become a major clearinghouse for anti-Saud propaganda and a sticking point in British-Saudi relations.

Osama's letter appears to be written more in sorrow than in anger. The tone is that of a man severely disappointed in his own government and especially the clerical establishment of Wahhabi Islam. Remembering the many earlier fatwas issued by bin Baz opposing any settlement with Israel, Osama says he knows the Saudi authorities pressured the elderly cleric to issue the one supporting Oslo. As one Saudi critic of the Saudi family has noted, "Bin Laden does not practice a splinter form of Wahhabi Islam; he practices the official Saudi ideology and has attempted to hold the Saudi royals accountable to it. Bin Laden only broke with the Saudi establishment over foreign policy."[22]

Abdul Aziz bin Baz was a major figure in the clerical establishment for decades before his death in 1999. He preached a very reactionary brand of Islam, proclaiming the earth is flat, banning high heels for women as too sexually provocative, barring men from wearing Western suits, and imposing other restrictions on behavior. He was particularly harsh with Shia Islam, which has always been a major target of Wahhabi extremists. In many ways, bin Laden was turning on the very institutions that had shaped him but felt he had to do so because the Wahhabi leadership had betrayed its principles on the single most important issue for jihadis, Israel.

The letter to bin Baz was followed in mid-1995 by one addressed to the "honorable scholars" of Islam, especially those in Saudi Arabia. It expanded the attack on the ruling family to new heights, accusing it of betraying not only Palestine but also the holy city of Mecca and the holy land of the peninsula by allowing the deployment of American forces against Iraq. A calamity has taken place, bin Laden declares, and "for the first time the Crusaders have managed to achieve their historic ambitions and dreams . . . by gaining control over the Islamic holy places and the

Holy Sanctuaries . . . turning the Arabian Peninsula in to the biggest air, land, and sea base in the region."[23]

Bin Laden then asks: "After the Crusaders' occupation of Saudi Arabia, the Jews' violation of Palestine and Jerusalem, and the destruction and slaughter of Muslims in Chechnya and Bosnia, can matters get any worse?" The answer: jihad must be the Muslim course, "so scholars rise up." This is Osama's first clear call for militant resistance that links the Crusaders in Arabia with the Israelis in Palestine as the enemies.

As 1994 and 1995 rolled along, Osama found himself facing serious problems in Sudan. Apparently he was the target of at least one assassination attempt at this time, and maybe others as well. A February 1994 attack on his home was conducted by some Libyans who may have been rented for the occasion, possibly by Saudi intelligence. Saudi officials deny this and blame the Sudanese government for staging the attempt to make it look like a Saudi job and thus frighten bin Laden into being more helpful to them. The truth is elusive here, as in so many other aspects of bin Laden's career.

However, the Saudis did up the temperature on bin Laden in other ways. In March 1994, even before he wrote his letter to bin Baz, the government took away his citizenship, in effect making him stateless. It urged his family to persuade him to give up his criticism of the House of Saud, and failing that, to restrict his access to family funds. Before long, his monthly stipend from the Bin Laden construction consortium ended and he was short of funds, although not destitute by any means. The family disowned him publicly, issuing a statement critical of his activities.[24]

Meanwhile, bin Laden renewed his friendship with Zawahiri in Khartoum. The Egyptian had become a wandering terrorist, on the run from Egyptian intelligence and its allies (including the CIA, which was very active in trying to catch him). He found Sudan the most opportune site to operate against Egypt from the outside, with easy transit over its long and largely unguarded border.

A determined jihadist, Zawahiri began to exert even greater influence on bin Laden. Although the two had direct contact before, Sudan appears to have brought them much closer, Zawahiri probably being the critical force in encouraging bin Laden to break completely with the House of Saud and to become active against it. Bin Laden also began supporting Zawahiri's own Islamic Jihad movement with more money and arms.[25]

In April 1995 Zawahiri tried to unite the various Egyptian jihadist groups under his leadership in Khartoum, with the support of the Sudanese government and probably bin Laden. The effort failed, leaving the two largest groups, Zawahiri's Islamic Jihad and al Gamaa al Islamiyya, deadly foes. Gamaa staged a spectacular attempt to assassinate President Hosni Mubarak on June 26, 1995, by ambushing his motorcade while he was visiting Ethiopia for a summit of the Organization of African Unity (OAU). Meeting with Mubarak in Alexandria less than a month after the attack, I could see that he was still a bit shaken by the incident. He had no doubt that the Sudanese government was directly involved in the plot and that Khartoum was a nest of radical extremists planning further carnage. Mubarak would almost certainly have been killed if not for the heavy armor on his limousine. The attack increased Egyptian and American determination to kill or capture all the Egyptian jihadists hiding in Sudan.

Evidence then surfaced confirming Sudanese involvement. Both Gamaa and Islamic Jihad were openly active in the capital, and the trail from Addis Ababa back to Khartoum was rapidly uncovered. The Ethiopians pressed Sudan for the extradition of Gamaa leaders so they could stand trial in Ethiopia, but Sudan refused. The Egyptians and Ethiopians appealed to the Organization of African Unity and the United Nations, and in January 1996 the UN Security Council passed Resolution 1044 condemning the attack and demanding that Sudan return three suspects to Ethiopia to face charges. The U.S. ambassador to the United Nations, Edward "Skip" Gnehm, said the resolution demonstrated "the Sudanese government's sponsorship of terrorism as part of its foreign policy."[26] This seemed even clearer when Sudan failed to comply.

In April 1996 the United Nations passed another resolution (UNSCR 1054), calling on all states to reduce their diplomatic presence in Khartoum and to restrict the entry of Sudanese officials into their own territory. In August 1996 it took a further step and passed UNSCR 1070, imposing a global ban on Sudan Airways, the national airline. Khartoum was now paying a price for harboring a smorgasbord of international terror. Zawahiri's Islamic Jihad and Rahman's Islamic Group were but the tip of the problem, and the world was ratcheting up the pressure from every corner.

Desperate to get out of the international cross fire, Sudan decided to give up to French intelligence the infamous Carlos, who had carried out several major terrorist attacks in the 1970s, including the mass kidnapping of the oil ministers of the Organization for Petroleum Exporting Countries in December 1975. Sudan had been giving him asylum for several years. Oddly, it appears that Carlos had a religious conversion later in life and became a self-appointed supporter of bin Laden after September 11.

By the early 1990s increasing attention was also focusing on bin Laden. The CIA was watching his activities more closely in view of his growing connections with other radicals like Zawahiri, a known terrorist. The agency believed bin Laden was a significant financier of Islamic Jihad and other groups but not directly associated with the planning and operations of terror himself. That changed during 1996. As George Tenet relates in his memoirs, "An al Qaeda defector told us that UBL [bin Laden] was the head of a worldwide terrorist organization with a board of directors that included al Zawahiri."[27] Though perhaps more dramatic than was the case in fact, this picture certainly pointed to where bin Laden was headed.

It was time for Osama bin Laden to move on. His anti-Oslo letter to bin Baz, his support for Islamic Jihad, and his role in other jihadist movements made him a liability for the Turabi regime as it sought to avoid UN condemnation and stricter sanctions. Despite allegations by some after 9/11, the Sudanese never offered to hand bin Laden over to the United States (a point made by the 9/11 Commission in its report). In any case, the United States had no warrant for the arrest of bin Laden and thus could not try him even if he were sent there.

Instead the Sudanese authorities approached the Saudis about him. The Saudi government was reluctant to take on the task of trying a prominent hero from the Afghan war. Prince Turki asked the Egyptians if they had any evidence that Osama had played a role in the plot to kill Mubarak. The Egyptians had none. Sudan then turned to Pakistan and the Afghan mujahedin. The Sudanese told bin Laden to leave, confiscated his construction equipment, and forced him to sell all his assets at a fraction of their worth. Khartoum suggested he go to Afghanistan.

Perhaps fearing that Sudan would turn him over to his enemies if he stayed much longer, bin Laden left Khartoum on May 18, 1996, on his own initiative. Osama's declaration of jihad against the Saudi regime for its betrayal of Palestine and its pro-American policies had made him a man without a country. He returned to Afghanistan where the chaos of the early 1990s was being replaced by the terror of the Taliban. Ironically, he landed at Jalalabad airport, the scene of the mujahedin's failure that had led to his departure six years earlier.

According to the 9/11 Commission's report, the ISI facilitated his arrival in Afghanistan and helped him get set up. ISI also was instrumental in arranging his first meetings with Taliban leader Mullah Omar, to be discussed shortly. Thus Pakistani intelligence maintained the contact begun with bin Laden in the 1980s well into the late 1990s at the least.[28]

Bin Laden may have been on the run, but he was defiant. Within a few months of his arrival in Afghanistan he issued a letter to the entire ummah, with special attention to the Muslim Brothers of the Arabian Peninsula. This was the manifesto declaring war on America. Written in anger, it recounts the "oppression, hostility and injustice [committed] by the Judeo-Christian alliance" against the ummah.[29] The letter makes reference to the April 18, 1996, "massacre" in Qana, Lebanon, during clashes between Israel and Hezbollah in which 102 civilian refugees were killed and more than 300 wounded when the Israel Defense Forces (IDF) mistakenly shelled a UN compound near the village famous for Christ's first miracle. Bin Laden then lists "Tajikistan, Burma, Kashmir, Assam, the Philippines, Fantani, Ogaden, Somalia, Eritrea, Chechnya, and Bosnia and Herzegovina" as places where Muslims have been massacred by their Christian enemies and their allies.

But the "greatest disaster to befall the Muslims" is the "occupation of Saudi Arabia, which is the cornerstone of the Islamic world, the place of revelation." This is the result, Osama argues, of the corruption of the House of Saud, which has sold out the holiest of Islam places, the noble Kaaba, to the Israelis and Americans. Saudi Arabia, he complains, "is the biggest purchaser of weapons from America in the world and America's biggest trading partner in the region," yet America uses this wealth to support Israel and its "Jewish brothers in the occupation of Palestine."

His letter then becomes more personal: the Judeo-Christian alliance killed his teacher and mentor Abdullah Azzam, arrested Hamas leader Sheikh Ahmed Yassin, and killed the blind Sheikh Omar Rahman (actually arrested in New York, not killed). At the behest of the United States, the Saudis arrested prominent ulema who criticized the corruption of the House of Saud and "hounded" bin Laden from Saudi Arabia to Pakistan, Sudan, and Afghanistan.

The only possible redress for all this perceived injustice is jihad against the Judeo-American alliance that has occupied holy Jerusalem and holy Mecca. Invoking several sayings from the Prophet on the importance of jihad, bin Laden concludes with a call to arms: "Your enemies are the Israelis and Americans. Cavalry of Islam, be mounted!"

Shortly after this letter was published, bin Laden sat for an interview with an Australian Muslim journal, Nida'ul Islam, in which he summed up his life to this point. He claimed he began his interaction with Islamic causes in 1973 as a direct result of the Israeli-Arab war, that his tutor was the Palestinian Azzam, and that he could take credit for the defeat of communism in Afghanistan and South Yemen. He spoke approvingly of the Khobar Towers attack on American troops in June 25, 1996, and the Riyadh bombing in November 13, 1995, but did not claim any responsibility for them. He then granted several other interviews, with CNN and Arab newspapers, as he sought to get out his message and prepare the world for what was coming: the most intense terror campaign ever waged against America.

## THE WAR AGAINST AMERICA BEGINS

In May 1997 bin Laden teamed up with Zawahiri, who had been wandering around Europe and the Middle East since he left Sudan in 1996, and with their supporters to form a close-knit group of jihadists. Zawahiri became its ideological leader, bin Laden its charismatic chieftain. From Afghanistan, Zawahiri and others supported the bloody attack on a tourist group in Luxor, Egypt, that killed over sixty tourists. He was now more than ever a wanted man who needed al Qaeda's protection and support.

Another fugitive came to visit bin Laden and Zawahiri shortly after they reunited in Afghanistan: Khalid Sheikh Mohammed, who had spent the 1990s plotting attacks against America around the world. He was the uncle of Ramzi Yusuf, the mastermind behind the 1993 bombing of the World Trade Center then hiding out in the Philippines. In Manila the two had devised a plot to blow up American jumbo jets flying across the Pacific and another to crash a small airplane into CIA headquarters in Langley, Virginia. Ramzi was a superb bombmaker; one of his test bombs killed a Japanese passenger on a flight from Manila to Tokyo. But another set off a fire in the Manila safe house, and Ramzi had to leave in a hurry.

The police found his laptop computer with considerable information about his plans that the CIA was able to download.

Khalid is a Pakistani born in Baluchistan but who spent much of his early life in Kuwait along with his nephew. They were among the hundreds of thousands of South Asians who found work in the Persian Gulf states. He became a fighter in Afghanistan in the late 1980s and may have met bin Laden there briefly in 1989. He is a consummate terror planner, inventing diabolical plots incessantly until his capture in Pakistan in 2003.

Khalid apparently briefed bin Laden in late 1996 on some of his schemes. Drawing on the plot he had developed in the Philippines, he outlined a plan to hijack multiple airliners in the United States and use them as suicide bombs. As I mentioned earlier, the idea was probably influenced by an Algerian jihadist operation in 1994 that hijacked an Air France plane and would have used it to blow up the Eiffel Tower if not aborted by French commandos in Marseilles. Khalid no doubt had only a vague notion of his plan when he first presented it to Osama in 1996. When bin Laden pressed him to join al Qaeda and pledge loyalty to him as its leader, Khalid demurred and left Afghanistan. He would return, however, after bin Laden proved his seriousness as an enemy of America.

In the winter of 1997–98 bin Laden and Zawahiri decided to declare war on America unambiguously and publicly. The two were joined by three other prominent jihadists: Rifa'i Ahmed Taha, who led a splinter group of al Gamaa al Islamiyya that had merged with Islamic Jihad; Sheikh Mir Hamza, secretary general of the Jamiat Ulema-e-Pakistan, a Pakistani jihadist group; and Maulana Fazi-ur Rahman, the leader of a Bangladeshi Islamist group. The five signed a declaration proclaiming the founding of the World Islamic Front, an umbrella group dedicated to uniting the global jihadist camp.

It was an unprecedented event. Never before had the Sunni extremists united in such a public and open manner to proclaim their intentions. The declaration cited three reasons for action: the American occupation of the holy Arabian Peninsula, the alleged massacre of Iraqis as a result of the UN sanctions imposed in 1991, and the founding of Israel and its occupation of Jerusalem. The three crimes were directed by the United States, they argued, their purpose being to protect Israel. All the attacks on Arab and Muslim countries were done to "serve the interests of the petty Jewish state, diverting attention from its occupation of Jerusalem . . . and to fragment all the states in the region, like Iraq, Saudi Arabia, Egypt and Sudan, into paper ministates whose weakness and disunity will guarantee Israel's survival."[30]

To defend the ummah from further U.S. and Israeli attack, it was "the duty of every Muslim in all countries to kill the Americans and their allies—civilian and military—to liberate Al Aqsa Mosque and the Holy Mosque of Mecca." The order is significant; Muslims would ordinarily never put Jerusalem ahead of Mecca, but al Qaeda was making a statement about its priorities. The occupation of the Arabian Peninsula was the work of Israel, the real master of the Zionist-Crusader enemy. Hence it was the ultimate target. First, however, the United States needed to be defeated and its "armies broken and unable to threaten any Muslim."

Behind the rhetoric was al Qaeda's first major plot, the planning for which was well under way at the time of the declaration. The target would be the American embassies in Tanzania and Kenya. The two would be attacked almost simultaneously by suicide truck bombers, the new modus operandi of the organization designed to create maximum terror: multiple operations in different locales carried out at the same time. The al Qaeda cells involved had been casing the targets for months if not years and dated back to bin Laden and Zawahiri's time in the Sudan. The 9/11 Commission says the targets were first surveyed in 1994, but that may be too early.

On August 6, 1998, Zawahiri sent a fax to the office of the Arabic newspaper *al-Hayat* in Cairo reporting that an Islamic jihad cell uncovered by the CIA in Tirana, Albania (a Muslim country), had been sent to Egypt, where the terrorists had supposedly been brutally tortured. He warned that the United States would soon be punished: "We should like to inform the Americans that, in short, their message has been received and that they should read carefully the reply that will, with God's help, be written in the language that they understand."[31]

The next day the two embassies were attacked in East Africa. More than 220 people were killed and 4,000 injured. The majority were not even Americans. The terrorists had forgotten that most Americans take leave in August, so fewer were on duty than usual. No matter. Al Qaeda's war on America had begun.

## CHAPTER FOUR

# The Host: Mullah Omar

The plane ride from Islamabad to Kabul was short but memorable. As we approached the Afghan capital, the pilot put the nose into a sharp dive and made a tight corkscrew turn toward the airfield to avoid possible antiaircraft missiles. We were the guests of Afghanistan's rulers, the Taliban, but the pilot was taking no chances that we might be unwanted by our hosts.

On board the small UN aircraft were the U.S. ambassador to the United Nations, Bill Richardson; the assistant secretary of state for South Asia, Karl "Rick" Inderfurth; and myself, then the special assistant to the president and senior director for Near East and South Asia Affairs at the National Security Council in the White House. Our mission from President Bill Clinton was twofold: end the civil war in Afghanistan and bring Osama bin Laden to justice. Also on board was NBC diplomatic correspondent Andrea Mitchell, who was to cover the story of America's encounter with the Taliban. This was the first and only high-level U.S. visit to Afghanistan during the reign of the Taliban, and it would be the only time a senior American official met face to face with the Taliban to press them to hand over bin Laden.

The visit was surreal. Our hosts had arranged an honor guard at the airport: a row of soldiers in fancy uniforms left over from an earlier government. On the streets of the city the real Taliban were everywhere in evidence—armed to the teeth but without uniforms. Women were covered from top to bottom in chadors. Religious police were out enforcing the Taliban's cruel fanaticism. They were eager to show us only one sight in the bombed and destroyed city: the lamppost from which they had hanged the communist leader of Afghanistan after dragging him out of his asylum in the UN headquarters and torturing and butchering him.

The meeting was equally surreal. The Taliban sat on the floor, shoeless, with their automatic rifles at hand. Many showed the scars of battle and were missing arms or legs. They were completely uninterested in any talk of a cease-fire with their Northern Alliance enemies or any negotiations to end the civil war. Their enemies were infidels to be killed. When the snow melted in the Hindu Kush, the mountain range between Pakistan and Afghanistan, war would resume.

As for bin Laden, he was their guest. They could not hand him over, nor would they. In truth, he was too valuable to them and especially to their leader, Mullah Omar, to give up. From their many excuses, it was clear that talking would get us nowhere.

## THE RISE OF MULLAH OMAR AND HIS TALIBAN

Today's jihadist movement in the Sunni Muslim world has its roots in Afghanistan, in the resistance to the massive Soviet invasion launched in December 1979. Elements of the Soviet Fortieth Army marched in after the Soviet intelligence service, the KGB, had the country's communist dictator assassinated for failing to deliver a stable Marxist government. In response, President Jimmy Carter ordered the CIA to support the mujahedin resistance, which President Ronald Reagan backed on an even vaster scale in the 1980s. At the time, few thought the mujahedin could win: the CIA station chief in Kabul predicted the Soviet forces would smash them in less than six months.[1] Instead the resistance smashed the Fortieth Army.

The mujahedin found their key support in Pakistan and its Inter-Services Intelligence Directorate (ISI), which trained the fighters and coordinated their operations. For its part, the CIA gave money—close to $6 billion all told—and helped arrange shipments of arms to the ISI.[2] Saudi Arabia stepped forward as well, matching U.S. funds dollar for dollar and providing intelligence help and hundreds of volunteers. Egypt, China, the United Kingdom, France, and Israel also sent help, either directly or through the United States. The CIA tried to maintain ties to all mujahedin groups, but the ISI controlled the situation on the ground far more. The ISI's role in the war has been brilliantly related by the head of its Afghan department in the 1980s, Brigadier Mohammed Yousaf. In *The Bear Trap: Afghanistan's Untold Story*, Yousaf lays out in detail ISI's method of managing the war. He also argues that at the end, when victory was complete over the Soviet invaders, the United States abandoned Pakistan, leaving Islamabad to fend for itself in trying to manage the difficult and ugly outcome of the holy war.

Indeed, many if not most Pakistanis believe the United States used their country in the 1980s to defeat the Soviet Union and then callously betrayed its ally, ignoring the consequences of the forces unleashed by the war. The betrayal came in the summer of 1990: the United States imposed sanctions on Pakistan, complaining that its nuclear weapons program had reached a sufficient point where a weapon had been produced, as determined by the CIA. U.S. military assistance to Pakistan, including the delivery of F-16 fighter aircraft already paid for by Islamabad, was summarily suspended. According to many Pakistanis, the CIA could have made this judgment at any time in the preceding decade but only did so when the United States no longer needed Pakistan's help in the Afghan war. They are, of course, correct.

Pakistan was left to deal with the aftermath of the war. More than 2 million Afghans had taken refuge in Pakistan. This large displaced population bred violence and extremism. The "Kalashnikov Culture" emerging along the borderlands occupied by the refugees and the mujahedin contributed to a growing breakdown in law and order in an area that had never seen strong central government authority.

Back in Afghanistan, the mujahedin tried to march on Kabul but failed to take the city. The ISI told then prime minister Benazir Bhutto that Kabul would fall in a matter of days.[3] The CIA's Special National Intelligence Estimate predicted "the Najibullah regime will not long survive the completion of Soviet withdrawal" and might collapse even before it ended.[4] Instead it took almost three years. Only when the communist government collapsed after the defection to the mujahedin of its most powerful commander, Abdul Rashid Dostam, did the city fall to Pakistan's clients. Dostam had been the most successful communist military leader in the northern part of the country, commanding a 30,000-man division of his fellow Uzbeks. Suddenly in 1992 he had a change of heart and became a friend of the West.

Most likely he had come to the conclusion that communism was a spent force and it was time to go with the winners. Unfortunately, the mujahedin leaders, joined now by Dostam, promptly went to war with each other, beginning a gruesome civil war that did far more damage to Kabul and other major cities than the war with the Soviet invaders had done. Kabul was completely destroyed in the battles. When I visited it in 1998, it looked like Berlin in 1945.

This internal conflict among the mujahedin parties paved the way for Taliban ascendance. The movement arose in the southern Pashtun provinces, led by a much-wounded veteran who had lost an eye in the jihad against the Soviet invaders, Mullah Omar. Omar proclaimed a new holy war had to be waged to purge the country of the warring parties and to install a pure Islamic government that would restore law and order.

Mullah Omar is a shadowy figure, even by the standards of the jihadist movement. What is known is that he comes from Afghanistan's Oruzugan Province, one of the poorest and most backward parts of a poor and backward country. He seems to have had little if any formal education outside of the religious schools, the madrassas, where the Taliban recruits its members. Omar is a graduate of one of the most famous madrassas in Pakistan, Darul uloom Haqqania. He was by all accounts a brave fighter in the anti-Soviet conflict but not a major figure in the mujahedin leadership. Instead he rose to prominence afterward.

Omar was outraged by the infighting of the mujahedin and even more so by their increasing depredations on the Afghan people as they became increasingly dependent on crime to finance their activities. Apparently the rape of two small boys by one mujahedin leader was the breaking point. Omar organized a group of followers to punish the criminals by hanging them from the gun barrel of a tank. That incident gave birth to the Taliban.

From the outset, the Taliban found support in Pakistan. While still keeping ties open to the other factions, the Pakistanis saw in the Taliban a mechanism to end the civil war and consolidate their influence over Afghanistan through a proxy. The ISI was confident that it could control the Taliban leadership and use the organization to solidify Pakistan's preeminence in the country. Pakistan became the first country in the world to recognize the Taliban government (only two followed: Saudi Arabia and the United Arab Emirates). The ISI cadre began to advise the Taliban militia, and the Taliban recruited heavily among the madrassas in Pakistan, especially in the border region.

Over time, Pakistan became increasingly tied to the Taliban. The extent of Pakistani assistance has always been a source of some contention, with Pakistan trying to cover its tracks and its enemies trying to exaggerate its role. In any case, Pakistani aid was vital to the Taliban military and to the prosecution of the war against the Taliban's rivals, who organized themselves into a new axis called the Northern Alliance after the Taliban took control of Kabul in September 1996. Pakistani advisers assisted the Taliban military, and Pakistani experts handled the logistics to maintain and operate the Taliban's more sophisticated weapons, including tanks and aircraft.[5] The ISI also used Afghanistan as a training base for Kashmiri jihadists needed to support the insurgency in Kashmir that Pakistan had been sponsoring since the late 1980s. By training operatives in Afghanistan, the ISI sought a measure of deniability to Indian charges that Pakistan was a state sponsor of terrorism.

Meanwhile the Taliban were also developing another patron, Osama bin Laden and his al Qaeda organization, which became in effect a state within the state. Mullah Omar was drawn steadily closer to bin Laden as the two collaborated. At first the two were wary of each other. When bin Laden arrived in Afghanistan seeking refuge with some of his old war comrades, a summons from Omar—delivered by the ISI—took him to Kandahar. In time he moved his family and infrastructure to Kandahar as well.

Kandahar was the real capital of the Islamic Emirate. Omar did not feel comfortable in cosmopolitan Kabul, long a center of multiple cultures and sects and not a Pashtun city. Even worse, it had a large Shia population, which was anathema to the extremely anti-Shia Omar. Kandahar, on the other hand, boasted religious significance: the Prophet Muhammad's cloak had for centuries been housed in the city's mosque. Omar took the highly symbolic step of removing the priceless relic from its holy site and donning it before a gathering of his followers. By this extremely provocative and dramatic act, Mullah Omar proclaimed himself the leader of the ummah, "Commander of the Faithful," in effect making himself known as the Prophet's heir.

Kandahar is named for Alexander the Great, whose army passed through it on the way to India. Lying in a flat depression without mountains to hide in, it proved the most dangerous battlefield for the mujahedin as Soviet aircraft carpet-bombed it to suppress the jihad. During the Soviet era its population fell from a quarter million to about 25,000, but it recovered quickly after the invaders left.[6]

Governing Afghanistan from Kandahar, Omar rarely met with non-Muslims (perhaps less than a half-dozen all told) and rarely with any foreigners, even fellow Muslims. The Pakistanis who did deal directly with him found him to be a frightening and difficult figure. Prime Minister Nawaz Sharif told Bill Richardson in 1998 that Omar was unstable and a crazed fanatic.

Crazy or not, Mullah Omar and his Taliban army gradually took over more and more of the country, advancing west and north from their base in the south with the help of Pakistani and al Qaeda reinforcements. In the summer after Richardson's visit, they confronted and defeated Dostam's Uzbek forces in the north. On August 8 the Taliban entered the north's major city, Mazar-i Sharif, and began to hunt down their enemies. Tajiks and Uzbeks loyal to Dostam or other Northern Alliance leaders were rounded up and many summarily executed. But the Taliban reserved its greatest enmity for Afghanistan's Shia minority, the Hazara, who were killed by the hundreds in the massacre that followed the fall of the city.[7] The next month the Taliban entered the Hazara stronghold of Bamian and killed thousands more Hazara civilians.

To the Taliban's ultimate discomfort, the victims at Mazar-i Sharif included ten Iranian diplomats and an Iranian journalist. At first the Taliban tried to cover up the crime, saying they did not know what had happened to the Iranians. When Mullah Omar finally said they were "probably dead," Iran blamed him personally for ordering their elimination and mobilized its army and Revolutionary Guard (IRGC) on the border.[8] In fact, the Iranians were killed by militiamen from a Pakistani Sunni group that specializes in killing Shia—the Sipah-e-Sahaba, which has long-standing ties to the ISI and a close relationship with both al Qaeda and the Taliban.[9]

By mid-September the Iranians had almost a quarter million army and guard troops on the border, commanded by IRGC's Brigadier General Azizollah Jaafari. Artillery skirmishes were becoming a daily event. Iran demanded the return of its diplomats and a formal apology. The Taliban were intransigent at first and threatened to attack Iranian cities if war broke out.

Seeing a disaster approaching on its western front, Pakistan quickly sought to defuse tensions by mediating between Tehran and Kandahar. Islamabad did not want a Sunni-Shia war on its border with its client outgunned by Iran. After several tense weeks, the bodies of the dead diplomats were returned to Iran between late September and mid-October 1998. Iran, which had publicly called for the overthrow of the Taliban regime, was appeased, and tensions eventually subsided.

The incident underscored the Taliban's extremism and isolation. Its Sunni leadership, especially Mullah Omar, saw the Hazara and Iranians as apostates for their Shia beliefs. Pakistan found itself tied to a regime having no support elsewhere in the Muslim world and engaging in increasingly violent and extreme actions against fellow Muslims.

With the Taliban's deepening isolation, bin Laden and Omar grew more and more dependent on each other. Bin Laden swore allegiance and fealty to the Commander of the Faithful, as did Zawahiri. They provided him with money and Arab troops to fight the Northern Alliance. These troops—while relatively small in number compared with the Taliban's Afghan and Pakistani forces—were extremely reliable and fanatic and played an increasingly important role in the combat with the alliance.

Not a major Islamist ideologue or a writer, Omar seemed to find in bin Laden as well as in Zawahiri the intellectual complement to his life of action. They provided the narrative that justified the Taliban's cruel and oppressive rule and government.

Bin Laden's worldview apparently also helped persuade the Taliban to destroy Afghanistan's most famous historical treasure, the centuries-old statues of Buddha in Bamian. To extreme Wahhabi believers like bin Laden, these were idols to a pagan god. To Mullah Omar and his followers, they were also symbols of a pre-Islamic past they wanted to obliterate. In 2001 the Taliban systematically destroyed them with the help of Pakistani military advisers, according to the residents of the region.[10]

By then al Qaeda was not only helping to recruit and train Arabs for the battlefield in Afghanistan, but it was also providing training venues for terrorist operations outside the country. On August 7, 1998, the day before the Taliban entered Mazar, al Qaeda carried out its first major terrorist attack, the bombings of the American embassies in Kenya and Tanzania. The investigation of those attacks was quickly able to trace them back to Afghanistan and bin Laden.

## THE AMERICAN RESPONSE

Responding to very time-sensitive intelligence information, President Bill Clinton ordered a cruise missile attack on a training camp in Afghanistan where bin Laden was expected to meet with some of his cadres. The attack failed in its mission when bin Laden did not appear at the scene at the exact moment of the attack. Some believe that he had just left a half hour before, others that he made a last-minute decision to stay in Kabul that day. Most of those killed or injured in the strike were in fact Kashmiris and their ISI trainers. Indeed, the majority of fighters in the camp were from the Harakat ul Mujahedin (HUM), a Kashmiri group very close to ISI. Probably twenty or so HUM fighters died in the attack.[11] This suggests not that the intelligence was wrong, but that bin Laden had such close contact with the Kashmiri group that he would visit its training camp. In any case, al Qaeda remained undamaged, and bin Laden's prestige soared. The Taliban feigned ignorance of his activities, while Pakistan protested the U.S. attack. Meanwhile, the connections between all of them deepened.

I was part of the small group in the White House that planned the attack on bin Laden. There was considerable argument over the targets. All agreed that attacking the camp bin Laden was going to visit made sense: killing him was the most important purpose of the attack. The proposed targets in Sudan were much less significant, but the consensus was that a hit outside Afghanistan was important to underscore the global nature of the growing al Qaeda threat.

In any case, the attempt on bin Laden failed. Worse still, the ties between Pakistan, the Taliban, al Qaeda, and Kashmiri terrorists grew even stronger. This was dramatically illustrated a year later when Kashmiri operatives hijacked Air India's Flight 814 following takeoff from Katmandu, Nepal, and diverted it to Mullah Omar's unofficial capital in Kandahar. The ISI station in Katmandu allegedly helped the hijackers penetrate airport security in Nepal. After eight days in Kandahar, the 155 hostages were released when India agreed to free three of its most wanted Kashmiri prisoners. One of them was Maulana Masood Azhar, leader of the Kashmiri HUM jihadist group whose facility the United States had bombed only months before in order to kill bin Laden. Azhar immediately traveled to Pakistan to meet with supporters and raise funds for the Kashmiri cause. ISI was his host for the victory tour in Pakistan.

Watching the hijack drama from the White House, I pressed hard for the United States to give India more help. I felt that the fight was as much ours as India's and that we had a vital interest in the outcome of the hijacking. To me the incident was an unmistakable wake-up call: this act of international air piracy—linked directly to the Taliban backed by al Qaeda, the Kashmiris, and the ISI—clearly indicated a threshold had been crossed.

According to India's foreign minister, Jaswant Singh, who negotiated the hostages' release on the ground in Kandahar and thus saw the terrorists up close, the operation was a joint one between ISI, the Taliban, the Kashmiris, and al Qaeda. Singh correctly notes that the hijacking was in some ways the "dress rehearsal" for 9/11 since it included many of the same characters in the planning of both operations.[12] Others have noted that bin Laden himself played a key role "behind the scenes" in the negotiations between the various parties, even hosting the victory celebration dinner.[13]

The United States and the international community reacted to the developing terror apparatus in Afghanistan and Pakistan with increasing frustration. Washington tried to break up the nexus and bring bin Laden to justice in both bilateral and multilateral forums. The bilateral approach came first.

Even before the embassy attacks in Africa, the United States tried to persuade the Taliban and Pakistan to arrest bin Laden and destroy his apparatus. In the spring of 1998 President Clinton dispatched Bill Richardson to South Asia with a specific mission: to visit Afghanistan. After stops in Bangladesh, India, and Pakistan, Richardson and a small U.S. team traveled to Kabul, as mentioned earlier, for the first and what would be the only senior U.S. engagement with the Taliban leadership. The Pakistanis had brokered the meeting at U.S. request and persuaded the Taliban to meet with Richardson at a senior level. I was part of the U.S. team.

The Taliban's number two, Mullah Mohammed Rabbani, headed the Taliban team. A meeting with Mullah Omar was not an option: as also mentioned earlier, he never met with foreign officials, rarely met with infidels, and seldom left Kandahar. The talks took place in the Afghan presidential palace over looking the city. Richardson began by trying to persuade the Taliban to agree to a cease-fire with the Northern Alliance to pave the way for a negotiated end to the civil war. The assumption was that ending the fighting would reduce the Taliban's need for Arab volunteers and would set the stage for an international relief effort to help Afghanistan recover from a quarter century of warfare.

The Taliban was not interested. The war against the Northern Alliance was a holy obligation and could not end until the Taliban had conquered the entire country. There was no point in negotiations or a cease-fire. Once the winter snow had melted in the mountains, the Taliban would press the military offensive, Mullah Mohammed Rabbani promised, and complete the conquest of Afghanistan.

Richardson next tried a different tack. As bin Laden's host, the Taliban was responsible for his actions. Bin Laden and al Qaeda had declared war on the United States and advocated the murder of its citizens. Thus it was the Taliban's responsibility to control his activity and turn him over to the Saudi authorities to prosecute him for sponsoring terrorism. The Taliban refused this request as well. Mullah Rabbani simply said bin Laden was their guest and they would monitor his activity themselves. As for his threats to kill Americans, bin Laden was not a qualified Islamic jurist and therefore no one would take his admonitions seriously. There was no reason to be alarmed. The talks ended with no agreement on the issues and no Taliban acknowledgment of its responsibility to restrain al Qaeda.[14]

Returning to Islamabad after a visit to the Northern Alliance in Sherbigan, Richardson and I urged the Pakistanis to pressure the Taliban. Pakistan was the Taliban's patron and sponsor, provided them with critical military aid, and was their only access to the rest of the world. Islamabad had to persuade the Taliban to behave as a responsible member of the international community if it wanted them to be accepted into that community. Prime Minister Sharif promised to work on the issue but gave little evidence of taking concrete steps in that direction. Rather, he stressed how unpleasant the Taliban could be to deal with and how difficult Pakistan's own relations with them were. Moreover, Pakistan had a vital strategic interest in a strong and friendly relationship with the Taliban as it faced a hostile India. Pakistan's 1,560-kilometer border with Afghanistan was largely unguarded, Sharif noted, and this allowed Pakistan to keep most of its military on the Indian border.

After the Indian and Pakistani nuclear tests in May 1998, the al Qaeda issue briefly shifted to the back burner of U.S.-Pakistani relations, only to move forward again when the two American embassies were attacked in

August. Clinton again pressed Sharif to rein in the Taliban and through the Taliban to get bin Laden. The chairman of the Joint Chiefs of Staff, General Joe Ralston, traveled to Pakistan to deliver the message directly to the Pakistani leadership and also to assure them that the cruise missile attack on the camp in Afghanistan was not a threat to Pakistan itself.

The Saudis, too, were leaning on the Taliban. Before the attacks on the U.S. embassies in East Africa, Saudi intelligence chief Prince Turki made another of his visits to Pakistan and Afghanistan. He met directly with Mullah Omar and pressed him to turn bin Laden over to the kingdom. Omar did not reject the request outright but asked for some time. When Turki returned with a planeload of commandos to arrest bin Laden and take him to the kingdom—this was after the East Africa bombings and the U.S. attempt on bin Laden's life—he found Omar had taken a "180-degree" turn. He refused to turn over bin Laden and was sharply critical of Saudi Arabia and its relationship with the United States. According to Turki, the meeting degenerated into a shouting match, with Omar delivering a "diatribe against the Kingdom as if it was scripted by bin Laden." Turki stood up, said he would not listen to any more "insults," and left.[15]

Clinton raised the bin Laden issue with Sharif directly during the prime minister's visit to Washington on December 3, 1998. Clinton told Sharif that Pakistan would shortly be compensated for several dozen F-16s held by the United States since August 1990, when it had determined Pakistan was building a nuclear weapon in violation of promises not to do so. This was a very welcome announcement for the prime minister. The president asked Sharif to use Pakistan's leverage with the Taliban to help fight al Qaeda. Sharif promised to review his options. The two spoke by phone again on December 18 to confirm the final details of the F-16 package and to get Sharif's update on bin Laden. Sharif suggested that the United States help train an ISI commando team to take care of the bin Laden problem. As he explained it, Pakistan could not be publicly seen to be taking a tough line on the Taliban—that would only help India—so Pakistan would work covertly with the United States on the al Qaeda issue.

The proposal seemed far-fetched to me and most of the U.S. team. The ISI was fully embedded in Afghanistan and had intimate relations with the Taliban. Why would it need U.S. assistance to bring bin Laden to justice? Sharif seemed to be offering a runaround, not a serious proposal. But eager to try anything, Clinton agreed to pursue the idea. It proved to be only a means of keeping the Americans occupied, not a serious proposal. Nothing came of it.

Clinton raised the issue again with Sharif when they met on the margins of the funeral of Jordan's King Hussein in Amman, Jordan, on February 8, 1999. The short discussion was dominated by the president's concerns about another possible al Qaeda attack. He urged the prime minister to act before more terrorism was committed. And again the Pakistanis made vague promises to address the issue but took no action with their clients.

The president had one more opportunity to raise the issue face to face with Sharif during their last encounter on July 4, 1999, at Blair House in Washington. Sharif had appealed to the president for help to end the bloody border war that Pakistan had started in May 1999 in the Kargil area of Kashmir. Pakistani troops backed by militants from the Kashmiri groups, especially from the HUM group that had been involved in the hijacking of the Indian airliner, moved across the Line of Control, which divided Kashmir and occupied key strategic positions threatening Indian supply lines in the province.[16] By early July the conflict was threatening to escalate to a larger conventional war along the entire border and perhaps even a nuclear exchange. The meeting in Blair House was therefore focused on the immediate danger of averting a larger war and possible nuclear crisis.

Nonetheless, Clinton urged Sharif to follow through on his previous promises and do something about Afghanistan and al Qaeda. The meeting was very testy, with sharp words from Clinton. He said Pakistan had done nothing to help with the Taliban and al Qaeda ever since Osama bin Laden had declared war against Americans. He wanted Sharif to know what a risk Pakistan was taking by supporting the Taliban. In the end, the Blair House summit succeeded in ending the Kargil war but failed to advance the search for bin Laden or resolve the Taliban problem.

Clinton and his team would have one more shot at trying to persuade the Pakistani government to do the right thing in regard to Afghanistan when the president traveled to Islamabad in March 2000 to meet with the new Pakistani leader, General Pervez Musharraf, who had assumed power in a military coup after the Kargil war. Clinton arrived in Islamabad after spending five days in India, where he held extensive discussions with Indian leaders, addressed the Indian parliament, and visited several major cities besides New Delhi. The Pakistan visit, in contrast, would last only five hours and be confined to a short visit to the capital, talks with Musharraf, and a televised speech to the Pakistani people. The abbreviated visit was a reflection of U.S. opposition to military dictatorships, a policy that had already led to further sanctions on Pakistan after the coup.

To add to the tension, the president's Secret Service advisers were deeply concerned about the potential for an al Qaeda attack on the president's party while he was in Pakistan. There had been a rumor of a planned attack in Bangladesh, at the start of the visit to South Asia, and the Secret Service worried that bin Laden would strike while the president was literally in his back yard. As a consequence, the city of Islamabad was virtually locked down during the brief visit.[17]

The ride into Islamabad from the airport was eerie. There were no people on the streets, only soldiers and policemen. But from every lamppost and overpass hung enormous posters with messages in English imploring Clinton to address the Kashmir issue. Some even asked the president to devote "only 10 percent" of the time given to Palestine to Kashmir. Others had grim photographs of victims of the conflict.

Clinton raised the Afghan problem directly in his meeting with Musharraf, pressing him to use Pakistan's leverage over the Taliban to persuade them to stop supporting terrorism and to arrest bin Laden and bring him to justice. I was with the president and was struck by the forcefulness of his message. Musharraf was equally direct and clear: he would do no such thing. Musharraf explained that Afghanistan was of vital interest to Pakistan. It gave Pakistan strategic depth in its struggle with India. With an unfriendly Afghanistan, Pakistan would have been wedged between two hostile neighbors and its army left to struggle on two fronts, which would have put it at a disadvantage against a stronger India. Therefore Pakistan had to maintain close ties with the Taliban and could not try to put pressure on them on America's behalf. Doing so would also be unwise, he noted, because the Taliban had the capability to cause serious unrest among Pakistan's own Pashtun tribes in the border region. Strategically, Musharraf stressed, Pakistan needed a quiet border with Afghanistan so that it could focus its resources, especially its army, on the Indian frontier.

By the end of 2000 the bilateral approach to the terrorism issue and Pakistan had reached a dead end. During those negotiations, the United States had also led an effort to use international forums, especially the

United Nations, to press the Taliban to give up bin Laden. The multilateral effort began immediately after the African bombings and the announcement of the UN Security Council's Resolution 1185 condemning the attacks, which, however, made no specific mention of the Taliban or bin Laden. In an energetic drive, U.S. diplomacy prepared a comprehensive intelligence case to demonstrate the ties between al Qaeda and the African bombings, the Taliban role as al Qaeda's host, and the threat al Qaeda posed to the peace and security of the international community.

The result was the passage of UNSCR 1214 on December 8, 1998, which covered a wide variety of issues related to Afghanistan but highlighted terrorism, especially the Taliban's role in "sheltering and training" terrorists in their territory. It demanded an end to the Taliban's practice of providing "sanctuary" for terrorists. It also called for an immediate cease-fire in the civil war and threatened sanctions if the Taliban did not comply. The resolution had unanimous backing. By the end of 1999, all of the permanent members of the Security Council saw the Taliban as a threat to regional stability and all were concerned about its role in sponsoring terror. The resolution also called upon all UN members to do their utmost to persuade the Taliban to comply with its terms—a clear message to Pakistan.

Not only did the Taliban remain intransigent and Pakistan refuse to change its approach, but Pakistani military assistance to the Taliban intensified. On October 15, 1999, within a year of Resolution 1214, the UN Security Council passed Resolution 1267, again demanding an end to the Taliban's provision of safe haven for terrorists. It specifically mentioned Osama bin Laden by name, noting that he was under indictment in the United States for the African bombings, and asked that he be turned over. In addition, the council imposed sanctions, including a ban on all flights into and out of Afghanistan and a freeze on Taliban funds abroad.

Still the Taliban refused to comply, and Pakistan stood by for another year without using its leverage. Thus on December 19, 2000, the council adopted UNSCR 1333 targeting Pakistan more directly: it called on all states to cease providing arms and ammunition to the Taliban, prohibit the training of Taliban fighters by their nationals, halt any advisory support to the Taliban military, and withdraw any advisers or volunteers fighting with the Taliban. Pakistan did not have to be named explicitly: it was the only country in the world providing military aid to the Taliban. The resolution also called for the closure of all Taliban offices worldwide and of the Afghan national airline, ARIANA, worldwide.

When neither the Taliban nor Pakistan complied with 1333, follow-up Resolution 1363 was passed on July 30, 2001, with the support of the new Bush administration in Washington. It created a monitoring team to oversee the implementation of 1333, thus becoming the last of five UN resolutions after the African bombings that called on the Taliban and Pakistan to take action against al Qaeda. The fact that still nothing had changed in the three years since UNSCR 1185 became all too clear on September 11, 2001.

Between 1998 and 2001 the United States, the United Nations, and the international community made a major effort to persuade Pakistan to rein in the Taliban and stop its support for international terrorism. Though it paid occasional lip service to the campaign, Pakistan took no action against the Taliban. If anything, it increased military assistance to the Taliban, in direct violation of a UN stricture. Two Pakistani governments, one elected and the other a military dictatorship, refused to use the leverage they had over their client to prevent terror.

Instead, Pakistan persisted in keeping Kabul friendly so as to maintain strategic depth against India. According to George Tenet, then director of Central Intelligence and the man most immediately focused on bringing Osama bin Laden to justice, "The Pakistanis always knew more than they were telling us and were singularly uncooperative [in this period]. My own belief, which was widely shared in the CIA, was that what the Pakistanis really feared was a two-front conflict with the Indians trying to reclaim Kashmir and the Taliban trying to export radical Islam across the border . . . that meant not cooperating with us in hunting down Bin Laden."[18] To this end, it had encouraged the growth of the Taliban in the mid-1990s, only to find itself strapped to a tiger that it could not fully control and whose polices were often embarrassing. The Pakistani leadership, especially in the army and ISI, would not change course until too late.

## SEPTEMBER 11: THE TURNING POINT, OR WAS IT?

On September 9, 2001, Osama bin Laden repaid Mullah Omar for all his help in hosting al Qaeda and all the difficulty it had led to. In a brilliant operation, the al Qaeda organization killed Omar's number-one enemy in

Afghanistan, the military leader of the Northern Alliance, Ahmad Shah Massoud. Massoud was the most capable and effective leader of the mujahedin in the Afghan war against the Soviet invaders, especially in the strategic Panshjer Valley north of the capital. More than a dozen Soviet offensives had failed to defeat Massoud's forces. After the fall of the communist regime in 1992, Massoud became defense minister in the new coalition government, but his followers quickly came into conflict with the other mujahedin leaders, and the city collapsed into civil war.

When the Taliban closed in, Massoud left Kabul and retreated to his strongholds in the Panshjer Valley and Badakhshan Province, in the remote northeastern corner of the country. As the Taliban gradually consolidated their control over the rest of the country, Massoud became the last bastion of resistance and the de facto leader of the Northern Alliance. His followers were primarily, though not entirely, from his own Tajik minority. He was an expert in guerrilla warfare, a student of Mao, and a great admirer of Charles de Gaulle.

Massoud was a very private man who avoided the limelight even though it sought him. He was expected at the meeting Bill Richardson had with the rest of the Northern Alliance but failed to show up, despite frequently saying he wanted more American support. He did not travel outside the country until April 2001, when he visited Belgium and France to ask for European support against the Taliban. He asked European leaders in the European Parliament in Strasbourg to pressure the Pakistanis to stop helping the Taliban, whose campaigns he felt "would not even last a year" without Pakistan's support.[19] He also met with CIA officers in Paris to discuss aid from America.[20]

By the time he returned, his followers controlled less than 10 percent of the country and constituted the last significant military force confronting the Taliban and their Arab allies. Al Qaeda planned his death carefully. An al Qaeda cell in Brussels, Belgium, organized the attack on the order of bin Laden. Belgium has a considerable community of Muslims, most from Morocco, Tunisia, or Turkey. Many live in rundown neighborhoods with high unemployment and are fertile recruiting fields for the jihad.

The plot was organized by a Tunisian named Tarek ben Habib Maaroufi who had been involved in jihadist activity for Tunisian and Algerian groups for almost a decade. Twice the Tunisian government had asked for his extradition, but as he was a naturalized Belgian citizen the requests were turned down. He was briefly arrested in 1995 but released in 1996. In late 2000 he visited Afghanistan and met with bin Laden to receive his instructions.

In Belgium, Maaroufi recruited two martyrs for a suicide operation: Abd Satter Dahmane and Bouraoui al Ouaer. Both were Tunisian immigrants but had lived in Belgium for some time. Dahmane was a Koran teacher who had visited Afghanistan in mid-2001 and met with bin Laden.[21] He and his wife stayed in the bin Laden family camp for several weeks while he and Ouaer trained for their assignment. They were taught to operate their explosive device and to handle themselves as journalists. Then they returned to Belgium. There they received new Belgian passports from a hoard of blank passports stolen from the Belgian consulate in Strasbourg and bought illegally by Maaroufi's accomplices. Next they traveled to London, where they received papers identifying them as journalists, and a letter was sent to Massoud asking for an interview allegedly based on the popular impression his European visit had made in the Belgian Muslim community. From London they went to Pakistan and then on to Tajikistan and across the border into Massoud's stronghold.

For some nine days they waited patiently for an audience. They did nothing to draw attention to themselves or to signal in any way that they were not the journalists they claimed to be. Finally, on September 9, 2001, they got their appointment. At noon they entered Massoud's office and set up their camera. They asked one question about Osama bin Laden. When Massoud replied, they detonated the explosives hidden in the camera. Massoud was fatally wounded and died within a few minutes. The cameraman died instantly; his companion was killed trying to run away. Osama had delivered his gift to Omar. Later bin Laden sent Dahmane's widow a letter with some money and a martyr's tape of her husband telling her of his love but indicating that he was "already on the other side" in heaven.[22]

The timing was critical. Bin Laden fully expected an American attack after 9/11 and wanted to remove the Northern Alliance's leader and thus weaken it before any such retaliation might come. This move indicates that the primary intention of the Manhattan Raid was to provoke an American invasion of Afghanistan. For bin Laden, such an invasion would recreate the scenario that had crippled the Soviet Union. He hoped to do the same to the United States and also eliminate a despised enemy. Even now his hatred for Massoud burns strong. In a message in late December 2007 he reminded listeners that "Ahmad Shah Massoud went to the Crusaders in Europe offering himself as a tool to topple the Islamic Emirate of Afghanistan. Some misled ones claim that he is a martyr."[23]

On September 11, 2001, Pakistan's policy of appeasing the Taliban and supporting its military came to a dead end, but only for the moment. Within hours of the attacks in New York and Washington, the CIA told the White House that al Qaeda was responsible and had planned the attack from its base in Afghanistan. In a few days, the UN Security Council issued a statement demanding that the Taliban hand over bin Laden. Jean-David Levitte, French ambassador and council president in September, said, "There is one and only one message the Security Council has for the Taliban: implement United Nations Security Council resolutions . . . immediately and unconditionally."[24]

By coincidence, the director of the ISI, Lieutenant General Mahmud Ahmed, was in Washington on September 11 making a series of calls at the CIA, State Department, and National Security Council. No one knew more about the extent of Taliban-Pakistan cooperation than Ahmed. No one was closer to Musharraf. In fact, Mahmud had been a key player in the coup that put Musharraf in power and had been a commander at Kargil. He was immediately summoned to the State Department to meet with Deputy Secretary of State Richard Armitage.

According to Musharraf's account of that meeting, Armitage told Ahmed that Pakistan had to choose whether to be with the United States or against it. Should Pakistan stand by its relationship with the Taliban, Armitage threatened to bomb Pakistan back into the Stone Age. Armitage has denied he threatened to attack Pakistan but has confirmed that he gave the ISI leader an ultimatum: either help America or be seen as an enemy. Indeed, those were his instructions from the White House.

Almost immediately Pakistan's policy toward the Taliban changed. Pakistan's ambassador in Washington, Maleeha Lodhi, who had been handpicked by Musharraf for the job, told the American administration that Pakistan would cooperate fully. More important, Musharraf sent a delegation to Afghanistan led by General Ahmed to present the international demands to the Taliban. Stalling for time, Mullah Omar convened a meeting of Taliban religious scholars to review the situation. The Shura

Council recommended that Omar try to persuade bin Laden to leave Afghanistan of his own will. Whether Omar did so or not is unknown. What is clear is that bin Laden did not leave, and the United States embarked upon Operation Enduring Freedom in October to assist the Northern Alliance in toppling the Islamic Emirate. General Ahmed was fired from his post a few days later, apparently for lack of enthusiasm in the new policy toward his former clients.

By September 2001 Pakistani aid to the Taliban was critical to the group's survival. Ahmed Rashid, a leading expert on the Taliban, estimated that up to 60,000 Pakistani Islamic students had fought in Afghanistan in support of the Taliban, dozens of Pakistani military officers were advising the group, and small units of the elite Special Services Group commandos (the unit Musharraf had once commanded) were engaged in combat operations with the Taliban forces. As he put it, "Pakistan's knowledge of the Taliban's military machine, storage facilities, supply lines and leadership hierarchy was total."[25]

Shortly after the start of military action, Pakistan deserted its Taliban ally. Its military advisers, pilots, tank crews, and other military personnel fled the country back to Pakistan. Some Pakistani troops had to be airlifted out of Afghanistan after being surrounded by the advancing Northern Alliance forces from Konduz in the northern part of the country. Others simply drove overland to Pakistan. Without their allies, the Taliban were even more hopelessly outgunned by the U.S.-backed Alliance. Their resistance quickly collapsed. By the end of the year the Islamic Emirate was replaced by a government installed by the Northern Alliance. Ironically, it was led by Mohammed Karzai, who had been the Taliban's first choice to represent the Islamic Emirate as its ambassador to the United Nations.[26] Most of the Taliban fighters simply faded away to their villages in the border region.

Explaining his decision to abandon the Taliban in his memoirs, *In the Line of Fire*, Musharraf said that war gaming prompted by Ahmed's conversation with Armitage led him to conclude that Pakistan could not prevail in a military conflict with the United States—moreover, that India would be the major beneficiary of continuing to stand by the Taliban:

I also analyzed our national interest. First, India had already tried to step in by offering its bases to the US. If we did not join the US, it would accept India's offer. What would happen then? India would gain a golden opportunity with regard to Kashmir. . . . Second, the security of our strategic assets would be jeopardized. We did not want to lose or damage the military parity that we had achieved with India by becoming a nuclear weapons state.[27]

In short, the decision to reverse a decade of Pakistani policy in Afghanistan was a derivative of the underlying Pakistani concern about India. For this, Pakistan was handsomely rewarded. Musharraf got a state visit to Washington in February 2002 and was promised economic assistance and debt relief. In 2003 Musharraf visited Camp David, and President Bush announced a five-year $3 billion economic and military assistance package. In 2004 Pakistan was designated a major ally outside of the North Atlantic Treaty Organization (NATO), which meant additional technology sharing between the two militaries. In 2005 Pakistan was promised the sale of F-16s again to demonstrate the bad old days were truly over. By 2007 Pakistan had received more than $10 billion from the United States, over half in unaccounted funds for the army, a sum equal to all the aid provided by the United States to Pakistan between 1948 and 2001.

Musharraf was careful to give only limited support to the United States in the war on terrorism, however. The Taliban apparatus in Pakistan's madrassas was not dismantled, and many Taliban officials continued to operate in Pakistani cities, particularly Quetta, the capital of Baluchistan. By 2004 they were openly fundraising in Quetta again. No major Taliban official has ever been arrested in Pakistan, while Afghan government authorities claim the ISI is again providing direct aid to the Taliban in its operations against NATO and Afghan army forces, a claim denied by both Musharraf and Mullah Omar.

Pakistan has been more active in arresting al Qaeda operatives, including the alleged mastermind of 9/11, Khalid Sheikh Mohammed, who was captured in March 2003 in a Kashmiri safe house in Rawalpindi (ironically the military capital of Pakistan). But the top leadership of al Qaeda has eluded capture. In response to the Pakistani crackdown on its operatives, bin Laden and his deputy Zawahiri have repeatedly called for Musharraf's overthrow and have plotted to kill him. Up to nine assassination plots have failed. But the al Qaeda leadership remains alive and active in Pakistan, a point confirmed to the Senate in January 2007 by then director of National Intelligence John Negroponte: "Al Qaeda's core elements are resilient. They continue to plot attacks against our homeland and other targets, with the objective of inflicting mass casualties. And they are cultivating stronger operational connections and relationships that radiate outward from their leaders' secure hideout in Pakistan."

Musharraf also promised to crack down on the madrassas and end their use by extremists to indoctrinate fanaticism. In addition, he said he would end the jihadi culture in Pakistan and halt all cross-border terrorist operations into Kashmir and India. None of this has happened. More than one and a half million students still attend unregulated madrassas in Pakistan, and the police authorities in Mumbai implicated the ISI directly in a bombing campaign on the Mumbai metro system that killed 186 people on July 7, 2006.

Nor were the Taliban destroyed by the American campaign in Afghanistan. Both the group and al Qaeda survived. All of this has developed remarkably closely to the script Mullah Omar outlined in late 2001 and early 2002, right after the fall of Kabul and Kandahar. Lamenting the "catastrophe" of the emirate's fall, he said his organization would survive and return to challenge the coalition and its Afghan backers.

Mullah Omar also was quick to predict that he would not be captured by the coalition and would still be able to lead the Taliban in its war: "I am considering two promises. One is the promise of God, the other of Bush. The promise of God is that my land is vast. If you start a journey on God's path, you can reside anywhere and will be protected. The promise of Bush is that there is no place on earth where you can hide that I cannot find you. We will see which promise is fulfilled."[28]

Mullah Omar also put the Taliban struggle after 2001 into a wider context now, associating it with other Islamic struggles against perceived foreign occupiers, especially in Palestine, Kashmir, and after 2003, Iraq. In a message on the Muslim holiday Eid in October 2006, Omar praised Muslim fighters everywhere, especially in Iraq, for fighting the United States.[29] A constant theme in his rhetoric is that the Taliban will defeat it and NATO just as the mujahedin defeated the Soviet Union and the Warsaw Pact. This history is important. Like most people, Afghans remember who promised what—validation occurs when you are seen to be right.

There are at least three key reasons for the Taliban resurgence. First, the Taliban were never fully defeated in 2001. After a few losses on the battlefield because of the Northern Alliance and coalition airpower, the Taliban dispersed. They did not fight for Kabul or Kandahar; rather, they followed classic guerrilla tactics and fled. By early 2002 they were definitely on the ropes, however, and vulnerable to a decisive takedown—which never came.

Instead, the cadres moved to remote areas of Afghanistan like Omar's home province of Oruzugan and went to ground. They bided their time and survived. This proved fairly easy as the new Karzai government and its coalition supporters had far too few security forces to secure and govern the country. And the Taliban adjusted its tactics, adopting new ones such as the use of suicide bombers and improvised explosive devices from the Iraq war. Al Qaeda provided key help in transmitting these techniques from Iraq to Afghanistan. Indeed, according to Taliban leaders, Osama bin Laden is actively involved in planning many of their operations, including the attack on Bagram air base when Vice President Dick Cheney visited Afghanistan in February 2007.

Second, the coalition and especially the United States took its eyes off the Afghan ball when the invasion of Iraq began. Afghanistan was then put on the back burner and given relatively little reconstruction assistance. U.S. aid to Afghanistan, a country devastated by a quarter century of war, totaled less than $1 billion in both 2002 and 2003. Compared with other reconstruction efforts, Afghanistan was simply done on the cheap. Lack of security and economic reconstruction fueled not only the Taliban's revival but also the return of the poppy crop and the drug culture. The Iraq war's impact on the fight against terrorism along the Afghanistan-Pakistan border has been enormous, says Gary Schroen, who led the first CIA team into Afghanistan to fight the Taliban and al Qaeda less than a month after September 11, with promising results initially:

However, as early as March 2002 the U.S. military began to withdraw many of the key units involved in this effort, in order to allow them to regroup and train in preparation for the coming war with Iraq. At the same time, the focus on Iraq also began to increase within the CIA and it became a magnet that drew away personnel and resources, making it increasingly difficult to staff the CIA teams in Afghanistan with experienced paramilitary officers. In late 2003 there was a public discussion in the media of a spring military offensive in the Afghan border regions to root out bin Laden. Spring came and went with no offensive. The U.S. military and the CIA were unable to shift the additional manpower resources to conduct the operation—the demands of Iraq simply did not allow it.[30]

Another senior CIA officer with years of experience in South Asia and counterterrorism, Robert Grenier, agreed: "The best experienced, most qualified people who we had been using in Afghanistan were shifted over to Iraq [in late 2002 and early 2003]. I think we could have done a lot more on the Afghan side if we had more experienced folks."[31] In fact the CIA station set up in Kandahar in late 2001 was closed down in March 2002, along with other stations in major Afghan cities.[32] In short, the Iraq war saved bin Laden and Mullah Omar.

Third, the Taliban benefited from a safe haven and help in Pakistan. Even when the group's long and well-established ties with the ISI and the Pakistan army were cut by Musharraf after 9/11, those with various militant Pakistani and Kashmiri groups remained very much intact. These ties had developed over the course of the 1990s and were most dramatically illustrated during the December 1999 hijacking of Air India's Flight 814 from Katmandu to Kandahar, perpetrated by al Qaeda, the Taliban, and Kashmiris mixed together.

The Afghan government goes even further, suggesting the Pakistani army and ISI still actively assist the Taliban. Afghan authorities say Mullah Omar spends a great deal of his time in Quetta. Musharraf says this is a lie. For his part, Mullah Omar has consistently denied any official Pakistani assistance and calls Musharraf a traitor who should be overthrown and executed.

One thing is very clear. The Taliban and al Qaeda apparatus that operates in Pakistan does so with very close connections to the Pakistani terrorist groups that the ISI helped create in the 1990s. Moreover, the ISI itself continues to have close and intimate ties with these two groups, as Gary Schroen points out:

During the 1980s and the early 1990s, the ISI arranged for Kashmiri militants and their Pakistani supporters to be trained in camps in Afghanistan, alongside foreign volunteers who had come to take part in the Jihad against the Soviets. Many of those foreigners were al Qaeda members and bonds of friendship and common cause were formed among those training together. Since early 2002, whenever a raid has been conducted in Pakistan against an al Qaeda safehouse, al Qaeda members are found being hosted by militant Pakistanis, primarily from Lashkar-e Tayyiba or Jaish-e Mohhammad groups, supporters of the Kashmiri insurgency.[33]

To underscore the point, the arrest of Abu Zubayda, the first senior al Qaeda lieutenant captured after 9/11, took place in a safe house belonging to Sipah-e-Sahaba, a Pakistani terrorist group that specializes in attacks on Shia in the country and has a long history of relations with the ISI.[34]

The Taliban insurgency has recovered with a vengeance. It carried out two martyrdom (suicide) operations in Afghanistan in 2002 and three in 2003. By 2007 they were occurring on an average of 1 every 72 hours, for a total of 140 in the year. With the Taliban-Qaeda alliance growing stronger and deadlier, more Americans died there in 2007 than in any previous year. Much of the country's Pashtun south is now under Taliban control, at least at night.

Furthermore, the Taliban has grown more powerful on the Pakistan side of the border as well. In 2007 there were fifty-six suicide operations inside of Pakistan, thirty-six targeting the Pakistani army. According to the CIA, the al Qaeda–Taliban connection in Pakistan is also responsible for the murder of former Pakistani prime minister Benazir Bhutto.[35] A Pakistani Taliban movement has emerged independent of Mullah Omar's Taliban but is closely affiliated with the Afghan group and al Qaeda. Along with the various Kashmiri groups, this nexus of terror has become a state with a state in the western badlands of Pakistan stretching from Baluchistan in the south to Kashmir in the north. In this hothouse of terror, bin Laden, Zawahiri, and Omar are lurking and planning their next attacks on the United States.

## CHAPTER FIVE

# The Stranger: Zarqawi

I got into the taxi in Baghdad without noticing it had no meter, a sure sign something was amiss. It was a hot morning, already well over 100 degrees Fahrenheit, and I was tired. My alarm bell should have gone off earlier but it didn't. My two colleagues got in the back seat and I sat in the front with the driver. We raced away from the curb, accelerating to 60 for a block and then stopping at the light.

The driver spoke some English, and I asked him to take us to the Ishtar Sheraton. He said, "No problem." Then he pulled out a pistol. He waved it at me: "Isn't this a beautiful weapon?" Not wanting to antagonize a man driving erratically and holding a loaded gun in my face, I replied that indeed it was a fine weapon.

He looked in the back seat at my two colleagues, both female, both terrified. "How about a trade," he suggested, "the pistol for one of your women?" Not your typical conversation with a cab driver in Washington. I demurred. He repeated the offer.

Fortunately, we were now almost at the Sheraton. "No, thanks, pull over," I said and gave him a wad of dinars. We jumped out of the cab and rushed inside. The incident was altogether typical of Saddam's Iraq. The whole thing was a setup: the Iraqi intelligence service knew we were visiting, and even though we were supposed to be "friends" in the late 1980s and had helped Iraq fight Iran, the Mukhabarat (intelligence service) loved to harass us and test our nerves.

There is an Arab word for Iraqis, *tabaghadadi*, which literally means to be from Baghdad. But it also has wider connotations. It means to be tough, brutal, and hard. Those are the traditional attributes of an Iraqi— my cab driver exemplified them. So did the founder and late head of al Qaeda in Iraq, Abu Musaib al-Zarqawi, a man so violent that his own followers nicknamed him "the stranger." Ironically, he was not an Iraqi at all but a Jordanian. All the same, he was the epitome of brutality.

## WHO WAS ZARQAWI AND HOW DID HE GET TO IRAQ?

As explained in chapter 4, the U.S. decision to invade and occupy Iraq was a lifesaver for al Qaeda. In the winter of 2001 and 2002 the movement was on the verge of destruction. It had lost its safe haven in Afghanistan once the Pakistanis pulled the plug on their support for the Taliban (at least temporarily). The CIA had developed extensive contacts with the Northern Alliance before 9/11 and was ready to quickly implement a plan to persuade the various militia warlords in the alliance to attack the Taliban. CIA money, Northern Alliance foot soldiers and cavalry, and American airpower overwhelmed the Taliban far more rapidly and effectively than bin Laden, Zawahiri, and Omar had ever anticipated. They thought they were going to fight the lumbering Soviet Fortieth Army again; instead they encountered a much more nimble enemy.

The successful invasion of Afghanistan was the product of years of planning by the CIA after the East African bombing. The agency carefully rebuilt its contacts with Afghan warlords like Ahmad Shah Massoud and Abdul Rashid Dostam, contacts that had languished in the 1990s while Washington lost interest in Afghanistan. The warlords were eager to renew old acquaintances and had been lobbying for more help for years. In 1996, for example, when I was serving as Deputy Assistant Secretary of Defense for the Near East and South Asia and first met Dotsam, he was asking for U.S. military assistance to his group. Dostam, an Uzbek with Mongol features, is a tough-looking warrior and a big man. His career has seen many transitions from communist general and Soviet ally to mujahedin fighter and despoiler of Kabul, and in the 1990s to a reborn supporter of the West against the Taliban and al Qaeda. He gave me a lovely carpet, bloodred.

In the CIA operation to destroy the Taliban, Gary Schroen, who led the first team of CIA officers into the Panshjer Valley to rally the Northern Alliance to fight the Taliban after the murder of Massoud, persuaded the Northern Alliance to trust the Americans again and to attack the Taliban and their allies.[1] Considerable cash helped Schroen make his case, as did the intense if not always accurate bombing support of the U.S. air force. George Tenet has rightly described the routing of the Taliban and al Qaeda in Afghanistan in 2002 as "one of the great successes in Agency history."[2]

Osama and Omar had not expected this kind of sophisticated attack, nor had they calculated that Pakistan would defect from the cause. They looked for a repeat of the Soviet crumbling but soon found themselves defeated along the front lines in the north, with the Northern Alliance spearheading the rapid fall of Kabul and Kandahar. As noted earlier, however, they pursued classic guerrilla tactics and melted away rather than fight against hopeless odds.

They made one last stand in the Tora Bora Mountains along the Pakistani border before going into Pakistan and beginning the long hideout they have maintained since 2001. How close they came to capture is hotly debated. Many in the CIA feel that the prize was actually within their grasp. Others, especially in the military, disagree. Like a number of others, I tend to believe the United States almost had them. Pakistan's ambassador in the United States, Mahmud ali Durrani, agrees: "I think al Qaeda was almost destroyed in an operational sense. But then al Qaeda got a vacuum in Afghanistan. And they got a motivational area in Iraq. Al Qaeda rejuvenated."[3]

The organization was clearly dealt a staggering blow by Operation Enduring Freedom. The imperative in 2002 was to finish the job and destroy al Qaeda and the Taliban while they were on the ropes. America would be a much safer place today had President George W. Bush continued to relentlessly hunt down Osama, Ayman, and Omar.

Instead he chose to go to war in Iraq. By the summer of 2002 the media abounded with speculation that the United States was considering an invasion of Iraq. The issue was openly debated in Washington, and the administration was clearly encouraging the idea. Al Qaeda noticed.

Even before the fall of Kandahar, al Qaeda embarked on several moves to forge a capability in Iraq and rally the faithful for the coming war there. As early as October 8, 2002, Ayman Zawahiri reported to the Muslim world that he, bin Laden, and Mullah Omar were enjoying "good health" despite the American attacks on them in Afghanistan and were preparing for an assault on Iraq. A "campaign against Iraq," he said, "has aims that go beyond Iraq to target the Arab and Islamic world. It aims at crushing any effective military force neighboring Israel."[4]

On February 11, 2003, bin Laden sent a letter to the Iraqi people, broadcast via al-Jazeera, warning them the Crusaders were planning "to occupy one of Islam's former capitals, loot Muslim riches, and install a stooge regime to follow its masters in Washington and Tel Aviv to pave the way for the establishment of Greater Israel." He advised the Iraqi nation to prepare for a long struggle against the Crusaders and in particular to engage in "urban and street warfare" and to "emphasize the importance of martyrdom operations which have inflicted unprecedented harm on America and Israel."[5]

Bin Laden even encouraged the jihadists in Iraq to work with "the socialist infidels," that is, the Baathists and others, against the Crusaders in a "convergence of interests." This overt message five weeks before the Anglo-American invasion was accompanied by more active measures months beforehand.

Thousands of Arab volunteers went to Iraq in the run-up to the invasion, some inspired by bin Laden's words. Most important, long-time bin Laden associate Ahmad Fadil al-Khalayilah, also known as Abu Musaib Zarqawi, infiltrated Iraq sometime in 2002 to begin preparations to resist the invasion. Zarqawi had been a partner in al Qaeda's December 2000 plot to blow up the Radisson Hotel and other targets in Amman, Jordan, and had built his own jihadist training camp in Herat in Afghanistan. In Herat he operated independently of al Qaeda but as a close complement to it. After the coalition overran Herat, he moved to Iraq, where he created an infrastructure to prepare for the Americans. His network carried out its first operation even before the invasion: on October 28, 2002, it killed a U.S. Agency for International Development officer, Laurence Foley, in Amman.

Zarqawi, one of four brothers and six sisters, was born in Jordan in October 1966, less than a year before the 1967 war. His family is a member of the large Bedouin tribe Bani Hassan, which has traditionally been a firm supporter of Jordan's Hashemite monarchy. His father was a retired army officer and mayor of Zarqa, a small tough and mean working-class city with small industries close to Amman. It has a large Palestinian population and a very large Palestinian refugee camp nearby created after the 1967 war, when tens of thousands of West Bank Palestinians fled the Israeli occupation of their homes. The camp is dirty, without adequate sewage or electricity. It breeds extremism and fanaticism.

Nowhere in the ummah is the situation more ripe for such growth than in the Palestinian refugee camps. Some founded in 1948, others in 1967, they are among the shameful legacies of modern civilization for allowing such human misery to continue for so long. Many are to blame: Israel, the Arabs, and the rest of the world have done far too little to find a way to end this appalling suffering. The Palestinian leadership has done its own part to perpetuate the horror.

Zarqa and the nearby Al Ruseifah Palestinian camp were overrun again with new refugees in 1991 when the United States and its allies liberated Kuwait from Iraq. The newly returned Kuwaiti government decided to expel the quarter million Palestinians who had resided in the emirate for decades because of their alleged sympathy with Saddam Hussein and the Iraqi occupation. Families that had called Kuwait home for years were suddenly homeless and went to Jordan, which they picked because many had families there and because the Kuwaitis were also angry at King Hussein's sympathy for Saddam. The future queen of Jordan, Rania, would be one of them.

More than half the Palestinians expelled from Kuwait ended up in Zarqa or Al Ruseifah, greatly expanding the population of both and adding many disgruntled and angry men to the local jihadist circles. It would be no accident that Zarqa would become the greatest recruiting ground in Jordan for Iraq's al Qaeda a decade later.[6]

In 1984, when Zarqawi was seventeen, his father died. Apparently the loss affected him tremendously and he dropped out of school. Zarqawi found refuge among other of society's dropouts in the Palestinian camp. Turning to alcohol, drugs, and violence, he became a petty criminal and a thug. Soon he was arrested and jailed for drug possession and sexual assault. In prison he found Islam.

Like many an inmate, Zarqawi became a more clever and dangerous criminal while in jail. He attracted a gang around him and became well known for his brutality, which made him an easy convert to extremist jihadism. After several years in prison, he was released in a general amnesty in 1988, whereupon he married and went to Afghanistan to join the mujahedin. Arriving in 1989, he was too late to see the Soviet invaders leave but did witness the struggle between the various mujahedin factions and the communist government in Kabul. He probably had some connections with Pakistan's Inter-Services Intelligence (ISI) during this period.[7]

Zarqawi actually spent most of this time in Peshawar, Pakistan, the primary location of the country's large Arab community. Like many of his jihadi comrades from Arab states, he was eager to find a new target for his struggle. His trip to Pakistan was facilitated by several Palestinians, including fellow expellee sheikh Abd al Majid al Majali, better known as Abu Qatadah, who would go on to be a radical cleric in London and make a name for himself as a defender of al Qaeda. Abu Qatadah was also closely linked to Abdullah Azzam, who had much influence on bin Laden.

In Pakistan Zarqawi hooked up with another expellee and Jordanian jihadist, Issam al Barqawi, whose nom de guerre is Mohammed al-Maqdisi, and the two of them formed a small Jordanian network of Afghan veterans. In 1992, when Kabul finally fell to the mujahedin, the two of them returned to Jordan to prepare for the next jihad. They began plotting against the Hashemite monarchy.

By the early 1990s Zarqawi had become fully indoctrinated in the jihadist and Wahhabi extremist philosophy. In addition, his time in jail and in Afghanistan had turned him against the Hashemites and their rule in Jordan. As the decade wore on, his hatred grew only deeper as Jordan moved into the peace camp with Israel in 1991 following the first Persian Gulf War.

The Madrid peace conference of that year produced the first real momentum toward an Arab-Israeli peace agreement since the signing of the Egyptian-Israeli agreement in 1979, which had sealed Anwar Sadat's fate. As the king of Jordan moved toward peace, the country's jihadist camp swelled with new recruits opposed to any deal with Israel, no matter what the terms. In Zarqa the "new wellspring" was so profuse that "dozens of clandestine jihad organizations emerged."[8]

The Hashemite Kingdom of Jordan has had a unique relationship with Israel from the beginning of the Zionist experience after World War I. The borders of the original League of Nations Mandate for Palestine extended from the Mediterranean in the west to the British Mandate of

Mesopotamia (modern Iraq) in the east, with the largest percentage of the territory lying east of the Jordan River. Winston Churchill, then secretary of state for the colonies, detached the river's East Bank from the West Bank to create the Hashemite Emirate of Transjordan to give one of England's wartime allies, Prince Abdullah of the Hashemite family, a small kingdom of his own. (Abdullah's brother Faisal got the bigger prize, being made king of Iraq.) Abdullah chose to accommodate the burgeoning Zionist movement of that period rather than to confront it. In effect, he and the Zionists became partners in managing Palestinian-Arab politics. Both saw Palestinian nationalism as a threat to their own ambitions: for the Zionists, it was a barrier to Israel's creation; for Abdullah, a barrier to the expansion of his small kingdom across the Jordan and into the Arab-inhabited sections of the mandate.

In 1947 and 1948 Abdullah colluded with the Zionists to carve up Palestine. However, their secret communications failed to prevent a war between the two conspirators. Fierce and intense fighting ensued as Jordan's small but very effective army proved a serious enemy for the new Israeli state. In the cease-fire and armistice negotiations that ended the war, Jordan took control of East Jerusalem and the rump West Bank and became the Hashemite Kingdom of Jordan. Only the United Kingdom and Pakistan recognized the Jordanian annexation of the West Bank and East Jerusalem.

The war produced the first wave of Palestinian refugees on both banks. Jordan was transformed into a majority Palestinian state with a large hostile population angry at their king. Abdullah resumed secret talks with Israel to conclude a permanent peace treaty. On July 20, 1951, while visiting the Al Aqsa Mosque in Jerusalem, he was assassinated for his efforts by a Palestinian with links to the Muslim Brotherhood. The king was shot three times in the head and chest and his grandson, Hussein, once in the chest, but the bullet was deflected by a medal Abdullah had insisted Hussein wear that day for their visit to the mosque. Within a year Hussein ascended to the throne.

As a young boy, I lived in East Jerusalem, where my father worked for the United Nations. We were among the few in the city who could travel freely to both sides, Jordanian East Jerusalem and Israeli West Jerusalem, through the heavily guarded checkpoints that divided the city. The Palestinians were unhappy with Hashemite rule but had no alternative. Periodically they would riot against the king and his pro-Western policies. When they did, our family would stay indoors in our home and hope the Arab Legion and Jordan's efficient intelligence service, the General Intelligence Directorate (GID), would keep the peace as best they could.

Hussein continued secret talks with the Israelis for the next thirty years, but he had learned dramatically the costs of a covert partnership with Israel and was careful until the mid-1990s not to be too public about his dialogue with Israel. In 1994, after the Oslo agreement had opened the door to direct Israeli-Palestinian negotiations, Hussein felt the moment was ripe to finally conclude his own treaty with Israel. Not surprisingly, the talks were conducted in secret by the intelligence services of the two states. Their foreign ministers were kept in the dark about the real negotiations until a deal was done and signed in October 1994.

By then Zarqawi's effort to organize an anti-monarchist jihadi underground in Jordan had already been foiled. As soon as he returned from Afghanistan, Zarqawi had begun publicly speaking out against the king and the impending peace agreement with Israel. In March 1994 the GID raided his home and discovered an arms cache. Found in his bed, Zarqawi pulled a pistol from under his pillow and tried to kill the arresting officer but failed, then tried to kill himself but failed there too.

Zarqawi then attempted to turn his trial into a political event, demanding that the king be indicted in his stead. The court found him guilty of belonging to an illegal organization and possessing illegal weapons and sentenced him to fifteen years in a remote desert prison named Al Sawwaqa, where he was joined by his comrade Maqdisi. There the two created a jihadist network, with Maqdisi as the ideological leader and Zarqawi the enforcer.

Abu Mohammed Issam bin Mohammed bin Tahir al Barqawi, alias al Maqdisi, was born in 1958 in a West Bank village near Nablus. At a young age, he and his family moved from Jordan to Kuwait, as did many Palestinians looking for jobs and money in the boomtowns of the Gulf. Maqdisi finished his secondary education in Kuwait and then studied science at Mosul University in northern Iraq, where he was introduced to some Islamic clerics and radical circles. From there he went to Pakistan and became close friends with Zarqawi. In 1991 his family was expelled from Kuwait and moved to the Al Ruseifah camp.

In their jailhouse, Zarqawi and Maqdisi attracted a following. To better outline his views on the jihad, Maqdisi produced a series of books, two of the more famous being *The Creed of Abraham* and *The Clear Evidence of the Infidelity of the Saudi State*. Both advocate the overthrow of apostate regimes that work with the United States and Israel against the cause of Islam. Maqdisi's works became extremely popular among young radical jihadists, most notably the group that killed five American military advisers in Riyadh in November 1995, which cited his works and bin Laden's in their confession after their arrest and called Maqdisi the most important influence on their thinking.

Maqdisi found his own inspiration in the 1979 attack on the Grand Mosque in Mecca by a small jihadist group believing the return of the Mahdi, the successor to Muhammad, was imminent. The group's radical Saudi leader, Juhayman al Utebi, even thought he had found the Mahdi. The attackers took over and held the mosque for days despite Saudi counterattacks, which eventually succeeded in subduing the radicals with French assistance. Juhayman was captured and subsequently executed, but his writings found their way into print, and Maqdisi drew on them for his own analysis of the corruption of the Saudi family and political system.[9] Zarqawi would later name one of his suicide missions in Iraq in honor of Juhayman. Ironically, the bin Laden family, probably including Osama, was active in assisting the Saudi authorities in their counteroffensive to retake the mosque from Juhayman.[10]

As the prison group's enforcer, Zarqawi kept himself physically and mentally fit by working out incessantly with rocks as weights and memorizing the Koran. He imposed strict rules on his Islamist inmates, forcing them to dress in Afghan style and wear beards, preapproving the books they could read, and forbidding contact with the other prisoners. Not above attacking the guards, he became famous throughout the prison as a very tough character.

King Hussein died on February 7, 1999. The next day he was buried with full honors and in the presence of many world leaders. I had the honor of accompanying President Bill Clinton to the funeral. It was a cold day in Amman with a light rain. Hundreds of thousands of Jordanians lined the streets to bid him a last farewell. In a short meeting after the ceremony, the new king, Abdullah II, told the president that he was going to continue his father's policies, which included offering pardons on special state occasions such as his father's funeral. Hussein had often pardoned his political enemies, even men who had tried to kill him, in the belief that pardons could transform enemies.

After less than five years in prison, Zarqawi and Maqdisi were both pardoned for their crimes. Instead of being transformed, however, Zarqawi began actively plotting a new terrorist attack. By now he was in contact with bin Laden and the al Qaeda movement. According to Seif al-Adl, one of the senior al Qaeda security officials in Afghanistan in 1999, the al Qaeda leadership had paid close attention to Zarqawi's court case and trial in Jordan. Thus upon his release Zarqawi came to Kandahar with some close aides and a letter of recommendation from his earlier mentor, Palestinian jihadist Abu Qatadah, who now operated out of London.

After extensive discussion, Osama bin Laden and Ayman Zawahiri agreed to let Zarqawi operate in close collusion with al Qaeda, but from an independent base camp in western Afghanistan near the ancient city of Herat.[11] The Taliban leadership, including Mullah Omar, also agreed to let Zarqawi set up a camp there for his Jordanian and Palestinian followers. Omar personally selected the area of the city for the base on the understanding that Zarqawi would be in charge of both the camp and its group, whose nucleus consisted of Jordanians and Palestinians from Zarqa. Initially, Zarqawi called his group *Jund al Sham* (Army of Greater Syria), which he later changed to *Tawhid wal Jihad* (Monotheism and Jihad). Bin Laden gave him some seed money to get things started. He brought his ailing mother with him at first, but she went home after a short stay.

At this point Zarqawi was not a member of al Qaeda but an ally, or an associate. This arrangement is not unusual for al Qaeda, which often establishes collaborative ties with other terrorists that choose to remain independent of its control. For Zarqawi, Herat offered a means of infiltrating operatives in and out of Afghanistan via Iran as opposed to Pakistan. The location may have made him feel more independent of the other jihadists and the Pakistanis, who may have been more eager to turn him over to Jordan than to work against bin Laden, given Osama's higher profile. For bin Laden, any security concerns he may have had about Zarqawi's group and its possible penetration by the Jordanian intelligence service could be addressed by keeping it in Herat. Zarqawi did not pledge allegiance to bin Laden or al Qaeda, nor was he informed of the ongoing preparations for the 9/11 plot in America, although he was closely involved in al Qaeda's more immediate plans.

The al Qaeda leadership was planning a special terrorist extravaganza for the end of the year, known as the millennium plot, or more accurately, the millennium plots. The group had a hand in multiple plots that it hoped to carry off more or less simultaneously and thereby create the impression of a global terrorist network with the power to make its acts coincide on several continents. By staging an attack just as one millennium was ending and another starting, it hoped to heighten the drama and terror surrounding the event.

One plot was to take place in the United States. An Algerian named Ahmed Ressam with long connections to the Algerian Islamist community in Canada was to bring a car bomb into Los Angeles International Airport and blow it up. On December 14, 1999, Ressam was arrested by an alert U.S. border guard at Seattle when he arrived by ferry from Vancouver carrying nitroglycerin and four timing devices in the trunk of his car. He was convicted in 2005 and sentenced to twenty-five years in prison. Ressam had moved to Canada in 1994 on a French passport, then traveled to Afghanistan in 1998 for training at an al Qaeda camp. There he came to the attention of a senior al Qaeda figure, Abu Zubayda, who gave him the Los Angeles mission.

Another plot was to take place in the harbor of Aden in Yemen. A group of al Qaeda operatives planned to attack a U.S. destroyer, the USS *The Sullivans*, while it was taking on fuel in the harbor. The plot failed when the small boat they planned to use sank before they could attack the ship. The plotters would try again a year later, with much greater success, against the USS *Cole*.

A third step of the plan was to hijack an Air India flight from Katmandu, Nepal, on December 24, 1999. Though successful, it was not considered part of the millennium attacks by most American terrorism experts at the time. Only the government of India saw clearly that the hijacking bore the imprint of al Qaeda, the Taliban, and the ISI. India's foreign minister Jaswant Singh negotiated with the terrorists, who were Kashmiris with long ties to the ISI, and wrote later in his memoirs that "this was not a simple hijack. . . . [I]t was rehearsal of sorts for what was to follow in New York . . . a kind of forerunner of 9/11."[12] Other observers on the ground also noted that bin Laden himself was involved in the negotiations and the plot.[13]

Zarqawi and his Herat group were to concentrate on Jordan. Their sleeper cells inside Jordan collected an arsenal of weapons and explosives for simultaneous attacks on a large number of targets on the eve of the millennium, one being the Radisson Hotel in Amman. Another two were tourist sites: the historic spot on the Jordan River where Jesus was baptized by John the Baptist and the ruins of a Byzantine church on Mount Nebo where Moses looked into the Promised Land. The GID uncovered the plot and found the cache of arms before it could be used on December 12. Apparently Zarqawi had briefly returned to Jordan to oversee the plans but fled back into Afghanistan. He was indicted in absentia for his role in the plot in 2002. Like the Algerian Ressam, the plotters had also been in touch with Abu Zubayda, one of al Qaeda's key operatives in Pakistan.

Throughout this period, the Clinton White House was on high alert. National Security Adviser Sandy Berger convened the principal members of the National Security Council virtually every day for a month to ensure all were doing their utmost to share and collect information that could protect the United States. Sandy hounded the FBI and the CIA to talk to each other and provide any tips that might foil al Qaeda's multiple plots. In the end, bin Laden's plan for multiple attacks fizzled out, leaving only the India operation to claim success.

After 9/11 and the U.S. intervention in the Afghan civil war on the side of the Northern Alliance, Herat quickly fell to the alliance. It had never been a Taliban stronghold and was far from their power base in the Pashtun south. Zarqawi fled into Iran. His activities then became very much a mystery.

In his famous address to the United Nations Security Council on Iraq on February 5, 2003, Secretary of State Colin Powell at one point digressed from his main topic—Iraq's weapons of mass destruction—to make the case that Iraq was an ally, even a partner, of al Qaeda, as indicated by the activities of Zarqawi. Powell said that in May 2002, after the coalition forces overthrew the Taliban emirate in Afghanistan, Zarqawi fled through Iran to Iraq in order to get medical attention in Baghdad. There he was allegedly hosted by Saddam Hussein's government, which allowed some two dozen of his followers to come to Baghdad as well to "coordinate the movement of people, money and supplies into and throughout Iraq for his network." This was said to have gone on for eight months. Other members of his network were supposedly operating in the Kurdish zone in northern Iraq, in an area outside of Saddam's control but allied with him against the mainstream Kurds. A small jihadist Kurdish group, Ansar al Islam, was fighting Saddam's main Kurdish enemies, the Patriotic Union of Kurdistan led by Jalal Talabani, the first president of Iraq after Saddam. There, according to Powell, Zarqawi's network was engaged in making poisons, including ricin.

Moreover, Powell painted a picture of a Zarqawi network operating from Iraq with links in several European countries, including France, the United Kingdom, Spain, Italy, Germany, and Russia. More than 116 operatives of this network had already been arrested in Europe, he said, several engaged in plotting terrorist operations. In Russia, it was active in the Chechen areas and across the border in Georgia in the Pankisi Gorge, making toxic weapons there as well. Powell also linked the network to the murder of American diplomat Laurence Foley in Amman in 2002. On learning that the captured assassin had received money and weapons for the attack, continued Powell, the Jordanians asked Saddam to turn Zarqawi over to them. Saddam replied he had no information on Zarqawi's whereabouts, but American officials later briefed the press on the medical attention Zarqawi allegedly received, which was to replace a leg severely damaged in the fighting in Afghanistan with a prosthetic device.[14]

Although parts of this story were true, major details were misleading or have since been refuted, such as the amputation. When Zarqawi was killed by a bomb three years later, both his legs were intact, with little sign of previous injury to either. More important, once the United States reached Baghdad and could review Iraqi documents and interrogate Baathist Iraqi intelligence officials, it became apparent that the U.S. administration had got it wrong. According to the Senate Intelligence Report on prewar intelligence in Iraq, "The Saddam regime did not have a relationship with, harbor, or turn a blind eye toward Zarqawi."[15] If anything, the postwar evidence indicated that the Saddam regime was already trying to find Zarqawi and his gang when the Jordanians asked for him but was unable to do so.[16]

The Powell speech also made a great deal of Zarqawi's alleged connection to the radical Kurdish jihadist group, Ansar al Islam, but later analysis has shown few ties with this group or its base camp in Kurdistan. The group never mentions him in its own propaganda, and his main base of activity was in the Sunni strongholds of Iraq, namely, Baghdad and Anbar Province.[17] A senior Jordanian GID official discounted the story as well: "We know Zarqawi better than he knows himself. And I can assure you that he never had any links to Saddam."[18]

But if Powell was wrong about the nature of Zarqawi's ties to Saddam and Ansar al Islam, he was dead right about Zarqawi's overall strategy. The Jordanian thug was laying a trap for the American occupation. His network was building an apparatus to deal with the coalition forces once they entered the country. Safe houses were identified, arms and explosives cached, and intelligence networks built for the day after the Americans defeated the Baathist enemy. And a network of outside supporters was put together in the Arab world and the Muslim diaspora in Western Europe to provide money and martyrs for the battle.

Zarqawi's efforts were coordinated with the al Qaeda leadership back in Pakistan. Either just before or during the U.S. attack, Zarqawi returned to Iran to meet with his established contact, Seif al-Adl (whose true name is Muhammad Ibrahim Makawi), and arrange for the entry of al Qaeda operatives into Iraq through Syria.[19] At this time Zarqawi was still independent of bin Laden and not a formal member of al Qaeda, but they were very much allies in setting the trap for America in Iraq. As noted earlier, bin Laden and Zawahiri were also publicly urging their followers to go to Iraq to challenge the American and British invaders.

Zawahiri even turned the story of weapons of mass destruction on its head to provide a rationale for jihadi resistance. In the early fall of 2002 Zawahiri reported that bin Laden and Omar were alive and preparing for the next round of the war in Iraq, which America was waging to "confirm Israel's uncontested monopoly over weapons of mass destruction in the region to ensure the submission of Arab and Islamic states."[20] A few weeks later bin Laden issued a longer message, urging his followers to go to Iraq and prepare to fight the invaders, who sought a "stooge government to follow their masters in Washington and Tel Aviv."[21]

In short, al Qaeda was far ahead of the United States and United Kingdom with a plan for postwar occupation in motion months before the war. Zarqawi set the infrastructure in place for an insurgency, and bin Laden and Zawahiri gave them their help to mobilize the ummah's assistance.

This activity raises a puzzling question. If the Bush administration was so worried about Zarqawi's efforts in Iraq before the war, why did it not bomb the Kurdish camp in northern Iraq that Powell referred to in his testimony? Indeed, it subsequently emerged that the U.S. military and the CIA very much wanted to bomb the camp, regardless of whether Zarqawi was there.[22] Apparently the Bush team simply underestimated the danger that Zarqawi and the nascent al Qaeda infrastructure in Iraq would pose to the occupation. That miscalculation would have disastrous consequences.

## Zarqawi's War and Its Implications for Al Qaeda

Zarqawi had an evil two-pronged plan for the occupiers, and he put it into action after the invasion. First, he sought to isolate the Americans by driving out all other foreign forces. This was done with systematic terrorist attacks, most notably the bombing of the UN headquarters and the Jordanian embassy in Baghdad in the summer of 2003. The assault on the UN offices on August 19 was carried out by a twenty-six-year-old Moroccan volunteer, Abu Osama al-Maghribi, who came from a relatively well-off family that owned a restaurant in Tangiers. When the war in Iraq began, he left his family and wife to perform his mission. As he was leaving Morocco, his wife told him she was pregnant, and on the day he struck the UN headquarters, she informed him it was a son whom she would name Osama after bin Laden. As Maghribi entered the car loaded with a bomb to drive it to his martyrdom, he reportedly said he was happy for the "two good pieces of news [for his family] in the same day."[23]

The UN bombing had particularly serious consequences. Among the dead was the UN secretary general's special envoy to Iraq, Sergio Vieira de Mello. The devastation also drove out of Iraq most of the international community of aid agencies and nongovernmental organizations just when the United States and nascent Iraqi state most needed their counsel. Zarqawi thus cornered America and the United Kingdom alone in Iraq.

Second, and more important, Zarqawi targeted the fault line in Iraqi political society—the Shia-Sunni divide—in order to provoke a civil war among the Iraqi people. His goal was clearly to isolate America, then destabilize Iraq and turn it into a quagmire. In a letter intercepted in January 2003 and later released by the CIA, Zarqawi called the Shia "the lurking snake, the crafty and malicious scorpion, the spying enemy, and the penetrating venom." Quoting from Ibn Taymiyya, he warned: "Beware of the Shia, fight them, they lie."[24] As a devout Sunni extremist, he felt that going after the Shia would be all too easy.

Zarqawi began his pursuit of civil war with a series of attacks on the Shia leadership in Iraq, its holy places, and ordinary citizens. In the summer of 2003 his operatives killed the senior and long-time leader of the Supreme Council for the Islamic Revolution in Iraq (SCIRI), Ayatollah Mohammed Baqir al Hakim. Next came the bombing of Shia shrines in Najaf and Baghdad in March 2004, in Najaf and Karbala in December 2004, and in Samarra in February 2006; the Samarra shrine was then struck again in May 2007. The attack on the popular and widely respected Ayatollah Hakim was carried out by the father of Zarqawi's second wife, Yassin Jarad. He was a Palestinian and fellow Jordanian who had been with Zarqawi's movement for years and was a graduate of the Herat camp.[25] Zarqawi had married his daughter as a second wife when she was fourteen. The attack was organized by another Zarqawi friend, Abu Omar al-Kurdi (also known as Oras Mohammed Abdul Aziz), who was later captured and hanged for organizing the operation.[26] The attacks on Samarra were planned by an Iraqi named Haitham al Badri.[27]

Even by the ruthless standards of al Qaeda, Zarqawi excelled in violence and brutality. He introduced the practice of beheading hostages and filming it for propaganda purposes. He conducted several beheadings himself, including that of an American contractor captured by his gang. In another case, he killed the intelligence chief of SCIRI with his own hands. As Zarqawi put it, "His stinking head was severed to expedite his departure to hell."[28] Because of his machinations, thousands of innocent Iraqis lost their lives simply for being in the wrong place at the wrong time. Within the movement, his extreme views gained him the name *al Gharib*, "the stranger," while one al Qaeda piece dubbed him the "Sheikh of the Slaughterers." For the moment, this savagery worked. It made Zarqawi famous and intimidated many in Iraq, especially in the Sunni community. But it would also sow the seeds of al Qaeda's undoing in Iraq.

From the beginning of the war, al Qaeda in Mesopotamia, as it was eventually called, played only a small part in the overall Sunni insurgency, yet was a key driver in many ways. It specialized in suicide bombings and mass causality attacks much more than any other group, and it had the best links to outside networks that provided it with the foreign recruits to carry out multiple attacks. A study of the first two years of the occupation, from April 2003 to April 2005, found that the Zarqawi network was responsible for only 14 percent of all insurgent operations but could claim 42 percent of the suicide bombings; in addition, those suicide attacks scored the largest mass casualties.[29] Another study concluded that al Qaeda makes up about 15 percent of the overall insurgency in the country.[30] Still further reports estimate that a total of 440 suicide attacks took place in Iraq between March 2003 and August 2006, at least 30 percent of which were claimed by Zarqawi's group.[31]

The targets of al Qaeda's attacks reveal a great deal about Zarqawi's strategy. More than three-quarters were Iraqi, especially Shia, targets consisting of either members of the new post-invasion government (which was dominated by the majority Shia) or Shia shrines, politicians, and marketplaces. A favorite target is the military wing of the largest Shia party in Iraq, the SCIRI. Named the Badr Corps or Badr Brigades after an early Muslim victory, the group has strong ties to Iran, which provided it with a safe haven during the Saddam era. Al Qaeda denounced SCIRI and the Badr Brigades as a group aligned with Iran and America that betrayed the Iraqi people and called the Badr Brigades the "al Ghadar brigades," or the "traitors." For its part, al Qaeda claimed some of its attacks on SCIRI in the name of the Omar Brigades, in memory of Omar, the third caliph of Islam, a symbol of Sunni orthodoxy.[32]

For Zarqawi, the real enemy in Iraq was the Shia, especially their organized political parties and militias and the Iraqi police and security forces, which are dominated by the Shia parties. The Shia collaborate with the occupation forces, benefit from the invasion, and represent a threat to the Sunni minority. Zarqawi justified attacks on them in one of his first major public messages, a letter addressed to the first Shia prime minister of post-Saddam Iraq, Iyad al-Allawi:

> We do not fight for a fistful of dust or the illusory boundaries drawn by Sykes-Picot. We are not fighting so that a Western evil would replace an Arab evil (i.e., Saddam). Ours is a higher and more sublime fight. We are fighting so that Allah's word becomes supreme and religion is all for Allah. Anyone who opposes this goal or stands

in the way of this aim is our enemy and will be a target for our swords, regardless of their name or lineage. . . . Why is it permissible to strike the enemy when he has blonde hair and blue eyes (i.e., an American), but it is not permissible to strike him when he has dark hair and black eyes (a Shia)? A Muslim American is our dear brother: an infidel Arab is our hated enemy, even if we both come from the same womb. We have revived the jurisprudence of our good ancestors in fighting heretics and enforcing Allah's law on them. Jihad will be continuous and will not distinguish between Western infidels and heretic Arabs until the rule of the caliphate is restored or we die in the process.[33]

In targeting the Shia, Zarqawi sought to instigate a civil war between Iraq's majority Shia and the minority Sunni Arab communities. He calculated that such a conflict would make Iraq ungovernable and erode the legitimacy of any U.S.-supported regime, even one elected by a majority of the Iraqi people. He would fan the deep-seated Sunni fear of Shia rule and of Shia relations with Iran, Sunni Iraq's traditional enemy.

Zarqawi was also reaching much deeper into the historical memory of his core supporters: Sunni Arabs with a strong Salafist and Wahhabi connection. For them, attacking the Shia was a maxim of their strict Islamic faith. The Wahhabis' first major operation outside the Arabian Peninsula in 1802 was to attack and destroy the Shia shrines in the Iraqi city of Karbala. Anti-Shia violence is a deeply ingrained part of extremist Sunni fundamentalism.

Zarqawi's violent attacks on the Shia and other Iraqi civilians, his use of beheading as a terror weapon, and the gruesome nature of his work drew criticism even within the jihadist community, and even from his old mentor Maqdisi. Instead of following Zarqawi to Herat or to Iraq, Maqdisi stayed in Jordan and was arrested again for his anti-Hashemite activities. From his cell in Qafqafa prison in Amman, he wrote Zarqawi a message of "support and advice" in late 2004 praising his disciple for attacking the occupation army, a legitimate target, but sharply criticizing the attacks on the Shia, who he argued are fellow Muslims:

Beware of the complacency on what we used to be strict regarding the protected status of Muslim blood, money and honor, even if they were mutineers or wantons: shedding protected blood is one of the predicaments of doomsday. We have studied and taught that allowing the bloodshed of Muslims is a grave danger. The clean hands of mujahedin should be protected from being tarnished with the blood of the protected people.[34]

Shortly after the statement was released, Maqdisi was freed from prison and put under house arrest, raising the suspicion that it was part of a Jordanian effort to undermine Zarqawi in the jihadist movement, especially since it had been widely circulated in the jihadi underground. Maqdisi was then rearrested for giving another interview in which he urged jihad against America despite criticism of Zarqawi. In early 2008 he was again freed.[35]

Responding to his former mentor, Zarqawi said that he wept when he read the criticism:

The crimes of the Badr Brigades are still fresh in memory, not to mention their wearing the disguise of the police and the pagan guards [that is, the Iraqi army]. As for saying the al Rafidah [those who refuse, that is, the Shia] in general are like the Sunni in general, this is a great injustice, by Allah. Can those who uphold the principles of monotheism be equated with those who uphold the principle of pleading with al Husayn and members of the family of Ali?[36]

The anti-Shia violence and the ferocity of Zarqawi's methods, including beheadings, even produced some second guessing in al Qaeda's core in Pakistan. It prompted Ayman al-Zawahiri to write a long letter to Zarqawi in July 2005 (later published by the CIA to underscore the relationship between the al Qaeda leadership in Pakistan's badlands and Zarqawi 's franchise in Iraq, but also to highlight the quarrel in the jihadist community over attacking the Shia). In it, Zawahiri speaks friend-to-friend, offering some open advice. He mentions the situation in Afghanistan and the recent arrest of a senior al Qaeda operative from Libya, Abu al Faraj, then congratulates Zarqawi for his success in "fighting the battle in the heart of the Islamic world" against America. Zawahiri sees the battle in Iraq as the first step in a multistage process. It will be completed when the Americans are expelled from Iraq. The second step will be to create an Islamic emirate in the Sunni areas of Iraq that will launch a struggle against the apostate regimes in the region and their Iraqi allies. The third and final step will be to export the successful jihad to the rest of the states neighboring Iraq, which will culminate in "the clash with Israel" and its destruction. Zawahiri writes that the al Qaeda movement in Iraq should be prepared for events to move quickly once the Americans decide to leave.

In this endeavor, says Zawahiri, it is essential not to "repeat the mistakes of the Taliban," who restricted their popular support in Afghanistan largely to Kandahar and the south and thus isolated themselves from the rest of the country. He urges Zarqawi to strive for the unity of the jihadist movement in Iraq, which brings him to the Shia issue. Although he fully agrees the Shia are traitors for helping the occupation, he fears that mass attacks on their community, especially on mosques and shrines, will be misunderstood both in Iraq and in the wider Muslim world and will alienate many: "Can the mujahedeen kill all the Shia of Iraq?" he asks, wondering, too, how Iran will respond and whether it will take "countermeasures." After all, Zawahiri notes, "we and the Iranians need to refrain from harming each other at this time in which the Americans are targeting us."[37]

Zawahiri continues with utmost tact, deferring to Zarqawi as the al Qaeda field commander in Iraq on the right strategy to pursue there and repeating that he is seeing the Shia "matter from afar without being aware of all the details." At the end, Zawahiri makes clear that he and bin Laden are merely expressing a few concerns to their battlefield commander. The decision on how to proceed and the right tactics to use, they leave up to Zarqawi.

This private airing of second thoughts about the war on the Shia has never come out in the public domain. Whatever doubts al Qaeda had about its lieutenants in Iraq and their decision to foment civil war, it kept them private. Publicly, Zarqawi was a hero of the movement.

At the same time, Zarqawi and bin Laden were on much closer terms by the time the CIA intercepted this communication. On October 17, 2004, after several months of discussion, Zarqawi proclaimed his allegiance to the al Qaeda center and to the "sheikh of the Mujahedin of our time, Abu Abdullah Osama bin Laden." The name of his group was changed from *Tawhid al Jihad* to *Tanzim al Qai'dat al Jihadi fi Bilad al Rafidayn*, or al Qaeda in Mesopotamia. In his statement of allegiance

Zarqawi taunted the occupation and the supporters of the invasion, saying it was "not the piece of cake" they expected and promising the ultimate victory of al Qaeda. He went so far as to say that al Qaeda's defeat of the Jews and "their compatriots on the extreme American right" in Iraq would incur loses larger than the casualties inflicted "from the blessed 9/11 attacks."[38]

The al Qaeda leadership in South Asia responded with warm words of approval for Zarqawi, who was proclaimed the prince of al Qaeda in Iraq and was given responsibility for al Qaeda operations there and throughout the surrounding Arab states, and into Turkey as well. Al Qaeda propaganda organs lavished praise on Zarqawi as a strategic genius for his successes in Iraq against the American and British forces and for the blows inflicted on the Shia. One Saudi jihadist analysis of al Qaeda's military policy in Iraq lauded Zarqawi for setting a trap for the occupation armies, then pursuing a well-organized strategic plan that drove out foreign and Arab diplomats, isolated America and Britain, and then attacked the Shia, "the symbol of heresy." The war should be pursued until the "elimination of the Badr forces, its commanders, members and clerics, including al Hakim [the son of the ayatollah killed in 2003] and Sistani [the leading Shia cleric in Iraq]." The author considers the Shia to be followers of Mu'ayyad al din ibn Al-Alqami, a Shia cleric who supported the Mongols in the thirteenth century and was accused by Ibn Taymiyyah of treason—yet another reference to the historical depth of jihadist revenge. Finally, the author promises that Zarqawi and his followers will be remembered as "the new generation" of al Qaeda trained on the battlefields of Iraq that would bring the jihad to every country in the Arab and Muslim world:

> Qa'idat al jihad in Iraq is the reestablishment of another al Qaeda, which will export Jihad to the rest of the world as the mother al Qaeda did in Afghanistan. Abu Mus'ab al Zarqawi has such capabilities that the mind cannot imagine. He prepared for fighting the Americans over a year prior to the American occupation in Iraq. He built the camps and arsenals, and recruited supporters from the Najd [the center of the Arabian Pennisula and heartland of Wahhabism], Hijaz [the western part and home of Mecca], and Yemen, to be his agents in each city of these regions. In addition he built his

camps in Herat and recruited people from al-Sham [meaning Syria, Lebanon, Jordan, and Palestine] who became his official advisers.[39]

In sum, Zarqawi was the trap master. In collusion with bin Laden and Zawahiri, he planned and prepared for the American and British invasion of Iraq and the subsequent occupation. He deliberately isolated his enemies from the international agencies that might have helped them stabilize Iraq (although their own hubris did this as well), then instigated a civil war to drown the occupation in a bloodbath.

On June 7, 2006, Zarqawi was killed in an American air strike after months of searching to find him. He was in the hands of the Iraqi police at least several times before his death and escaped without their figuring out whom they had. He may also have been captured by American forces at least once and escaped without detection. In the end, Jordan's GID played a central role in uncovering the clues that led to his death. But by then he had already done his damage. In the pantheon of al Qaeda, he was truly an evil genius.

Zarqawi's death failed to destroy al Qaeda in Mesopotamia, however. He was quickly replaced by an Egyptian member of the group. Within a few months the new leadership took the dramatic step of announcing the creation of the Islamic State of Iraq in the center of the country, which boasts a Sunni majority. In effect, the Sunnis seceded from the rest of the country, symbolically attaining Zarqawi's goal of fostering civil war and creating chaos.

Both Zawahiri and bin Laden issued glowing testimonials to Zarqawi after his death. Zawahiri said he was "a soldier, a hero, an imam and the prince of martyrs who defined the struggle between the Crusaders and Islam in Iraq."[40] Bin Laden called him a "knight, the lion of jihad" and justified his attacks on Shia as payback for their collaboration with the Crusader occupiers.[41]

At the same time, Zarqawi's extremism did have consequences beyond what he expected, and his critics have been proven at least partly right since his death. A wave of revulsion against al Qaeda and its violence gradually gained momentum within the Sunni community itself. Sunni tribal leaders who felt threatened by the nihilism of Zarqawi and his cutthroat lieutenants began to fight al Qaeda in some of Iraq's Sunni strongholds, including Anbar Province, and even made deals with the occupation forces against al Qaeda. Although these deals did not extend to the Shia government in Baghdad, which felt uneasy about the Sunni change of heart against al Qaeda, they have dealt a serious blow to the organization in Iraq.

It was also probably a mistake to create an Islamic state in Sunni Arab Iraq because this suggested its people were not really Iraqi nationalists. By seceding from the rest of the country, even if only on paper, al Qaeda seemed willing to renounce Sunni primacy over all of Iraq. Most Sunni Arabs are not yet prepared to do so.

For its part, al Qaeda has fought back hard against the Sunni backlash, assassinating key tribal leaders, including one who had just met with President George W. Bush. The terrorists have also tried to move their lairs away from Anbar to friendly territory in the north. Bin Laden and Zawahiri have made a public appeal to Sunnis in Iraq, urging them to unite behind al Qaeda and not desert the movement.

Until the Sunni adverse reaction, al Qaeda was spectacularly successful in its primary goal in Iraq, namely, to turn the occupation into a costly quagmire for the United States and Great Britain. Hence they bought critical time for the al Qaeda core in Pakistan to rejuvenate itself and build a new safe haven in the Afghan badlands. Al Qaeda in Iraq is far from a spent force as this book goes to print, but whatever its future, it has already been a role model in its demonstration of how to trap a superpower.

## BEYOND BAGHDAD:
## AL QAEDA'S SAUDI OFFENSIVE AND THE WAR IN IRAQ

Iraq was not the only focus of bin Laden's attention after 9/11. He also opened a major offensive in his own homeland, Saudi Arabia, aimed at toppling the Saudi monarchy. Before September 11, bin Laden had been careful not to carry out violent operations there. In 2002, after the fall of Kandahar, several hundred Saudi members of al Qaeda returned to the kingdom and worked with sleeper cells that had been operating covertly for several years under bin Laden's direction.

The extent of al Qaeda's infrastructure in the kingdom's underground would come as a surprise to the Saudi authorities—and to the American intelligence services. There had long been suspicions of a significant al Qaeda presence, but no one even imagined what was really there.

Bin Laden ordered the start of the uprising at roughly the same time that the United States and United Kingdom invaded Iraq. Subsequent accounts from al Qaeda operatives in the kingdom suggest they felt the order was premature because they needed more time to prepare, but bin Laden was intent on moving ahead in the spring of 2003.[42] Senior Saudi officials believe the order reflected bin Laden's sense that the Anglo-American invasion of Iraq offered a unique opportunity to overthrow the Saudi monarchy by appealing to the intense anti-American reaction it provoked among the Saudi population. Al Qaeda members in the kingdom apparently also felt the invasion and fall of Saddam's Baathist government would be a good omen for their own insurrection and perhaps presage the fall of all the monarchies in the peninsula.[43]

Bin Laden forecast the insurrection in a major address to the Muslim world on February 14, 2003, on the very eve of the Iraq invasion. This is the first and so far only statement in which he framed his argument in the form of a sermon: it was delivered on the holy day of Eid al Adha, the Feast of the Sacrifice, just a few days after his letter to the Iraqi people urging them to get ready to fight the invaders. Clearly, bin Laden was preparing for an epic battle.

Much of the sermon is a review of contemporary regional history based on the familiar al Qaeda formula laid out by Zawahiri. He accuses the House of Saud of betraying the Ottoman Empire to the British in the First World War. He argues that the goal of the Crusaders is to divide the Saudi kingdom into smaller states so as to dominate the region more easily and accuses the Saudi family of complicity in this endeavor. The purpose of the Crusader invasion of Iraq and of the Crusader military presence in the Arabian Peninsula is, of course, to consolidate Greater Israel, incorporating "large parts of Iraq and Egypt within its borders, as well as Syria, Lebanon, Jordan, the whole of Palestine and a large part of the Saudi Arabia."[44]

Osama then called for the overthrow of all the monarchies of the peninsula: in Kuwait, Bahrain, Qatar, Saudi Arabia, and the others, all of whom are nothing but traitors or "quislings," a reference to the Norwegian Nazi who betrayed his country to Hitler. The Saudis must be overthrown for many reasons, but above all because they have betrayed the Palestinian cause to "Jews and Americans." Bin Laden rails against then Saudi crown prince Abdullah for proposing at the Beirut Arab summit in March 2002 that all Arabs sign a permanent peace agreement with Israel if it withdraws to the 1967 lines, an act that would "betray the ummah."

Bin Laden admits the Saudis will be difficult to topple in view of their American support but reminds his listeners that no one anticipated the fall of the Soviet Union in Afghanistan. America has been defeated before, he says, in Lebanon in 1982, in Somalia in 1993. The mujahedin have also inflicted many blows on the Crusaders: in Aden in 1992, in Riyadh in 1995, in Khobar in 1996, in Tanzania and Kenya in 1998, again in Aden in 2000, and most spectacularly on September 11, 2001. He clearly takes credit for 9/11, if not for the other attacks, calling it a "brave and beautiful operation, the likes of which humanity has never seen before[,] destroying the idols of America" and striking "the very heart of the Ministry of Defense and the American economy" in payment for "the unjust policies of the American government on the Palestinian issue." "America," he concludes, "is a superpower . . . built on foundations of straw."

At the end of the sermon he brings to all Muslims—particularly those in Palestine, "the good news that [their] mujahedin brothers are sticking to the path of jihad to target the Jews and Americans and that the Mombassa operation was just the beginning of the deluge." This is a reference to an al Qaeda attack in Kenya on the Israeli-owned Paradise Hotel on November 28, 2002, in which ten Kenyans and three Israelis were killed by a car bomb and an attempt was made to shoot down an Israeli chartered passenger jet at the nearby airport en route to Ben Gurion Airport in Israel using a surface-to-air missile. The message is clear: the war to overthrow the apostate Saudi monarchy is part of the struggle to liberate Palestine.

The first act in this war came less than ninety days later, when multiple suicide car bombs attacked several Riyadh housing compounds used by American and other Western contractors working in the city. Seven Americans were among the 30 killed; another 200 were wounded.

What followed would be the longest, most violent, and sustained internal struggle against the Saudi monarchy and establishment since the founding of the modern Saudi state in the early years of the twentieth century. Not even the uprising in the Grand Mosque in Mecca in 1978 was as serious a threat to the House of Saud as the al Qaeda challenge, which was better organized and occurred not only in one location but throughout the kingdom.

Gun battles between Saudi security forces and bands of al Qaeda operatives became frequent, almost daily incidents in the next few months.
Clashes occurred in Riyadh, Mecca, Jidda, Khobar, Yanbu, Taif, and other
cities and towns. Al Qaeda used car bombs to target Western facilities and
also kidnapped and murdered individual Westerners. There would be
occasional episodes of relative calm when it appeared the security forces
had defeated al Qaeda insurgents, followed by new eruptions of violence.

One of the most violent attacks occurred at the U.S. consulate in Jidda
on December 6, 2004. Nine people were killed when an al Qaeda band
penetrated the consulate grounds and almost succeeded in capturing a
young female diplomat. The vast majority of the al Qaeda operatives were
Saudis, although they also had the help of Arab volunteers from Yemen
and elsewhere.[45] Many of the Saudis had fought in Afghanistan and had
experience in combat.

After the shock of the first rounds of battle subsided, the House of
Saud mounted a very effective and complex counteroffensive. Lists of the
top al Qaeda operatives were published in the press, and the secret police
and other security forces went after them relentlessly. The results were
impressive: many on the lists were either captured or killed in shootouts
across the kingdom. The lists were updated periodically to take note of
new operatives and the death of experienced ones.

At the same time, the kingdom went to great lengths to paint the al
Qaeda menace as a perversion of Islam and to rally the Wahhabi establishment against it. Senior Wahhabi clerics denounced attacks on the Saudi
nation by bin Laden and his followers, and some working for the monarchy attempted to turn captured jihadists against the organization. The
Ministry of Interior, led by Prince Nayif, and the Ministry of Islamic
Affairs, led by Sheikh Salih Bin Abd al Aziz al Sheikh, a descendant of the
original founder of Wahhabism, made extensive use of clerical support to
fight al Qaeda. They set up a reeducation and rehabilitation program to
turn captured terrorists into quiet citizens, sending them to special camps
where pro-Saudi clerics held detailed discussions to persuade them of the
errors of supporting al Qaeda.

At first the reeducation program operated in secret, but it proved so
successful that it was eventually brought out into the open. Approxi-
mately 100 clerics and scholars formed the nucleus of the program, aided
by 30 or so psychologists who provided counseling. Since its inception in

2004, the program has handled roughly 2,000 prisoners, of which 700 have renounced their jihadist beliefs and been returned to their families. Another 1,000 are still in the program, while 1,400 refused to participate and remain in regular Saudi jails. Less than a dozen of those released have returned to the al Qaeda camp.[46]

As the counteroffensive grew more and more effective, bin Laden found it increasingly difficult to communicate directly with the al Qaeda bands inside the kingdom. Still trying to provide direction and inspiration to the uprising, he presented a long analysis of the faults of the peninsula's monarchs in a message urging the peoples of the Muslim world to "resist the new Rome." He catalogued the betrayal of the Saudi and Hashemite families in supporting the British in World War I and mocked the Saudi and Gulf leaders for having to ask American soldiers to defend them from Iraq in 1990 (a reflection of his effort to persuade the Saudi leadership to let him do the job instead). He linked the battle against the occupation of Iraq to the struggles against the House of Saud, seeing them as one continuous battle aimed at defeating the Crusader-Jewish conspiracy.[47]

December 2004 brought another call to depose the "tyrants," this time in the form of a letter to the "Muslims in Saudi Arabia in particular and Muslim[s] elsewhere generally" bearing a blistering attack on the Saudi monarchy. It, too, recounts the family's alleged perfidy with the British in 1914–18 and is particularly critical of King Fahd for continuing to reign for several years after a debilitating stroke: "The idea that the entire length and breadth of the land is ruled in the name of a king who for a decade has no longer known what is going on is incredible."[48] He complains of the royal family's corruption—one of their royal palaces he charges is larger than the country of Bahrain—and he accuses the Saudi leadership of having colluded with the Bush administration to invade Iraq, particularly in Ambassador Prince Bandar's meetings with Vice President Dick Cheney. The battle in Iraq and the battle in Saudi Arabia, he emphasizes, are all one conflict.

This became the case increasingly on the ground as well as in al Qaeda propaganda. Former intelligence chief Prince Turki saw evidence of connections between the two as early as mid-2004: "Much of the equipment we have seized during raids on al Qaeda cells in the Kingdom has come from Iraq. There is no doubt that as a result of the Iraq war it is easier for al Qaeda to sell its point of view to potential recruits in the Kingdom. Al

Qaeda has become stronger and more active since the Iraq conflict."[49] Furthermore, a growing number of Saudis went to Iraq to join the insurgency there and fight alongside Zarqawi and al Qaeda in Iraq. According to U.S. estimates for 2007, at least 45 percent of the foreign fighters in Iraq came from Saudi Arabia and were the ones most frequently involved in suicide attacks.[50] Iraqi sources put the figure even higher, reporting that nearly half the foreign detainees in Iraq were Saudi citizens.[51] One cache of documents found in an al Qaeda safe house that served as a transit point for foreign volunteers showed that out of 602 registered foreign fighters 244 were Saudis.[52] The majority fought with the Zarqawi group, but some Saudi opposition sources claim up to 5,000 Saudis were participating in the insurgency by as early as October 2003.[53]

Al Qaeda's cells in Iraq also benefited from the support of parts of the kingdom's Wahhabi establishment. If some clerics were critical of al Qaeda's attacks on Saudi targets, others were openly supportive, and several even provided religious blessing for attacks on the Shia and Shia shrines.[54] Others organized conferences to rally support for the Sunni insurgency and to highlight the threat posed by the Shia in Iraq and by Iran. A group of three dozen Saudi clerics issued a statement in December 2006 supporting the Sunni insurgency in Iraq and urging all Sunnis to back it. The statement denounced the occupation as a joint U.S.-Iranian conspiracy, a "Crusader-Safavid" alliance, harkening back to the sixteenth- and seventeenth-century Safavid Empire that established Shiism as the official faith of Iran.

Nearly four years after the occupation of Iraq, the clerics concluded, it has become clear that the Crusaders and the Safavids intend to take over Iraq in a partnership that will enable them to realize their ambitions in the Middle East, protect the Jewish occupiers, remove Sunni influence, encircle the Sunnis in the entire region, and create a Shia crescent.[55] Their statement was enthusiastically greeted by the al Qaeda Islamic State of Iraq and by other jihadist groups. It was followed by a conference in Istanbul, Turkey, in December 2006 attended by clerics from the kingdom and elsewhere in the Arab world who endorsed the insurgency as well.

Al Qaeda even sought to expand the war beyond the boundaries of Iraq and Saudi Arabia. Zarqawi's group attempted several attacks in Jordan, many of which were foiled by the GID. In April 2004 he planned to hit

GID headquarters with several truck bombs loaded with more than 20 tons of chemical explosives. The GID nipped the plan in the bud, accusing Zarqawi of trying to use a chemical weapon against his homeland. Though he admitted to the bomb plot, Zarqawi denied the chemical weapons charge, boasting that if he had such a weapon "we would not hesitate one second to use it on Israeli cities." Zarqawi was more successful in November 2005 when his operatives bombed the Radisson Hotel (on his target list since 2000) and two other large hotels in Amman, killing dozens, including a wedding party. However, the bombing generated a backlash against him and his group among many Jordanians.

Turkey, another target of attacks, suffered several hits in Istanbul in November 2003, which included the British consulate and Jewish firms and killed or wounded more than 800 people. Since then al Qaeda has been relatively quiet in Turkey, although several senior al Qaeda operatives in Iraq have been Turkish jihadists.[56]

Al Qaeda has had even greater ambitions. In the questioning of detained al Qaeda senior lieutenant Khalid Sheikh Mohammed (KSM), it was learned that al Qaeda in Saudi Arabia had formulated a plan to recruit some pilots in the Royal Saudi Air Force and have them fly their own aircraft to attack the Israeli southern port city of Eilat. The goal would be to incite an Israeli counterattack on Saudi Arabia and push the two countries into war, turning the region into a cauldron of violence and pitting two American allies against each other in a military conflict. Fortunately, the idea never got off the ground before KSM was captured by the CIA.[57]

There is also some evidence that al Qaeda considered instigating a war between the United States and Iran to increase the scale of conflict in the region. Indeed, as the war in Iraq progressed, the Iraq contingent identified Iran and its Shia allies in Iraq as the group's main long-term enemy. The United States and United Kingdom, it believes, will withdraw from Iraq sooner or later, but Iran will remain a long-term threat to Sunni interests in Iraq.

In his public statements, bin Laden was initially reluctant to attack the Shia in Iraq, perhaps out of concern for al Qaeda operatives who fled to Iran after the rout of the Taliban in Afghanistan in 2002, some being family members. Perhaps he also wanted to avoid opening another front with another enemy too soon after the loss of Kandahar.

Since the death of Zarqawi, bin Laden's forbearance seems to have ended. He has openly sided with Zarqawi's position that the Shia are a legitimate target because they are "agents of the Americans."[58] The Islamic State of Iraq went even further in mid-2007, threatening to attack Iranian targets in Iraq (especially SCIRI and the Badr Brigades) and in Iran if Iran did not cease its interference in Iraq on the side of the Shia. Some al Qaeda senior figures are more scathing still. Notable among these is Abu Yahya al-Libi, who was captured in Operation Enduring Freedom but escaped from Bagram prison in July 2005, along with three other senior al Qaeda operatives. A frequent commentator for al Qaeda, al-Libi has lashed out at the Shia and Iran in particularly harsh tones:

> Since the establishment of the Ayatollah Khomeini's rejectionist Magi nation in Iran in 1979, the nation has been living on the hope of establishing the great Persian nation after placing its foundation in Tehran. The idiot Khomeini invented the concept of wilayat al faqih for them to end the years of straying which obligated them to lie in wait through the ages, generation after generation until the return of the imaginary inhabitant (the hidden Imam). As soon as they tasted the sweetness of power of which they deprived themselves for long centuries spent in waiting and wailing, hitting their faces and tearing their clothes, they salivated, their appetites increased and their imagination expanded to the establishment of a great rejectionist Persian nation to become a maddening abomination, a source of deviation and misguidance, relying in this on their counterparts the Jews.

Al-Libi even accuses the Saudi monarchy of partnerering with the Shia and Iran because it allows Shia and Iranians to perform the hajj pilgrimage to Mecca, thus accepting them as real Muslims. Real defenders of the holy mosques, Libi argues, would not admit Shia.[59]

By 2006 the Saudi counteroffensive against al Qaeda was having significant results. The Saudis foiled more than a hundred attacks and killed or captured over 260 operatives, including all but one of the twenty-six most wanted. Even a major attack on the Abqaiq oil-processing center in the Eastern Province on February 24, 2006—the facility where 60 percent of Saudi exports are handled—failed when the attackers were killed by Saudi guards.

Nonetheless, bin Laden still has many followers in the kingdom, as the constant arrests by the Saudi intelligence service affirm. In December 2007, for example, the Saudis reported foiling a major al Qaeda plot to disrupt the annual pilgrimage to Mecca. In February 2008 another group planning an attack was arrested and discovered to be carrying a message from Zawahiri in a cell phone. Although attempts to overthrow the House of Saud have so far been much less effective than the push for civil war in Iraq, it would be premature to think the threat to Saudi Arabia has ended.

## CHAPTER SIX

# Al Qaeda's Plans

It was early afternoon on March 18, 2000, and I was preparing to leave the next day with President Bill Clinton on his long-planned trip to South Asia, the first by an American president in a quarter century. Kathy Cooper, my special assistant, rang me to say that National Security Adviser Sandy Berger wanted to see me immediately in his office. No good could come of this, I thought. Sandy was usually too busy to have time for a chat—a summons to his office meant something important was up.

When I arrived, I could see trouble right away. Sandy and his deputy, Jim Steinberg, were meeting with CIA director George Tenet and the president's chief of staff, John Podesta. Also present were Strobe Talbott, who, as deputy secretary of state, was representing the State Department, and the president's Secret Service team chief. I knew instantly this was going to be another discussion about the dangers of the president's imminent trip. For months, the Secret Service had been arguing against a Pakistan stop because of the risk of an assassination attempt on the president from the al Qaeda terrorist organization in neighboring Afghanistan. The Secret Service and the CIA had received no specific warning in connection with the trip or al Qaeda but were justifiably worried that it was too ideal an opportunity for Osama bin Laden to miss. At first I assumed we were going to have one last discussion about canceling the stop in Islamabad.

I was wrong. The threat now was specific, but in a different locale. George Tenet opened the meeting by reporting he had information about an al Qaeda plot to shoot down the president's plane as it landed in Dhaka, Bangladesh—in only forty-eight hours. Al Qaeda allegedly had a team in place on the ground with a surface-to-air missile ready to fire on *Air Force One* as it landed at Dhaka airport.

Sandy asked for reactions from the team he had assembled in his office. Noting the seriousness of the situation, he said he wanted to place all the issues on the table before going out to the president. How good were the data, what measures could be taken to reduce the risk, what were the security conditions on the ground in Dhaka, what would be the regional implications of canceling the Bangladeshi stop at this late moment, and what would be the larger geopolitical and strategic fallout of not going forward?

Tenet felt he had to take the information very seriously. The Secret Service said it was not going to recommend whether the intelligence warranted canceling the stop, but everyone there knew of its deep concerns about the Pakistani leg of the trip. The stop in Bangladesh was tricky. The airport was small, and the president was supposed to fly by helicopter to Jaypura, a remote village in the interior, to see rural life and especially the operation of microcredit in the field. That created an additional opportunity for a surface-to-air to strike.

Sandy asked me what I thought. It had been largely my idea to go to Bangladesh—one of the largest Muslim countries in the world—to acknowledge and show support for the Bangladeshi democracy. Though desperately poor, it had made tremendous strides since breaking away from Pakistan in 1971 to alleviate its poverty and reduce illiteracy. Now headed by Shaika Hasina, a female prime minister and thus a rare commodity in the Islamic world, it was also a poster child for the microcredit concept developed by Clinton's long-time friend Mohammed Yunus in his Grameen Bank in Bangladesh. Furthermore, the country did not support terrorism, did not seek to acquire weapons of mass destruction, and was not a threat to regional peace. In other words, it was the kind of Muslim democracy America wanted to support.

I quickly reviewed these arguments but could not make a judgment on the intelligence. If we did decide to cancel the Bangladesh stop, I felt we had to rule out Pakistan as well. If it was too dangerous to visit a democracy with no previous record of terrorism, how could it be safe to go to a military dictatorship where al Qaeda was known to be widely entrenched and on intimate terms with many in high positions?

My Secret Service friends obviously took to this argument, but Sandy did not. Actually, we had wrestled over the Pakistani stop for some time, and the president himself had been angry with me when we had gone at it in the White House Map Room a few days earlier.[1] Sandy did not want to reopen that debate, but he knew I had a point. Jim added a key argument as well: if the president failed to visit a friendly democracy for fear of a terrorist attack, it would represent a strategic victory for al Qaeda and all terrorists, indicating not only that he could not travel in safety but that no one could. Moreover, key parts of the world would now be considered off limits for American leaders.

After considering the issues, Sandy went to see the president in the Oval Office. George laid out our intelligence, and the Secret Service reviewed the trip's particulars, including the schedule and the vulnerability of both the initial landing at Dhaka and the helicopter flight to Jaypura and back. Some "new looks" already devised for the flight into Pakistan could also be used at Dhaka, he said, but that could expose them prematurely. Sandy discussed the regional implications as I had outlined them and Jim's point about not letting terrorists intimidate America.

The president listened intently, well aware of the time pressure—we were due to leave the next morning, arrive in New Delhi later that day, stay there overnight, then fly to Dhaka the first thing in the morning. We would only spend the day in Bangladesh, returning to Delhi for the night to begin the president's official visit to India. It had to be a day trip for a simple reason: presidential travel now requires huge numbers of press, communications, and security personnel, not to mention aides, and Bangladesh did not have enough hotel space for everyone. Thus the tight schedule. The president asked Chief of Staff John Podesta for his view. John said we should go forward but take whatever precautions possible to reduce the risks. Sandy agreed. I added one last point: we could not let a people down who were struggling hard to make their country a better place and who were jubilant that a president of the United States was about to make the first-ever official visit to their country.

Clinton said he would talk to his wife, Hillary, and let us know. I went home that night half expecting to be called back to revise the schedule or go over the issues again but heard nothing until the next day, when we were summoned to board *Air Force One* and head for India. As he explained in his autobiography, Clinton decided he "didn't want to give in to a terrorist threat."[2]

After a night's sleep in Delhi, we left for Bangladesh early the next morning. The Secret Service had come up with two precautionary steps. First, the trip to the village of Jaypura was canceled so there would be no helicopter flights. Instead, the entire village would be brought to the U.S. embassy in Dhaka to meet the president and tell him about their lives and the changes microcredit was making for the better. Second, instead of taking the large Boeing to Dhaka, we would fly on a small aircraft with only a handful of passengers. A smaller target, it might not even be recognized as the president's jet by a terrorist on the ground. The press and other passengers would follow later in another aircraft.

On board the aircraft were the president, his Secret Service detail leader, Secretary of State Madeleine Albright and her South Asia expert, Assistant Secretary Rick Inderfurth, Sandy, and myself. It was crowded but comfortable.

Since the flight from New Delhi to Dhaka would now take longer than planned, everyone had more time to think about what lay ahead of us. Shortly before landing, I briefed the president on the political and economic situation in Bangladesh, and we went over the issues and points the president would want to make with Prime Minister Sheika Hasina. Albright and Sandy also commented on the purpose of the trip and what we wanted to accomplish during our brief visit. The trickiest issue was Hasina's strong desire to have the president visit the site of her father's assassination, which had occurred in 1975. Though seemingly innocuous, this would have put the president in the middle of Bengali internal politics and entirely on Hasina's side, against her political opponents, which is what we had assured the prime minister we would not do. The president laughed and said, "Let's hope that is the only assassination problem we have to deal with today."

The landing was smooth but seemed to take forever. As we approached the ground, we could see hundreds of Bangladeshi soldiers lining each side of the runway, with scarcely a yard between them. They were there to provide one last line of protection should someone try to fire at the jet. I could not help noticing that most of the soldiers were looking over their shoulders at the descending aircraft rather than away into the distance, as they should have been if they were on the alert for any sudden movement and needed to get into a firing position to shoot.

Once on the ground, we were quickly taken up with the tight schedule. Sure enough, Hassina managed to speak to the president alone for ten minutes and spent the whole time lobbying hard for a visit to her father's memorial. Clinton tactfully sidestepped the request, moving ahead to the embassy, and the meeting with the villagers, the highlight of the visit. We had so many press and security people with us in the embassy that I told Sandy it was a good thing we had not visited the village itself or we would have destroyed it with our overwhelming numbers.

After a long day and a state diner, we headed back to New Delhi. The president mentioned that his daughter Chelsea and his mother-in-law would be staying in India while he visited Bangladesh and Pakistan, a gesture to the gravity of the threat as he saw it.

The trip to Pakistan a week later was almost anticlimactic. We again found ourselves in a small, unmarked aircraft while a larger one followed with the press. As we flew over Pakistani air space, the Secret Service leader told me the press aircraft had taken evasive action in response to a heat source detected below. This was a standard procedure to divert any incoming missile. Later we determined the heat was probably from open fires in the Indus River Valley below, but at the time his news added to the tension. The Pakistanis had gone to great lengths to ensure no one could threaten the president once we were on the ground. The streets of Islamabad were deserted except for soldiers. The soldiers and huge posters urged the president to support the struggle for the liberation of Indian-controlled Kashmir.

Meeting with Pakistan's new military dictator, Pervez Musharraf, the president pressed for an end to its support of the terrorist groups in Kashmir, which had just murdered thirty-five Sikhs while he was in India, and of the Taliban, which hosted Osama bin Laden and al Qaeda. Terrorism, he warned, would consume Pakistan if the country continued to back jihadism in the region. Musharraf flatly refused, saying he could not afford to alienate the powerful Pashtun tribes along the Afghan border by being tough on the Taliban, although he was slightly more positive concerning al Qaeda but promised nothing concrete. He asked the president to pressure India to leave Kashmir. It was not a productive stop except for the president's televised speech to the Pakistani people.

Leaving Islamabad, we flew on a small aircraft once again, stopping in Oman to change planes before proceeding to our final stop, Geneva, where we would see Syria's president Hafez al-Asad. We thus paid a one-hour visit to Muscat and met with Sultan Qabus, on another first-ever presidential visit to Oman.

How serious was the threat to the president? No one will probably ever know. Al Qaeda was certainly capable of such an operation. In 2003 it fired a surface-to-air missile at an Israeli aircraft in Kenya, just narrowly missing it. The president did the right thing in continuing with the trip despite the threats, whatever their veracity. That visit proved to be a turning point in U.S. relations with South Asia in general and India in particular.

All the same, any such threats cannot be viewed lightly. Al Qaeda has an ambitious agenda for the new century. Its ultimate goal is to create (or in its view restore) the Islamic caliphate from Spain to Indonesia, uniting all the lands of the modern Muslim world and some territories lost in Christian reconquests over the past centuries. Although it has no blueprint for governing the caliphate, it plans to impose *sharia* (Islamic law) on the model of the Taliban's Islamic Emirate of Afghanistan, whose government barely functioned in its brief history. However, no one in the organization has conducted a substantial analysis into either a method of governance or of appointing the ruling leader.

This is not surprising. Al Qaeda's leaders are well aware that they are not close to achieving this objective and are not taken up with its practical implications for the time being. They are well aware that they do not have a mass following in the Muslim world and that they are not on the verge of taking over even a single Muslim country. They regard themselves as a vanguard movement, a small group of "knights" showing the way for the ummah. They are focusing on a more immediate concern: how to defeat the United States just as they defeated the Soviet Union, how to overthrow U.S. allies in the Muslim world, and how to destroy Israel. As mentioned at the outset of this volume, theirs is a three-pronged strategy: first, wear down the United States and its Western allies in the "bleeding wars" in Iraq and Afghanistan just as the mujahedin wore down the Soviet invaders; second, consolidate their safe haven in South Asia while creating new al Qaeda "franchises" or allies across the Muslim world to fight the West in their areas and attack the local apostate regime; and third, build an infrastructure of supporters in the West, especially in Europe, that can be used to stage "raids" into the West, perhaps even armed with a weapon of mass destruction to spread terror and fear throughout the Western world. These raids would also serve to bait the West into more quagmires.

## BLEEDING WARS

The "bleeding wars" are the crucial first step. The al Qaeda leadership is convinced it can reproduce the communist collapse by defeating the Western powers in Afghanistan and Iraq. As I have already noted, this was the main purpose of the Manhattan raid: to start the first bleeding war in Afghanistan. Iraq was an unintended but welcome bonus.

Afghanistan is al Qaeda's top priority for a number of reasons. First, the odds of success are better in Afghanistan than anywhere else. The organization has a long history there and thus many deep connections and alliances—particularly with the Taliban, whose Pashtun roots also run deep—on both the Afghan and Pakistani side of the border. Despite the Taliban's brutal excesses and the attraction of a genuine democratic alternative in the Karzai government, the group has a strong following and has recovered from the setback inflicted by Operation Enduring Freedom in 2001 to the point that it has become a threat to the Karzai regime. Al Qaeda has assisted the Taliban in this resurgence with critical advice and fighters, and Osama bin Laden is even credited by the Taliban leadership with planning an attack on a base that Vice President Dick Cheney visited in 2007. Al Qaeda tactics clearly have been adopted by its Taliban ally: in all of 2002 Afghanistan sustained two suicide attacks; in 2007 that figure jumped to more than one every three days.

The country's demographics are also in al Qaeda's favor. Unlike Iraq, Afghanistan is a predominately Sunni country with a long history of fundamentalist Sunni influence. Its Shia minority, the Hazara, constitute only 15 percent of the population and have traditionally been minor players in its politics.

Perhaps most important, Afghanistan is situated next to al Qaeda's most important safe haven, Pakistan. Since 2002 al Qaeda has thrived there. Although the Musharraf government has tried to prevent the rise of al Qaeda and has, according to President Musharraf, arrested some 600 al Qaeda operatives, including key individuals such as Khalid Sheikh

Mohammed, it has failed to capture the senior leaders or prevent them from having access to their followers. Indeed, the al Qaeda propaganda machine, al-Sahab ("the clouds"), has only grown more influential and robust. Its output of video messages has doubled in each of the past two years, and its technical expertise has increased at an impressive rate. Even its logo now appears on coffee mugs, just as at CNN or Fox. A new message comes out every seventy-two hours now.

Behind this propaganda façade, the al Qaeda apparatus in Pakistan has become increasingly effective in organizing operations on a global scale. Messages from bin Laden and Zawahiri circulate around the world. According to the British intelligence services, "The command, control and inspiration" for every major terrorist operation in the United Kingdom since 2003—including the July 2005 attack on the London underground and the August 2006 plot to simultaneously blow up ten jumbo jets over the North Atlantic—were directed and commanded by the al Qaeda core in Pakistan."[3] Danish and German authorities have also reported foiling plots linked to the Pakistan core, while al Qaeda franchises around the Islamic world reportedly receive their guidance from bin Laden.

Moreover, since 2003 al Qaeda and the Taliban have become all but inseparable. Al Qaeda appears to have every reason to trumpet its success in Afghanistan against the North Atlantic Treaty Organization (NATO) and Karzai. Indeed, Zawahiri has said the jihad has gone so well "against the Crusaders in Afghanistan" that "Musharraf and his regime are reeling; they are in their final days."[4] Large parts of the southern half of Afghanistan are now effectively under Taliban control at night or too dangerous for NATO forces to operate in, except in large numbers and with airpower to back them up quickly.

Al Qaeda is also pleased with the results of the struggle in Iraq, despite the setbacks to the Mesopotamia franchise after Zarqawi's death. Although admitting some disappointments in 2007, for example, Zawahiri believes "the state of the jihad in Iraq today is good, thank God. . . . The most recent reports . . . indicate that the mujahedin are gaining further strength while the Americans are in a deteriorating situation. Let us just remember the decisions of the British to escape [Basrah]."[5]

Al Qaeda is well aware that the demographic balance in Iraq works against its Sunni Arab base, as does the long-term threat of a stronger Iran emerging out of Iraq's chaos. Its leaders decry what they see as the rise of

Safavid power in the Persian Gulf, a reference to the last great Iranian empire in the seventeenth century, which converted Iran to Shiism and briefly dominated the region of modern-day Iraq before being evicted by the Ottoman Empire. Al Qaeda leaders ridicule George W. Bush and America for invading Iraq and thereby allowing the revival of the Safavids at the expense of Washington's own interests.

To Zawahiri, these actions spell collusion: "Iran achieved an agreement with the Americans before the latter's entry into Iraq. The agreement provided for partitioning the country" and giving Tehran control over the Shia majority. Iran, says Zawahiri, uses the Shia militias and Shia government in Iraq to attack Sunni interests in coordination with the U.S. military. Tellingly, he argues Iran and its Shia allies in Iraq have never issued a "single fatwa from a single Shia religious authority inside or outside of Iran urging jihad against the Americans in Iraq or Afghanistan."[6] Bin Laden and his colleagues often encourage their followers to believe the jihad is on the path to success by emphasizing the heavy price in lives and money paid by America, Britain, and others to keep forces in two battlefields. This is bound to become unsustainable and create the conditions for collapse, bin Laden argues, just as it did for the Soviet Union.

If anything, al Qaeda wants the wars to continue and has no interest in an early American withdrawal from either. In its view, the "bleeding wars" offer the best opportunity to defeat the United States. The American and allied armies are far more vulnerable in Afghanistan and Iraq than they would be offshore or in isolated bases in Saudi Arabia, say, where the bulk of American forces were deployed before the Iraq war and after the Khobar attack. It is much easier to kill the enemy in Mesopotamia and Afghanistan's traps.

## BUILDING SAFE HAVENS AND FRANCHISES

Al Qaeda's second priority is to consolidate its safe havens in the badlands of Afghanistan and Pakistan and to build new franchises in the rest of the Islamic world. To entrench itself ever more deeply in Pakistan, al Qaeda has used its long-standing ties to groups such as Lashkar-e-Tayyiba (LeT) and Jaish-e-Mohammed (JeM) to burrow into the fabric of militant Pakistani Islam. These groups and the milieu in which they operate have grown progressively stronger since 2002 in part because the Musharraf government's rigged elections that year put Islamist parties in charge of western Baluchistan and the North-West Frontier Province. Military operations to control the Islamic extremists have failed repeatedly, leaving the borderlands ever more closely tied to al Qaeda's allies.

Musharraf himself has been a target of the al Qaeda apparatus in Pakistan. At least two attempts have come close to killing the Pakistani leader (he may have been targeted up to nine times). Both showed strong indications of inside jobs, suggesting that al Qaeda has successfully penetrated deep into the Pakistani military and security services.

Al Qaeda was probably also involved in the murder of former prime minister Benazir Bhutto in late 2007. She had been the target of previous attempts by al Qaeda some going back to the mid 1990s, one of which occurred shortly after her return to Pakistan and killed 140 innocent onlookers. She knew the risks all too well—as she wrote before her death, she had been "targeted twice before by al Qaeda assassins."[7]

Al Qaeda's goal in Pakistan is to consolidate its stronghold there and use it as a base for global operations by exploiting the large Pakistani diaspora around the world, especially in the United Kingdom, where there are some 800,000 citizens of Pakistani origin. In time it hopes to see Musharraf driven from power, the army break apart, and the secular middle of Pakistani society collapse. Then its Islamic allies will take power, and Pakistan and Afghanistan can form the core of the caliphate in South Asia, wresting Kashmir from India.

Al Qaeda is the first truly global terrorist organization in history. From its South Asian base, it has been creating franchises or supportive networks in the rest of the Islamic world. Like a large corporation, it has a central headquarters in South Asia with affiliates and franchises around the Islamic world from which it can stage raids into the Christian and Hindu worlds beyond: the Zarqawi network in Iraq, al Qaeda in Mesopotamia, and now the Islamic State of Iraq are spectacularly successful examples. The al Qaeda apparatus in Saudi Arabia is a close second. While both the Iraqi and Saudi franchises are now on the defensive, others in Yemen, North Africa, Libya, Turkey, and the states of the Levant are in their growth phase. As in any corporation, the various franchises will be stronger or weaker at any given time depending on local circumstances. The most critical factor is the health of the center—the lair in South Asia.

Groups that take on the al Qaeda franchise label must pay a cost, of course: they become a target of the U.S. global war on terrorism. Those that do adopt the label—whether because they are on the run and need help or are doing so well they can risk the West's attention—are obviously ready to take the resulting heat.

One of Al Qaeda's next major goals after Iraq, the Kingdom of Saudi Arabia, and Afghanistan is to create an Algerian franchise that can serve as a node for jihad throughout North Africa and in the Maghrebi Diaspora of Western Europe. For some two years or more, bin Laden and his deputy Ayman al-Zawahiri negotiated with the Algerian Salafist Group for Preaching and Combat (GSPC) on the terms and conditions for its joining the movement. In late 2006 bin Laden had the group renamed al Qaeda in the Islamic Maghreb (AQIM), and it began conducting attacks in that name in late 2006 and early 2007 with a series of strikes on police stations and Western oil targets.

On April 11, 2007, AQIM carried out multiple suicide bombings, previously unknown in Algeria, targeting the prime minister's offices and police headquarters in Algiers, killing almost three dozen. Another truck bomb was apparently defused. The group later produced a martyrdom video of three suicide bombers who had died in the "Badr raid" (as it was named after the famous early Muslim victory).

On December 11, 2007, AQIM struck the UN headquarters in Algiers, a target clearly selected by the leadership in Pakistan for its symbolic value. To al Qaeda, the United Nations epitomizes Western domination of the Islamic world. A key target, UN facilities have now been attacked in Iraq and Algeria and should be considered at risk around the world. Dominated by four Christian Crusader states (the United States, United Kingdom, France, and Russia) and a communist fifth (China), the UN Security Council symbolizes al Qaeda's grievances. It imposes sanctions on Muslim states like Iraq and Libya and authorized the creation of Israel. It is a fairly easy soft target around the globe.

The new Maghrebi franchise should target France in particular, says Zawahiri, so as to be "a source of chagrin, frustration, and sadness for the apostates [of the regime in Algeria], the treacherous sons of France," and urges the group to become "a bone in the throat of the American and French crusaders."[8] French intelligence officials anticipate GSPC attacks on French targets in North Africa and probably in France itself sooner or later. As of

February 2005, the French domestic intelligence agency, Renseignements Généraux, estimated that about 5,000 GSPC sympathizers and militants now reside in France, grouped around 500 hard-core members.[9]

Zawahiri's warning should be taken very seriously. American and Israeli targets have already been on the list of disrupted Algerian attacks in France and Belgium, and it includes NATO or EU installations elsewhere in Europe. Remember, too, that the first-ever plot to hijack an airliner and crash it into targets on the ground was hatched in Algeria in 1994 when an Air France jet was seized with the idea of crashing it into the Eiffel Tower (see chapter 1). Like Pakistanis in the United Kingdom who have become British citizens, Maghrebis in France, Belgium, or Spain who have acquired French, Belgian, or Spanish citizenship have European passports that make it much easier to enter the United States and attack the American homeland.

## THE ULTIMATE FRANCHISE: PALESTINE

The franchise that bin Laden and Zawahiri would most like to develop is a Palestinian one, preferably in alliance with the Hamas movement. With its record of resistance to Israel, including dozens of martyrdom attacks, Hamas has more credibility as a Sunni jihadist movement than any other organization in the region. Hamas has serious reservations about such a relationship, however, as the comments of its late founder and spiritual leader, Sheik Yassin, indicate.

Asked about al Qaeda after his release from prison in 1997, following a botched Mossad assassination attempt in Amman, Yassin responded: "We support and sympathize with any movement which defends the rights of its people to enjoy self governance and independence but we are not prepared to seek an alliance with those movements."[10] At the same time, there is evidence of operational links between the two groups. In 2004–05 Hamas operatives apparently helped an al Qaeda cell in the Sinai carry out attacks on Israeli and Western targets in the Sharm al-Shaykh and Taba holiday resorts. Upon uncovering these connections, Egypt's intelligence service was furious with Hamas for bringing terrorism to the country's booming tourist centers.[11] Although the extent of these connections is very unclear, some contact is certain, particularly between the military wing of Hamas and al Qaeda.

Nonetheless, Hamas jealously guards its independence from outsiders, well aware of the sorry fate of Palestinian movements that align themselves with Arab patrons and become pawns in the inter-Arab political conflict of the Middle East. Hamas has only developed close relations with Syria and Iran in recent years, out of need for military assistance and increased economic aid. Publicly, most Hamas officials have been careful to distance the organization from al Qaeda violence, especially outside of Iraq or Afghanistan, and it has joined the electoral process in Palestine with great success.

For its part, al Qaeda has been increasingly critical of Hamas participation in the electoral process and its success in winning a majority in the last Palestinian parliamentary elections. Since Hamas is a descendant of Egypt's Muslim Brotherhood, al Qaeda has regarded it with suspicion from its birth. Zawahiri is particularly wary of its connection with the Brotherhood, and both he and bin Laden have warned Hamas not to let political power and government jobs seduce it into abandoning or scaling back the jihad against Israel.

Zawahiri had harsh words for Hamas on hearing of its March 2007 agreement to form a national unity government with Fatah, especially as the deal was brokered in Mecca by Saudi Arabia's King Abdullah. Hamas, he sadly claimed, had "fallen into the quagmire of surrender," and the leadership had "sold out" to the king: "The leadership of Hamas has committed an aggression against the rights of the Islamic nation by accepting what it called respecting international agreements [a code word for the Oslo process]." Extending his condolences to this Islamic nation, Zawahiri emphasized that "nobody, be he Palestinian or not[,] has the right to relinquish a grain of Palestinian soil." He was particularly upset to hear Hamas had negotiated with Fatah security chief Mohammed Dahlan, whom al Qaeda regards as a spy for Israel and America.[12] In a May 2007 video interview, Zawahiri criticized Hamas yet again, pointing to maps of Palestine illustrating Israel's increasing control over the country from 1948 to today and accusing Hamas and the Muslim Brotherhood of doing too little to fight this expansion.

In response, Hamas has denied any moderation in its commitment to the Palestinian cause: "We are a movement of Jihad and of resistance. . . . We in the Hamas movement remain loyal to our positions and dream of dying as martyrs. We assure Dr. al-Zawahiri and all those who remain unwavering in their attachment to Palestine that today's Hamas is the same Hamas you have known since its founding."[13]

Since this exchange, Hamas has in fact abandoned the Mecca process and in the three-day war in June 2007 evicted Fatah from Gaza, creating in effect at least a temporary three-state outcome to the Palestinian-Israeli conflict. How long this uneasy state of affairs—an Israel with a Fatah West Bank on one side and a Hamas Gaza on the other—will last is unclear.

Interestingly, al Qaeda's criticism of Hamas's flirtation with the political process and acceptance of a truce with Israel reveals some important and fundamental concerns about al Qaeda's long-term sense of its own vulnerability. The Palestinian "cause" is the centerpiece of al Qaeda's narrative about Western Crusaders' aggression against the ummah. The defeat of the Ottoman Empire in 1918 and the creation of the British Mandate in Palestine set in train the events that would lead to the creation of Israel after World War II. For Zawahiri, this has been the West's most evil act, making the "Zionist entity . . . a foothold for the Crusader invasion of the Islamic world. The Zionist entity is the vanguard of the U.S. campaign to dominate the Islamic Levant. It is a part of an enormous campaign against the Islamic world in which the West, under the leadership of America, has allied with global Zionism."[14]

As Zawahiri argues, "After the fall of the Ottoman Caliphate a wave of psychological defeatism and ideological collapse spread" throughout the Islamic world.[15] This defeatism made possible the Zionist victory in the 1948 war, which Palestinians consider to be the great disaster of their history, the *naqba*, or catastrophe. For Zawahiri, the issue is profoundly personal as well: he began his career in terror as a junior participant in the 1981 plot to assassinate Anwar Sadat for making peace with Israel.

Thus any sign that the Palestinian movement is turning away from jihad, however tentative, is a concern for al Qaeda. It worries that movement toward a peace agreement will undermine a critical plank of its narrative and alienate it from the ummah. Bin Laden provided two revealing commentaries via al Qaeda's propaganda machine on the sixtieth anniversary of Israel's creation in May 2008. In one he said to Americans, "The main root of the conflict between our civilization and your civilization is the Palestine question. I stress that the Palestine question is my nation's central issue. It was, therefore, a key factor that has, since childhood, provided me and the free 19 men (the 9/11 hijackers) with an overwhelming feeling of the need to punish the Jews and those supporting them. This is why the incidents of September 11th took place."[16]

In the second message on the sixtieth anniversary, bin Laden urged the Muslim world to overthrow the corrupt regimes that have made peace with Israel, especially Egypt, and join in helping the Palestinian struggle, especially in Gaza. He laments again that "the Ottoman state—its big faults notwithstanding—was protecting the ummah from the Crusader Western wolves" until it was betrayed by the Hashemite and Saudi families. Finally, he even attacks the Shia Hezbollah group for not being tough enough in fighting the Crusaders in Lebanon and accepting a cease-fire with Israel.[17] Al Qaeda has also accused Hezbollah of spreading the false rumor that Israel was really responsible for the 9/11 attacks as part of a secret pact between the Shia and Israel. Only al Qaeda is truly firm in standing clearly against any deal with Israel—everyone else is too soft.

## RAIDS INTO THE UNBELIEVERS' DENS

Of course, an important part of al Qaeda's strategy today is to launch more raids on the West, especially on the United States. Since 9/11 the group has focused on Europe, which it probably regards as a softer target than North America and which it hopes will be the springboard for attacks into the United States. Al Qaeda has made repeated efforts to orchestrate massacres in the United Kingdom, a notable success being the attacks on London's public transport system in July 2005. British security officials were at first reluctant to credit al Qaeda's leaders with planning the attacks but changed their tune as the evidence began pointing strongly in al Qaeda's direction. The organization itself released the martyrdom wills of two of the four terrorists, with commentary by Zawahiri to underscore its direct role.

Al Qaeda had planned an even more devastating attack for 2006: the simultaneous hijacking of ten jumbo jetliners leaving the United Kingdom for Chicago, New York, San Francisco, Montreal, and Toronto on the eve of the fifth anniversary of 9/11 and their destruction midair over the North Atlantic. Evidence presented at the trials of the accused terrorists in 2008 included martyrdom videos by six of them explaining their motives and suggesting that the mission of carnage include some of their wives and children on board so all could become martyrs together. Twenty killers had been selected for the operation, and their weapon was to be a new liquid explosive that could be smuggled onto the aircraft in pieces undetected and then assembled on board. After the plot was uncovered by Britain's MI5, the explosive was tested and found to be extremely deadly.

Had the 2006 plot succeeded, it would probably have been more devastating than 9/11. With all the forensic evidence of the crime at the bottom of the Atlantic, the terrorists would be able to repeat it without fear of discovery once air travel resumed—and could keep on replicating it indefinitely. The likely date for the attack was the five-year anniversary of 9/11, which would also be just a few weeks before the U.S. congressional elections. Both the 2005 and 2006 plots were run out of Pakistan by an al Qaeda operative known as Abu Ubaida al Masri, an Egyptian with very close ties to Zawahiri dating back to the early 1990s.[18] But Pakistan arrested only one man in connection with the 2006 plot, and he subsequently escaped from ISI's custody. Some of the plotters in the United Kingdom also escaped the police crackdown and are still missing.

The foiled August plot shows that al Qaeda remains determined not only to attack the U.S. homeland but also to target the most protected part of its transportation system, international and domestic air travel. No part of the infrastructure of America has been given more security than air travel in the days since 9/11, and al Qaeda still believes it can find a weakness in air traffic to cause carnage.

Al Qaeda was probably involved in the March 2004 attack on Madrid's metro system as well, the largest terrorist attack in Europe since World War II. Bin Laden and Zawahiri now routinely claim this as one of their "raids" into the West and point to its impact on the Spanish election that followed as a role model for creating a backlash against Western intervention in the Islamic world. In this case, the evidence of direct command and control is less abundant than for the U.K. attacks, although at least one journalist close to al Qaeda and author of a major book on the organization has claimed he knows that bin Laden was directly involved.[19] Note, too, that one of the alleged masterminds of the Madrid attacks, Karim Mejjati, was killed in an al Qaeda safe house in Saudi Arabia in April 2005, which strongly suggests a link. His widow now lives in Morocco and makes no secret of her admiration for al Qaeda.

Remarkably, the Madrid attack was previewed in a document prepared in Iraq and distributed on jihadist websites in December 2003. It provided a strategic analysis of Spain's vulnerabilities and pointed out that the Spanish government's support for the war in Iraq was not matched by public support, arguing that "painful strikes" in Spain would put an end to the deployment of Spanish troops in Iraq, especially if timed to coincide with the elections scheduled for March 2004. That, of course, is exactly what happened. The document represents unique and important insight into the sophistication of al Qaeda's targeting strategy.[20]

In 2007 security officials in several other European countries reported disrupting plots that had direct links to al Qaeda's leaders in Pakistan. Denmark's security service, for one, uncovered a plot apparently intended to coincide with Danish elections and may have been modeled on the Madrid attack, with the same hoped-for results. Another plot, foiled by German authorities, would have attacked a major U.S. air base near Ramstein and killed hundreds of American soldiers. Both plots were publicly ascribed to al Qaeda in Pakistan.

Americans, of course, are relieved to have avoided further assaults since 9/11. Improved counterterrorist practices are almost certainly part of the reason why. The creation of the Department of Homeland Security and the National Counterterrorism Center have substantially improved national security, through better interdepartmental cooperation and coordination, toughened airport security procedures, and heightened awareness of the threat at the national, state, and local level.

But a big part of the reason seems to lie with al Qaeda's own priorities, the first of which is to trap the United States in bleeding wars, as outlined earlier. Al Qaeda does not expect to defeat America via raids, even a devastating one on the order of 9/11 or one deploying a weapon of mass destruction. The United States must be worn down, just as the Soviet Union was in Afghanistan.

Second, al Qaeda seems to think it must outdo 9/11. What it considers small attacks—such as a bombing in a shopping mall or on a subway system, as in London and Madrid—are too insignificant for America. Apparently both bin Laden and Zawahiri want the next raid into America's heartland to be a substantial strike. Hence the attempt to down ten jumbo jets across the Atlantic.

What else would match 9/11? The obvious answer is a raid with a weapon of mass destruction. In his memoirs, former CIA director George Tenet lays out in detail al Qaeda's prolonged efforts to acquire a nuclear device. Procuring such a device, Tenet concludes, is among al Qaeda's highest priorities.

The most likely place for al Qaeda to acquire a nuclear weapon is Pakistan, which has been the focus of the organization's attention, as Tenet notes. According to most accounts, Pakistan possesses up to 200 nuclear weapons. Although the security surrounding them has improved significantly in the past decade, at least on paper, the growing presence of al Qaeda and its allies in Pakistan should serve as a cause for deep concern. The greatest possible threat is that al Qaeda will recruit a senior Pakistani military officer in control of some part of the national arsenal, who may then secretly pass one or two weapons to the terrorists and use his senior position to cover up the theft.

Al Qaeda would almost certainly choose to use such a device on Israel if it could get the bomb into Tel Aviv or Haifa, the nation's two largest cities. By one estimate, a nuclear attack on Tel Aviv would kill 125,000 people.[21] Jerusalem would be spared, given its large Arab and Muslim population and the sanctity of its holy places. If it could not develop a workable plan to attack Israel, al Qaeda would then probably use its nuclear option against the United States. The only warning of such an attack would no doubt be the explosion.

## CHAPTER SEVEN

# How to Defeat al Qaeda

After weeks of intense work since the start of the second intifada in Gaza and the West Bank, it was nice to spend a quiet day in late January with my wife. The offices of the National Security Council were closed for the inauguration of a new president after the most unusual election in modern American history. Elizabeth and I were enjoying a day's outing in Baltimore, an escape from the pressures of Washington.

Five minutes past noon my cell phone rang. It was the new deputy national security adviser, Steve Hadley, calling with my first instructions from the new team. The president and Condoleezza Rice wanted all U.S. negotiators at the Taba talks between Israel and Palestine withdrawn immediately. I told Steve we were not a party to the Taba talks, which were bilateral meetings between the two sides. He said, "Then get any observers or facilitators or whatever out of Taba—we don't want to be associated with the negotiations or their outcome."

I dutifully called our ambassadors in Tel Aviv and Cairo to ensure that no U.S. diplomats were on the ground in Taba in any capacity. With that, the United States ceased being an active partner in the Arab-Israeli peace process, ending a streak that began a quarter century earlier with Richard Nixon. Six years later, the Bush team would belatedly realize its mistake and try to renew the negotiations with a summit conference in Annapolis. In the meantime, the fires of al Qaeda's jihad would burn brightly, leaving the United States in urgent need of a grand strategy to quell them.

In the seven years since 9/11, al Qaeda has remained a deadly foe and is still planning further attacks on the United States, despite some serious blows to its network. Many key operatives have been killed (most notably Zarqawi) or captured (like Khalid Sheikh Mohammed) by brave American soldiers and intelligence officers. With the help of its allies, including some not well known to the public, the United States has foiled dozens if not hundreds of terrorist plots to attack targets throughout the world. The Saudis alone claim to have foiled 180 terrorist plots in the kingdom since 2003.[1]

The obituary of al Qaeda has been prematurely written several times along the way, most notably after the fall of Kandahar in 2001. Now some are suggesting that criticisms of bin Laden and Zawahiri by former jihadists jailed in Egypt, Saudi Arabia, or Jordan suggest the movement is coming apart. Others claim it no longer provides a central leadership for the movement, which it is argued is now more about copycats and imitators that a single united organization. Still others argue that the defeats in Iraq and Saudi Arabia signal al Qaeda's demise. Many take solace from the lack of another attack in America since 9/11.

Unfortunately, history suggests this wishful thinking is premature again. In the twenty years since bin Laden first used the term "al Qaeda" and, more important, in the ten years since he declared war on America, al Qaeda has seen many critics of its nihilism and violence within the ummah. As we have seen in this book, the movement has quietly criticized itself on occasion and learned from past mistakes. It is remarkably adaptive, even with its two top leaders as the most wanted men in the world with a $50 million reward on their heads. The core constituency of al Qaeda, which is a small minority in the ummah, is not easily swayed by former jihadists speaking from prisons or intimidated by setbacks on any single battlefield.

At the same time, the past seven years have demonstrated that a primarily military strategy will not eradicate this foe. Instead, the botched occupations of two Muslim countries, Iraq and Afghanistan, have unwittingly played into the hands of the jihadists—bolstering their propaganda that the United States wants to kill Muslims and control their world to exploit its resources. Never has the United States been as unpopular in the Muslim world as it is today. In allies like Pakistan, Saudi Arabia, Egypt, and Turkey, and in many other Muslim countries, its credibility has plummeted. As a direct result of the Iraq occupation, large majorities of Muslims and Arabs now say they distrust and dislike America.[2]

A new grand strategy against the al Qaeda movement must recognize the damage that the Bush policies have done to America's international reputation and start to repair it. Above all, it needs to reach out to Muslims and demonstrate by actions as well as words that the United States respects Muslim culture and values Muslim life.

The strategy must also integrate all aspects of international counterterrorism and homeland security. Diplomacy needs to be harnessed more effectively to resolve the quarrels that fuel al Qaeda's recruitment in the Muslim world. To this end, it is essential to find a just, two-state peace between the Israelis and the Palestinians. Intelligence collection and analysis needs to be more sharply focused to track down al Qaeda's leaders and break up its cells before they act. Defenses at home need to be closely integrated with alliance structures abroad. And the United States must earn back the confidence of its allies around the world.

## Defeating the al Qaeda Narrative: The Critical Step

As reflected in the activities and ideology of Ayman al-Zawahiri, al Qaeda has developed a complex narrative to explain and justify its war on America. The U.S. government needs to counter that narrative—through actions, not words. It is fruitless to argue over history, which is a path to endless disputes best left to the historians. The better way to counter the narrative is to act swiftly to address the core concerns that al Qaeda taps into in the Islamic world today and that facilitate its recruitment of terrorists.

The Israeli-Palestinian conflict, which is the crux of the narrative, is the obvious place to start. This is not because one can hope to dissuade al Qaeda from opposing the existence of Israel or seeking its destruction, but because the greater Muslim community can be shown a better alternative to endless conflict: namely, a viable and just solution to the Arab-Israeli conflict in all its manifestations.

The Bush administration made a fundamental error in judgment when it decided early in its term to put the resolution of the conflict on the back burner of U.S. foreign policy. The decision was based on a calculation that peacemaking had little chance of success—not an unreasonable conclusion in view of the failed attempts with Syria and Israel in Geneva in May 2000, and with the Palestinians and Israelis at Camp David in July 2000. With the start of the intifada in September 2000, those chances grew even dimmer. Now, after seven years of neglect, peacemaking is exceedingly difficult to revive. Hamas has become stronger, dividing the Palestinian movement and rendering its capacity to make peace more problematic. Hezbollah has also grown stronger, thanks largely to its success in the 2006 war with Israel. Thus the opponents of peace are stronger today than they were when Bush came into office.

As the president and his advisers, especially Condi Rice, have come to understand, their decision to abandon the peace process was decidedly unwise: it alienated key Arab and Muslim allies, especially Saudi Arabia and Egypt, and left the propaganda field open for al Qaeda and its allies to paint America as an insensitive giant that does not care about peace or the pursuit of justice in the region, yet preaches about the need for change. The appearance of callous hypocrisy toward the most important issue for Muslims and Arabs doomed the administration's efforts to advance a democracy and reform agenda as well.

The Bush team tried to replace action with words, but it did not work. In his first address to the UN General Assembly (just after 9/11), the president said the United States would support the creation of a Palestinian state living at peace next to Israel. I drafted those remarks and believe they were an important move forward for American diplomacy. They made explicit what President Clinton had made implicit in supporting the Oslo peace process. But words without action are not effective public diplomacy, let alone diplomacy in general.

Photo ops are no substitute for real diplomacy, either. The summits in Sharm al-Shaykh and Annapolis were slick media events but lacked substance, for the most part. They created more cynicism and skepticism about America's commitment to peacemaking than positive momentum toward resolving the conflict. And the president's first trip to Israel, after seven years of staying away, only reinforced the sense that this president did not really care about the outcome of the conflict. His second trip, on the sixtieth anniversary of Israel's birth, prompted an outpouring of bin Laden's hatred.

So what needs to be done? The next president needs to be as actively engaged in promoting peace as Jimmy Carter, George Bush senior, and Bill Clinton were. Fortunately, the basis for agreement is better understood today than at any time in the past, thanks largely to the failed summits of 2000.

On the Syrian front, a deal was almost within reach in 2000. Israel would return the Golan Heights to Syria, which would agree to a full peace with the exchange of ambassadors, extensive demilitarized zones on both sides of the border, and U.S. early-warning sites on Mount Hermon to monitor the security arrangements. The deal was stymied because Israel insisted on retaining a couple of hundred yards of beach along the northeastern shore of the Sea of Galilee, territory that Syria insisted on claiming even though the Sykes-Picot borders granted it to the British Mandate in Palestine, not to the French mandate in Syria in the 1920s. Prime Minister Ehud Barak balked at giving up the strip, and Clinton did not press him on the matter. Barak was right in principle—Syria had no legal right to the land—but wrong in his strategy.

Today creative diplomacy can remove this hurdle. The disputed land—tiny in size but grand in symbolism—can be ceded to Syria but made part of an international archaeological park under UN and U.S. auspices to ensure that both Israelis and Syrians have access to the area, that it is totally free of any military presence from either side, and that no water is stolen or transferred out of the lake to other lands without joint agreement of the two states. The larger issue of water resources in the extremely dry Levant can be resolved by a multibillion-dollar project to create desalinization plants to increase the amount of fresh water available to all the peoples of the region. This would be part of the broader American role outlined in the following paragraphs.

On the Palestinian issue, the proposals President Clinton made at the end of his presidency, the so-called Clinton parameters, should be the basis of a deal. Again, I helped draft those ideas and believe they are a fair and just basis for a settlement. Israel would return all but a small sliver of the West Bank and Gaza to the Palestinians and would compensate the Palestinians with equivalent land swaps in the Negev or Galilee for lost land. Palestine and Israel would share the city of Jerusalem and the holy basin at its core, assigning what is Jewish to the Israelis and what is Arab to the Palestinians. Palestinian refugees would have the option of either returning to the West Bank and Gaza or receiving generous compensation from an international fund, again led by the United States. And water desalinization plants would be built to ensure a greener future for all.

The United States would play a crucial role in convening the parties and using all official leverage possible to secure an agreement. It would have to appeal directly to the peoples of the region to back a deal and get them to help make it happen. The United States would also have to lead the international effort to pay the costs of water desalinization plants, refugee compensation and resettlement, improved Israeli security requirements, and other expenses.

I was in charge of negotiating these issues with an Israeli team at Camp David for President Clinton. The estimated costs in 2000 were about $35 billion. A Syrian deal would push that estimate up to perhaps $45 billion to $50 billion. The United States would not fund it alone but would cover a substantial part. It would be a cheap price to pay for putting the Arab-Israeli issue into the peace column and out of the war column.[3]

That plan, some will argue, will never fly in the aftermath of Hamas's takeover of Gaza in 2007. Although this undoubtedly makes the idea harder to implement, the key to success will be to persuade Hamas to become part of the process. To do that, the parties to the conflict must take the following action: Israel must open a dialogue with Hamas, as some prominent Israeli security experts (including the former head of the Mossad, Efraim Halevy) have already suggested; and the Arab states (particularly Syria and Saudi Arabia) must exert their influence to get Hamas to the table. It is essential to move on both fronts simultaneously, to create incentives for all players to help rather than spoil the process.

Without moving some of Hamas into the allied camp, the battle with al Qaeda will only be prolonged. Indeed, al Qaeda is very worried that the most successful Sunni Arab jihadist movement in history may settle for a deal. As already mentioned, the Mecca agreement between Hamas and Fatah infuriated al Qaeda. Its cries of treason underscored its vulnerability on this key issue. If Palestinians choose to make peace with Israel, the most fundamental point of al Qaeda's narrative becomes irrelevant.

In other words, making peace between Israelis and Arabs is not only wise policy in its own right but also an extremely useful strategy for pulling the rug out from under al Qaeda. As it has made abundantly clear to the world, al Qaeda opposes the very existence of Israel. That is why Zawahiri joined the plot to kill Sadat, and that is why bin Laden became a terrorist when Saudi Arabia endorsed the Oslo process. If the Arab countries and the larger Islamic community can come to accept Israel because Palestinians themselves are willing to make peace with it, then the crucial center-piece of al Qaeda's narrative and rationale for terrorism will crumble.

Al Qaeda will obviously continue to argue that any deal is treason and that not one inch of Palestine should be given to the Jews for their own state. Al Qaeda will try to rally the extremist wing of the Hamas movement and other disaffected Palestinians to its camp. But a real peace based on fair and just proposals will leave it more and more isolated from the ummah and will encourage the Arab and Muslim peoples to resist the extreme. That is precisely why al Qaeda fears this approach so much.

Of course, the conflict over Palestine is not the only issue drawing recruits to al Qaeda, but it is by far the most evocative and has the deepest resonance in the world of Islam. From Morocco to Indonesia, the Palestinian cause has repeatedly mobilized vast Muslim support.

Another conflict in urgent need of U.S. attention is the sixty-year-old Kashmir crisis, which, like Palestine, is a product of the dissolution of the British Empire. Kashmir is not as central to the al Qaeda narrative as Palestine by any means—it is mentioned far less often in the messages from bin Laden and Zawahiri—but it is an important issue for a key state of South Asia, Pakistan.

As explained in earlier chapters, al Qaeda's fortunes depend on the outcome of the battle for the soul of Pakistan. No country has provided the organization with a more critical lifeline than Pakistan. This was true before 9/11, when Pakistan helped engineer the alliance between al Qaeda and the Taliban and ensured the Taliban's safety in Afghanistan. It is even truer today, as Pakistan has become the new safe haven for bin Laden and al Qaeda's core leaders.

Pakistan's relations with al Qaeda have been shaped in large part by the country's national security agenda since partition, which revolves around the threat posed by India. The natural way to deal with the threat, its leaders argue, is to give the military a disproportionate slice of the national income to build a large modern military with nuclear weapons and terrorist surrogates. Since the country is under a military regime, the army also determines the parameters within which diplomacy with India can be pursued: it makes the critical foreign and security policy decisions, which are only then implemented by the Foreign Ministry. The army has decided that Pakistan's main enemy is India and that its defeat can be achieved in great part by supporting jihadi groups.

Extensive work on this issue has led former CIA director George Tenet to conclude:

> What the Pakistanis really feared was a two-front conflict, with the Indians seeking to reclaim Pakistan and the Taliban mullahs trying to export their radical brand of Islam across the border from Afghanistan. A war with India also posed the grim specter of nuclear confrontation, but from the ruling generals' point of view, the best way to avoid having their nation Taliban-ized was to keep their enemy close. That meant not cooperating with us in hunting down bin Laden and his organization.[4]

To make matters worse, the Pakistani army has a very deep distrust of the United States, which it considers a fair-weather friend. A common Pakistani joke is that the United States sees Pakistan as a condom, used and then thrown away. An on-and-off arms relationship, symbolized by the F-16 saga, has left a bitter taste in the officer corps, which is convinced that the United States will invariably abandon Pakistan when its interests no longer require a close relationship.

This preoccupation with India and the disproportionate role of the army in decisionmaking have profound implications for the international community, especially since India is clearly an emerging world power and one of the community's most important economies. Washington and New Delhi, now the capitals of the two largest democracies on the planet, are drawing increasingly closer, leaving Pakistan in the shadows feeling even more deeply threatened by the rise of India.

In a best-case scenario, the international community, led by the United States, should seek to allay Pakistan's anxiety about India by resolving the underlying dispute between the two countries, which is centered in Kashmir. From the Pakistani perspective, the optimal solution would be to unify the province—or at least the Muslim-dominated Valley of Kashmir and the capital of Srinagar—with Pakistan. This would reduce, if not remove, the need for a nuclear arsenal or jihadist backup to compel India to withdraw from the Valley—and is precisely the outcome that Pakistani leaders have in mind when they urge American leaders to devote diplomatic and political energy to the Kashmir issue.

Needless to say, it is a completely unrealistic scenario. India has no intention of withdrawing from Kashmir. On the contrary, it has already made a major concession, it argues, by accepting the de facto partition of the state between itself, Pakistan, and China. India is probably prepared to accept the Line of Control (roughly the cease-fire line of 1948) as the ultimate border with Pakistan, but not a fundamental redrawing of borders that would put the Valley under Pakistan's sovereignty.

But this does not rule out an option of more realistic proportions, which would complement the ongoing Indo-Pakistani bilateral dialogue. That dialogue has already produced several confidence-building measures: the two countries have reopened transportation links, set up hot lines between military commands, and held periodic discussions at the foreign secretary level on all their divisive issues. Unfortunately, the two parties seem unwilling to bridge the significant gulf created by Kashmir, made all the wider by India's refusal to negotiate while still a target of terrorist attacks planned and organized in Pakistan.

The United States has been reluctant to engage more actively in the Kashmir dispute in light of India's posture that outside intervention is unwarranted as Kashmir is a purely bilateral issue. Hence American diplomacy has put the Kashmir problem in the "too-hard" category and left it to simmer. The results are all too predictable. The Kashmir issue will continue to boil over periodically, and the United States and the international community will have to step in to try to prevent a full-scale war. This was the case during the Kargil crisis in 1999 and after terrorist attacks on the Indian parliament in 2001, when India mobilized its army for war on the Pakistani border.

A unique opportunity for quiet American diplomacy to help advance the Kashmir issue toward a better, more stable solution may exist in 2009. The U.S.-India nuclear deal agreed to during President Bush's July 2005 visit to South Asia should create a more stable and enduring basis for U.S.-Indian relations than at any time in their history. The deal removes the central obstacle to closer strategic ties between Washington and New Delhi: the nuclear proliferation problem, which has held back the development of those ties for two decades.

In the new era of a U.S.-Indian strategic partnership, Washington should be more prepared to press New Delhi to be more flexible on Kashmir. It is clearly in the U.S. interest to try to defuse a lingering conflict that has generated global terrorism and repeatedly threatened to create a full-scale military confrontation on the subcontinent. It is also in India's interest to find a solution to a conflict that has gone on too long. Since Kargil, the Indians have been more open to an American role in Kashmir because they sense Washington is fundamentally in favor of a resolution on the basis of the status quo, which favors India.

Currently the United States is enjoying better relations with both India and Pakistan than at any time in the past several decades. The rapprochement with India, begun by President Clinton and advanced by President Bush, is now supported by an almost unique bipartisan consensus in the American foreign policy establishment and Congress. Legislation with bipartisan support has also removed the sanctions that poisoned U.S.-Pakistani relations for decades. It is a unique moment for U.S. foreign policy. To take full advantage of it, the new administration should press forward on Kashmir.

A Kashmir solution would have to be based on a formula that would make the Line of Control both a permanent and normal international border (perhaps with some minor modifications) and a permeable frontier for the Kashmiri people on the two sides so they could live more normal lives. A special condominium might be created to allow the two constituencies to work together on internal issues, such as transportation, the environment, sports, and tourism.

Pakistan and India are unlikely to agree to such a formula on their own, given the mistrust that pervades both parties. A quiet American effort led by the next president is probably essential to move them toward an agreement. Resolution of the Kashmiri issue would certainly go a long way toward making Pakistan a more normal state, and one less preoccupied with India. It would also remove a major rationale for the army's disproportionate role in Pakistan's national security affairs. That, in turn, would help to restore genuine civilian democratic rule in the country. Equally important, an agreement on Kashmir would reduce the arms race between the two powers and the risk of nuclear conflict. Last, but certainly not least, it would free Pakistan of the need to fight an asymmetric war against India with allies like the Taliban, Lashkar-e-Tayyiba, and al Qaeda.

Of course, some tensions would still plague the two neighbors, and the Taliban would still be a problem in Afghanistan. Nonetheless, a Kashmir solution would set the stage for a new and friendlier era in the subcontinent, and for more productive interaction between the international community and Pakistan.

The alternative is to let Kashmir simmer and the Indo-Pakistani dialogue remain at a standstill. In the long run, this approach is virtually certain to lead to another crisis in the subcontinent. Sooner or later, the two countries will again find themselves on the precipice of war. In a worst-case scenario, a terrorist incident on the order of the July 2006 metro bombings in Mumbai or the hijacking of Air India 814 could spark an Indian military response against targets in Pakistan, allegedly involved in the planning and orchestration of terrorism. And that could lead to nuclear war.

The next president must adopt a more sophisticated approach to Pakistan and its terror nexus. That means going beyond threats and sanctions, beyond commando raids and intelligence cooperation, beyond aid and aircraft sales. It is time to come to grips with what motivates Pakistan's behavior and to make peace. Such a move would also help eliminate al Qaeda's hold on Pakistan and thus strike another major blow to the terrorists' narrative. Conflict resolution, not conflict management, would also paint a new and more fitting picture of America, not as a supporter of Israel and India in the subjugation of Islamic peoples, but as a peacemaker promoting justice and freedom for all peoples, including Muslims.

Al Qaeda's narrative cannot be defeated by conflict resolution alone, of course. The rise of democracy in the Islamic world will have a large impact on the organization as well. President Bush has spoken eloquently on this issue many times, perhaps most notably in Abu Dhabi, during his first tour of the region in 2008. But his actions have not been consistent with his rhetoric. When Hamas won the parliamentary elections in Gaza and the West Bank, the Bush administration shunned any contact with its leaders and organized an international campaign to isolate the Hamas government. This was seen as hypocrisy all over the Islamic world. As a prominent critic of the Mubarak government, Saad Eddin Ibrahim, has written, "The Bush Administration and the neoconservatives swiftly retreated from their democracy promotion policy. By 2008 George Bush had backslided to exactly the position he had warned against and vowed never to do in January 2005."[5]

Worse still, the Bush administration has failed democracy in Pakistan. A nation of 170 million people with a history of alternating military regimes and elected civilian rulers, Pakistan would appear to be the perfect candidate for an American liberation strategy, as Bush called it in his second inaugural address in 2005. Unlike Saudi Arabia or many other Arab states, Pakistan has political parties with considerable voter support, a history of elections (albeit always surrounded by controversy), and a tradition of functioning civil institutions and society.

Unfortunately, U.S. administrations, both Republican and Democrat, have usually backed Pakistan's military dictators over its democratic leaders. Dwight Eisenhower, the first president to visit South Asia, embraced Pakistan's first military leader, Ayub Khan. John F. Kennedy embraced him as well, holding a lavish state dinner for him at Mount Vernon, the only time the first president's mansion has been used to host a foreign leader. Lyndon Johnson and Richard Nixon supported the dictators as well; Nixon even gave his assent to their brutal war in Bangladesh, which led to the death of hundreds of thousands and the breakup of the country. Jimmy Carter and Ronald Reagan both endorsed Zia ul-Haq's war in Afghanistan against Moscow (although Carter was deeply angered by Zia's execution of the democratically elected Zulfikar Ali Bhutto).

When Musharraf seized power in his 1999 coup, Bill Clinton imposed sanctions and pressed for an early end to the military regime. He worked to see that Prime Minister Nawaz Sharif did not meet the same fate as Bhutto. But he also became the first head of state to visit Pakistan after the coup and thus provided some measure of legitimacy to the coup maker.

George W. Bush went much further, not only repealing the sanctions but also providing Musharraf with over $11 billion in aid, more than half through direct funding to the army with little or no accounting. When Musharraf staged phony elections in 2002 and 2007, Bush did not object. When he sacked the head of the Supreme Court and the nation's lawyers took to the streets to demand his return, the Bush team backed the general. The cost has been the alienation of the Pakistani people. Polls show U.S. approval in Pakistan at an all-time low today.

Obviously, democracy-promoting policy is fraught with difficulties. Unless a civil society has emerged before a state embarks on elections, the results will only favor entrenched antidemocratic forces. Many have written extensively on how best to promote the process, but in the face of a determined spoiler like al Qaeda, the important point to bear in mind is consistency between one's message and action. Calling for democracy means supporting democratic forces when they are challenging a dictator. The United States has failed to do so in Pakistan, much to the advantage of al Qaeda and its narrative.

If Pakistan is the most important and difficult nation to deal with in order to destroy al Qaeda, Saudi Arabia is probably second on the list. Saudi Arabia is bin Laden's home, and the majority of the 9/11 attackers were his countrymen. At the same time, the House of Saud has for decades been a strong and reliable U.S. ally on many issues. Saudi support was critical in defeating the Soviet forces in Afghanistan and has helped advance the Middle East peace process. In fact, without the Saudis' pushing the Bush administration, the president is unlikely to have become a supporter of the two-state solution in 2001.

But the kingdom is built on an alliance between the Saudi royal family and the Wahhabi clerical establishment (ulema) that dates from 1744. A militant branch of Islam, Wahhabism has been exploited by bin Laden and others to justify their actions. The Saudi leadership must always take into account the views of the ulema and their supporters, now a powerful lobby in the kingdom that often sets the standard for the Islamic answer on issues of great emotional resonance in Arabia, the first and foremost being Palestine. The Wahhabi clerics are also preaching to the converted. Having met with King Abdullah many times, I can attest that the Palestinian issue is one deep in his heart.

In the summer of 2001, for example, I accompanied then secretary of state Colin Powell to Paris to see the king at the George V Hotel. The king showed the secretary a file containing photos of dead and wounded Palestinians who had been killed or injured by the Israelis in the intifada. His voice trembling with anger, he kept pressing Powell to do something to halt the violence. This was a genuine glimpse inside the man's worldview: he was not putting on an act but was truly upset that the United States was not doing enough to help. Thus a critical aspect of advancing the Arab-Israeli peace process will be its beneficial effect on U.S. relations with key Arab partners such as Saudi Arabia, Egypt, and Jordan.

Advocating democracy in Saudi Arabia, however, is more problematic. Unlike Pakistan, the kingdom has no history of political parties, an independent judiciary, a free press, or elections. It has a deeply conservative and traditionalist population. If given the choice to express their views, the majority will probably not be supportive of American policy on key issues like the peace process. The king, ironically, is among the more reform-oriented members of the family. He believes in increasing consultation between the royal decisionmakers, the ulema, and the general population—but in a cautious and careful manner.

In short, there is no single formula for defeating the al Qaeda narrative. It will take an intricate and complex strategy to manage U.S. alliances with the key Islamic countries. But the most critical step will be to advance peace.

## Destroying the Leadership, Sanctuaries, and Branches

The second major element of a new grand strategy will be to focus on the enemy's leadership, the core team huddled around bin Laden and Zawahiri in South Asia. The target of U.S. military and clandestine warfare strategy needs to be that leadership. It provides the inspiration and direction for the violent jihad. As long as its members are alive and active, they symbolize the success of resistance to America and attract new recruits. It is not good enough to have them "on the run" or "hiding in caves." That is a recipe for defeat, if not an acknowledgment of failure. The death or capture of Osama bin Laden and his senior associates in Pakistan and Afghanistan will not destroy the al Qaeda movement but will deal it a serious setback. The question is, how to do it?

First, the hunt for bin Laden needs to proceed under a clear chain of command. Today, none exists. I raised this issue indirectly with the director of national intelligence (DNI), Admiral Mike McConnell, by putting the question to author Lawrence Wright in a sketch of the DNI he was writing for the *New Yorker* magazine. Pointing to some recent intelligence successes—the capture of Mir Amal Kansi, who murdered two CIA employees outside the gates of the agency in January 1993, and the arrest in Pakistan of Ramzi Yusuf, the mastermind behind the February 1993 bombing of the World Trade Center—I said, "They were in some ways harder targets," and asked, "Who in the American government is now responsible for the apprehension of Osama bin Laden? There's the director of the National Counterterrorism Center, but I doubt that is his job. The DNI? Who does the president think is responsible?"

McConnell responded: "If the president picked a single person, he'd probably point to Mike Hayden, the CIA director. At another level he might say secretary of defense. Depends on where bin Laden might be."[6]

The DNI's response is illuminating. The U.S. head of intelligence does not know who is in charge—clearly, he is not. As a result, the hunt under way for al Qaeda lacks a sheriff to lead the posse. The next president needs a grand strategy and a clear chain of command to kill or capture the worst mass murderer in American history. The longer bin Laden and his understudy Ayman al-Zawahiri survive, the more they will take on mythic proportions above the law and out of the reach of America.

The director of the CIA should be made responsible for a global manhunt to track down and either bring to justice or eliminate the senior leadership of al Qaeda and its franchises. Working with friendly foreign intelligence services, the CIA should have the task of bringing these individuals to justice or taking justice to them. The CIA has a fair record of success in tracking down individuals such as Ramzi Yusuf and Khalid Sheikh Mohammed. The next president should select a CIA director with experience in clandestine operations, especially human operations, to get the job done and then should give him the resources to do it.

The al Qaeda propaganda apparatus should also be shut down. Al-Sahab has grown rapidly over the past several years, either tripling or doubling its output each year. This year Zawahiri has used it to take hundreds of questions from its audience around the world, in effect running a call-in talk show to the ummah. It stands to reason that an active public media outlet would be vulnerable to espionage that could penetrate its inner workings and then countermeasures to put it out of action.

In addition, the al Qaeda sanctuary in South Asia should be closed permanently. Pakistan and Afghanistan have been the home of bin Laden and Zawahiri for most of their adult lives. They and their supporters have thrived in the badlands along the border between the two for far too long. But another big question is how to shut it down.

*A critical first step is to enhance U.S. commitment—military, political, and economic—to Afghanistan.* North Atlantic Treaty Organization (NATO) forces along the Afghanistan-Pakistan border will have to be increased significantly in order to defeat the resurgent Taliban, and that will require American leadership. This war cannot be won on the cheap, as the president has tried to do for six years. It is urgent for the United States to redirect its military and intelligence effort away from Iraq (which is not a haven for al Qaeda's core leadership) and toward the Afghanistan-Pakistan border regions (where bin Laden and his henchmen are ensconced).

When America's allies see that this country has finally gotten its priorities straight—that it is again committed to smoking out the al Qaeda leadership where it does reside—they will provide enough troops and equipment to overwhelm the Taliban and al Qaeda. It is essential to fully engage Muslim countries in this effort: to the extent that the troops rooting out al Qaeda and the Taliban are Muslims, the jihadists will be unable to portray the effort to defeat them as part of the usual "West against Islam" syndrome. The United States should therefore encourage its Muslim and Arab partners—especially Egypt, Jordan, Tunisia, Algeria, and Morocco—to offer troops to help stabilize Afghanistan.

America should also vastly increase its effort to build a larger and stronger Afghan army and air force. In the Korean War, the United States and its UN allies built a South Korean army from almost nothing to a force of 700,000 men in less than three years. By the end of the war, the Koreans were manning much of the front line. It has done far less in Afghanistan, partly because its ambitions have been low and partly because it has not put the resources into the job. Recruiting and training more soldiers should become a major priority, along with supplying them with state-of-the-art equipment and building an airlift capability to get them where they need to be. To this end, and to provide firepower for its army, Afghanistan needs help in constructing an air force. The Soviet invaders built an Afghan communist air force consisting of more than 400 fixed-wing aircraft and 100 helicopters; in six years the United States has built virtually no air capability there. Overall, today in Afghanistan NATO has fewer troops on the ground to stabilize the country than the Soviet Union deployed there in the 1980s and has created an Afghan army to assist it that is also fewer in numbers than the one created by the Soviet client's Marxist regime in the 1980s.

NATO should create a contact group led by a senior NATO diplomat to engage with all of Afghanistan's neighbors in identifying ways to stabilize the borders, especially the 1,500-mile-long Pakistan border. This group should include Iran, which has been a generally helpful player in Afghanistan in the past few years (in contrast to its role in Iraq). NATO should also reach out to India, which has already provided a half billion dollars in aid for Afghanistan and has a national interest in defeating Islamic terrorism, having been a target itself for far too long.

One immediate objective of a contact group would be to help Afghanistan and Pakistan agree on the demarcation of their border. The current line, called the Durand line after a British officer, has never been formally accepted as the official border by Afghanistan. This perpetuates the border confusion and makes it easy for the jihadists to move back and forth across the line. Former ambassador to Afghanistan Ronald Neuman rightly characterizes the current situation as "borderline insanity" and suggests that resolving its ambiguity is part of the required "big think" solution to the problem of the world's most dangerous badlands.[7]

*Beyond a military and security buildup, the United States should take the lead in formulating a major economic reconstruction program.* The international community has delivered far less aid per capita to Afghanistan than it has to other recovering states, such as Bosnia or Kosovo. This calls for nothing less than *a multilateral Marshall Plan for Afghanistan,* a country ravaged by three decades of war against the Soviet Union and then the Taliban. The effort must be on the scale of what rebuilt Europe after World War II. The United States should lead a coalition to rebuild this country, inviting Russia, Japan, Europe, India, and many others to contribute.

The next president should reach out to key leaders to help fund and develop such a program. King Abdullah of Saudi Arabia should be a key partner. For decades, the Saudis have been the most generous donor of aid to Pakistan, spending billions to oust the Soviet forces next door. Riyadh understands the importance of the task more than most, but it will take an energetic president and an early visit to the kingdom to get the job done.

The president should also enlist the help of Moscow in this venture. Its Soviet parent was responsible for the first Afghan war, and though the communist government is gone, it still bears responsibility for the hardships it created. Just helping to clear the massive minefields scattered across the countryside would be a major contribution. In southern Afghanistan alone there are 15 million mines left over from the Red Army—they are the basic ingredient in most Taliban explosive devices.

Such a Marshall Plan must include a major effort to provide all Afghan children with high-quality education and free lunches. Too many children fall into the hands of Islamic schools, some of which teach violent jihad, because it is their only educational option. Since the liberation of Kabul in 2001, 1,500 new schools have been built and 3,000 repaired, but the country needs at least 7,000 more.[8] The long-term defeat of al Qaeda depends on teaching hope, rather than hate, to the next generation.

Afghanistan's infrastructure also needs vast improvement. Three decades of war have devastated the country, which was one of the poorest in the world before the Soviet invasion. Since 2001 almost 2,000 miles of road have been built or repaired, but 11,000 more miles need to be completed, according to its development program.[9] Roads are essential to security and to developing agriculture. In the absence of highways and access to markets, farmers have turned to poppy cultivation and the production of heroin and opium, which today account for more than 90 percent of the world's supply. These crops have had devastating effects on the integrity of local government. To make matters worse, the Taliban plays a large role in the drug trafficking.

*These efforts must also extend into Pakistan.* The tribal regions along the border where al Qaeda thrives are poverty-stricken breeding grounds for jihadism and training outposts for jihadist fighters. U.S. economic assistance must be tied to more aggressive efforts by the Pakistani government to crack down on the Taliban and al Qaeda. Assistance to the borderlands of Afghanistan and Pakistan should focus on developing this area into a zone of peace and prosperity, not of terror and drugs.

The United States and its partners, including NATO, need to take a firmer line with Pakistan, insisting that it crack down aggressively and systematically on all terrorists: Arabs, Afghans, and Kashmiris. For their part, Pakistanis need to support the restoration of democracy. Not just elections, but real democracy based upon a renewed and strengthened civil society is ultimately the best way to undermine the Taliban and al Qaeda forces in Pakistan.

Democracy, some say, could bring radical Islamists to power. That is a canard. Polls show that most Pakistanis favor the mainstream parties. Moreover, the narrow political base of the Musharraf government is a key reason for the growing influence of the Taliban and al Qaeda. Pakistan needs a representative government and a free and vibrant civil society if it is to resist the siren call of the jihadists. To those who say the United States cannot afford to support Pakistani democracy more aggressively, I say it cannot afford not to.

As noted earlier, the United States also needs to pay more attention to the Kashmir problem if it hopes to help and win over Pakistan. With a legitimate and democratic government in place, Pakistan could be encouraged to work with its Indian counterpart to resolve the Kashmir issue fairly. This would give Pakistani democracy a major boost and perhaps send the army back to the barracks for good.

The hardest part of trying to defeat al Qaeda lies in meeting the challenges in Pakistan. This will not be easy and will take time, energy, and a sophisticated approach. But the alternative is too terrifying to consider, as Benazir Bhutto recognized just before her death: "I now believe al Qaeda could be marching on Islamabad in two to four years."[10] Though probably still an exaggeration, this scenario can no longer be easily dismissed.

Yet another component of a grand strategy to defeat al Qaeda must surely be the elimination of its branches around the world: the franchises in Iraq, Saudi Arabia, the Maghreb, Yemen, and elsewhere. Here there is some reason for optimism. Although effective in setting up regional franchises or merging with existing groups such as the Algerian Salafist Group for Preaching and Combat to create terror, al Qaeda has repeatedly encountered a backlash to its extremism and violence that seems to hurt the franchises as they try to develop and mature. That does not mean they are not dangerous. They are. However, the backlash can be used to advantage to counter these groups and strengthen the forces opposed to al Qaeda.

Jordan provides a good example of how this might work. Zarqawi enjoyed widespread support and popularity in Jordan, especially among its Palestinian population, when he attacked Americans in Iraq. But when he targeted Jordan's major hotels in Amman, he triggered a backlash from his own countrymen who did not want their land turned into a killing field like Iraq.

Similarly, bin Laden was widely admired in Saudi Arabia, even after 9/11, and considered a hero, a true knight fighting the Zionist-Crusader enemy. But when al Qaeda began killing innocent Saudis and other Muslims in the kingdom, he lost some of this luster, and the negative reaction assisted the House of Saud in fighting al Qaeda.

In Egypt, too, the carnage perpetrated by Ayman Zawahiri and the other Egyptian jihadists in the 1990s, especially the massacre at Luxor, alienated most of the population from the extremists. This helped the Mubarak government obtain more and better intelligence on its enemies.

As for Iraq, a backlash against Zarqawi's brutality has emerged there, although it is far from clear whether the reaction is strong enough to defeat al Qaeda completely. Though a critical battlefield in the fight against jihadism, Iraq has also become a quagmire for the United States that prevents it from fully engaging the core al Qaeda leadership in Afghanistan and Pakistan. America's enemies want it to remain bogged down there.

Clearly, the time has come to start disengaging from Iraq's civil war. The withdrawal should be orderly, phased, and complete. The key to an exit strategy is to exit. The United States should not entertain a South Korea–like solution, as the Pentagon has sometimes suggested, which would leave behind an open-ended military base. That would only alienate succeeding generations of Iraqis and other Muslims. The Iraqis do not want it, and neither should the United States.

This is not the place to review the litany of mistakes and misjudgments that led to this disaster. Suffice it to say the war was not necessary, its prosecution has been disastrous, and U.S. diplomacy has been inept and counterproductive. American troops must now be extricated from the quagmire and the Iraqis allowed to settle their conflicts. The Iraqi government should be given credit for the departure, so as to enhance its own legitimacy, and the United States should do all it can diplomatically to persuade other nations to help stabilize Iraq and fund reconstruction.

In the long run, al Qaeda will have to answer to the vast majority of Muslims who never wanted their religion to be exploited to justify mass murder and carnage on a global scale. When a smart grand strategy has turned the tables on al Qaeda and exposed it for what it really is—a small fringe of fanatics who have no real plan for a better life for the billion Muslims around the world—then the ummah will destroy al Qaeda far more relentlessly and effectively than the United States can ever do.

As early as 2004, the secretary general of the Arab League, Amre Moussa, warned that the war in Iraq and al Qaeda's brutal attacks on the Shia were opening "the gates of hell" for the Muslim world.[11] Like many others, Moussa was appalled that Zarqawi's violence would create the worst tensions in Shia-Sunni relations in the modern history of the ummah. He criticized the Bush administration for letting the situation drift toward civil war but also called on all Muslims to fight extremism and terrorism. In effect, he called upon the ummah to reject al Qaeda.

Other Muslim leaders have also rallied against al Qaeda's narrative and ideology. In late 2004 King Abdullah II of Jordan issued a detailed statement, the Amman Message, countering al Qaeda's argument that it is permissible to declare some Muslims (such as the Shia) apostates in order to justify their murder. Several senior Muslim clerics, including the Sheikh of Al-Azhar University in Cairo, Ayatollah Sistani in Iraq (the leading Shia ulema in the country), and Sheikh Qaradawi in Qatar (a very popular Sunni cleric) subsequently endorsed the Amman Message and its rejection of al Qaeda.

America's goal should be to help make that happen as quickly as possible. A wise strategy that attacks the al Qaeda narrative, its leadership, its sanctuary, and its branches can do so. There is no reason for despair or defeatism. Al Qaeda has serious vulnerabilities, as I have pointed out. It lacks a cohesive vision of the future and a workable plan for government. It has often overplayed its hand and created strong blowback. It does not have the support of the vast majority of Islam but relies on a small group of fanatics. Wise action will gain Islamic support against it. Failure to take this road will only lead to another catastrophe worse than 9/11.

Some have suggested the United States is facing an enemy that will take decades, even a century, to defeat. If it pursues wrong policies that antagonize the world's Muslims, that statement may well turn into a self-fulfilling prophecy. More blunders like Iraq and more prison camps like Abu Ghraib and Guantánamo Bay can only help al Qaeda.

At the end of day, al Qaeda is not Nazi Germany, Imperial Japan, or the Soviet Union. It is a relatively small organization that can be defeated by wise and smart policy. Though it is responsible for the worst day save one in U.S. history, its demise should not take decades to achieve.

# Notes

## CHAPTER ONE

1. This figure is based on the estimate of nonterrorist deaths provided by the 9/11 Commission, which lists 2,749 for the World Trade Center, 184 for the Pentagon, and 40 for ill-fated United Airlines Flight 93 in Pennsylvania. See *9/11 Commission Report: Final Report of the National Commission on Terrorist Attacks upon the United States* (July 22, 2004), notes to chapter 9, n. 188 (http://govinfo.library.unt.edu/911report/911Report_Notes.pdf).

2. Institute for the Analysis of Global Security, "How Much Did the September 11 Terrorist Attack Cost America?" (www.iags.org/costof911).

3. Michael D. Huckabee, "America's Priorities in the War on Terror: Islamists, Iraq, Iran and Pakistan," *Foreign Affairs* 87 (January/February 2008): 156.

4. "Poll 70% Believe Saddam, 9-11 Link," Associated Press, September 6, 2003.

5. "9/11 + 5 Finds a Nation Badly Divided as GOPers Back U.S. War on Terror, Wiretapping, and Saddam's Role in 9/11; Dems, Indies Suspicious of All Three," Zogby International, September 5, 2006.

6. Gary Schroen, interview, "The Dark Side," PBS *Frontline*, January 20, 2006 (www.pbs.org/wgbh/pages/frontline/darkside/interviews/schroen.html).

7. The most authoritative account of the plot is from the 9/11 Commission's report, especially Staff Study 16, "The Outline of the 9/11 Plot" (www.fas.org/irp/congress/2004_rpt/staff_statement_16.pdf).

8. See "The Wills of the Heroes of the Raids on New York and Washington: The Will of the Martyr Abu Musaib Walid al-Shehri," al-Sahab media, September 11, 2007. Translated by Open Source Center.

9. Malika al Araud, *Les Soldats de Lumiere*, unpublished (2003).

10. See Schroen, PBS interview.

11. Pervez Musharraf, *In the Line of Fire: A Memoir* (New York: Free Press, 2006), pp. 239–40.

12. Ibid., pp. 241–42.

13. Quoted in Michael Abramowitz, "Rove Redux," *Washington Post,* October 29, 2007, p. A13.

14. Gary Schroen, *First In: An Insider's Account of How the CIA Spearheaded the War on Terror in Afghanistan* (New York: Ballantine Books, 2005), pp. 359–60.

15. Mahmud Durrani, interview, "Pakistan: Fall Guy or Failure," *Washington Diplomat,* November 2007, p. 13; see also the account by Schroen, *First In.*

16. Musharraf, *In the Line of Fire.*

17. Benazir Bhutto, *Reconciliation: Islam, Democracy and the West* (New York: HarperCollins, 2008), p. 5.

18. Huckabee, "America's Priorities in the War on Terror," p. 165.

## CHAPTER TWO

1. Montasser al Zayyat, *The Road to Al Qaeda: The Story of bin Laden's Right-Hand Man* (London: Pluto Press, 2004), p. 34. Zayyat, an Egyptian jihadist, has written the most detailed biography of Zawahiri in Arabic. The two were in prison together after the Sadat assassination, but Zayyat later broke with Zawahiri.

2. Perhaps the best account of Sayyid Qutb's life and views is by Emmanuel Sivan, *Radical Islam: Medieval Theology and Modern Politics* (Yale University Press, 1985).

3. Ayman al-Zawahiri, *Knights under the Prophet's Banner* (London: Al-Sharq al-Awsat, December 2001), p. 62. *Al-Sharq al-Awsat* serialized excerpts from the book in late 2001, which were subsequently translated and published by the Foreign Broadcast Information Service (FBIS), now known as the Open Source Center (OSC). Henceforth FBIS will be cited as FBIS (OSC).

4. Lawrence Wright, *The Looming Tower: Al Qaeda and the Road to 9/11* (New York: Alfred A. Knopf, 2006), p. 40. Wright has written the most detailed account of Zawahiri's life available in English. See also Zayyat, *The Road to al Qaeda.*

5. Ayman al-Zawahiri, *Allegiance and Disavowal,* published by al Qaeda's al-Sahab media center and distributed on jihadist websites; trans. OSC, December 28, 2006.

6. Sivan, *Radical Islam,* p. 127.

7. Giles Keppel, *Muslim Extremism in Egypt: The Prophet and the Pharaoh* (University of California Press, 1985; trans. from original French: Paris, 1984), pp. 192–204.

8. Ibrahim M. Abu-Rabi', "Ayman al-Zawahiri as I Knew Him," Introduction in Zayyat, *The Road to al Qaeda*, p. 11.

9. Zawahiri, *Knights*, p. 31.

10. Wright, *Looming Tower*, p. 185.

11. Zawahiri, *Knights*, p. 18.

12. Ibid., p. 82. For an in-depth study of Napoleon and the invasion of Palestine in 1799, see Nathan Schur, *Napoleon in the Holy Land* (London: Greenhill Books, 1999), esp. chap. 13, which deals with the question of Napoleon's plans for the Jews in Palestine.

13. Ayman al-Zawahiri, "Realities of the Conflict between Islam and Unbelief," produced by al Qaeda's al-Sahab media; trans. OSC, December 21, 2006.

14. Ayman al-Zawahiri, "The Emancipation of Mankind and Nations under the Banner of the Koran," audio statement and text released January 30, 2005; trans. FBIS (OSC).

15. Ayman al-Zawahiri, "The Advice of One Concerned," audio statement and text, July 5, 2007; trans. OSC.

16. Zawahiri, "Emancipation of Mankind."

17. Ayman al-Zawahiri, interview by al-Sahab media, September 11, 2006, marking the fifth anniversary of 9/11; trans. OSC.

18. Ayman al-Zawahiri, interview, al-Jazeera TV, October 8, 2002; trans. FBIS (OSC).

19. Ayman al-Zawahiri, audiotape, read on al-Jazeera TV, September 28, 2003; trans. FBIS (OSC).

20. Ayman al-Zawahiri, audiotape, read on al-Jazeera TV, March 25, 2004; trans. FBIS (OSC).

21. Zahid Hussain, *Frontline Pakistan: The Struggle with Militant Islam* (Columbia University Press, 2007), p. 139.

22. Ayman al-Zawahiri, "Obstacles to Jihad, Four Years after the Raids of New York and Washington," lecture posted on jihadist websites, December 2005; trans. FBIS (OSC).

23. Ayman al-Zawahiri, video statement, al-Jazeera TV, Doha, September 1, 2005.

24. Ayman al-Zawahiri, interview, al-Jazeera TV, September 19, 2005.

25. Ayman al-Zawahiri, audiotape, posted jihadist U.K. website, March 5, 2006; trans. FBIS (OSC).

26. Islamic State of Iraq, statement on the Islamic Muhajirun Network, November 29, 2006; trans. OSC.

27. Ayman al-Zawahiri, "Lessons, Examples, and the Great Events of the Year 1427," al-Jazeera TV, February 13, 2007; trans. OSC.

28. Saad Eddin Ibrahim, "Egypt's Unchecked Repression," *Washington Post,* August 21, 2007.

29. Ayman al-Zawahiri, videotape, al-Jazeera TV, August 5, 2006.

## CHAPTER THREE

1. Steve Coll, *The Bin Ladens: An Arabian Family in the American Century* (New York: Penguin Press, 2008), pp. 87–92.

2. Osama would later remember his early education in Lebanon when Israel invaded Lebanon in 1982 and laid siege to Beirut that summer: "I became sure that the oppression and intentional murder of innocent women and children is a deliberate American policy." See ibid., p. 158.

3. Quoted in Jason Burke, *Al Qaeda: Casting a Shadow of Terror* (London: I. B. Tauris, 2003), p. 8.

4. For an insightful look into the generational struggle in the kingdom, see Mai Yamani, *Changed Identities: The Challenge of the New Generation in Saudi Arabia* (London: Royal Institute of International Affairs, 2000).

5. George Tenet, *At the Center of the Storm: My Years at the CIA* (New York: HarperCollins, 2007), p. 101.

6. Benazir Bhutto, *Daughter of the East: An Autobiography* (London: Simon and Schuster: 2007), p. 405.

7. Ibid., pp. 411–13.

8. Benazir Bhutto, *Reconciliation: Islam, Democracy and the West* (New York: HarperCollins, 2008), p. 205.

9. John Wilson, *Lashkar-e-Tayyeba*, Pakistan Security Research Unit Brief 12 (University of Bradford, May 21, 2007).

10. Lawrence Wright, *The Looming Tower: Al-Qaeda and the Road to 9/11* (New York: Alfred A. Knopf, 2006), p. 102.

11. *PBS NewsHour*, January 21, 2002.

12. Wright, *Looming Tower*, p. 133.

13. Robert Gates, *From the Shadows: The Ultimate Insider's Story of Five Presidents and How They Won the Cold War* (New York: Simon and Schuster, 1996), p.139.

14. Robin Wright and John Broder, "U.S. Bidding to Regain Stingers Sent to Afghans," *Los Angeles Times*, July 23, 1993.

15. Wright, *Looming Tower*, p. 153.

16. Ironically, a few years later the Saudis would support the south when it rebelled against the new united government led by President Salih and sought to reestablish an independent South Yemen. Saudi anger in 1994 was a reflection of Salih's support for Saddam in 1990. Bin Laden was harshly critical of the Saudi regime for backing the southern communists in 1994 and wrote a couple of scathing letters to Prince Sultan for arming them. See Vahid Brown, *Cracks in the Foundation: Leadership Schisms in al Qaida from 1989 to 2006* (West Point, N.Y.: West Point Combating Terrorism Center, 2007), p. 28.

17. Burke, *Al Qaeda*, p. 125.

18. For a thorough review of the evidence in Somalia and Yemen, see ibid., p. 135. The 9/11 Commission relied heavily on the testimony of al Qaeda defector

Jamal al Fadl, who left the group over a quarrel about money in Sudan and provided much information to the CIA. It was later determined that some of this information had been exaggerated to enhance his importance.

19. The issue of al Qaeda's role in Khobar has been thoroughly researched by Thomas Hegghamer, "Deconstructing the Myth about Al Qaeda and Khobar," *CTC Sentinel*, vol. 1, no. 3 (February 2008).

20. For the full interview, see Bruce Lawrence, ed., *Messages to the World: The Statements of Osama Bin Laden* (London: Verso, 2005), p. 52.

21. This key letter can be seen in ibid., pp. 4–14. Lawrence rightly notes: "The letter makes . . . plain that Palestine, far from being a late addition to bin Laden's agenda, was at the centre of it from the start."

22. As'ad Abu Khalil, *The Battle for Saudi Arabia: Royalty, Fundamentalism, and Global Power* (New York: Seven Stories Press, 2004), p. 69.

23. Lawrence, *Messages to the World*, p. 16.

24. The statement can be found in Coll, *The Bin Ladens*, p. 408.

25. Burke, *Al Qaeda*, p. 139.

26. UN Press Release, April 26, 1996.

27. Tenet, *At the Center of the Storm*, p. 102.

28. 9/11 Commission Report, p. 64.

29. Lawrence, *Messages to the World*, pp. 24–30.

30. Ibid., pp. 58–62.

31. The *al-Hayat* message is referred to in CNN, "Egyptian Doctor Emerges as Terror Mastermind" (www.cnn.com/CNN/Programs/people/shows/zawahiri/profile.html).

## Chapter Four

1. Robert Kaplan, *Soldiers of God: With Islamic Warriors in Afghanistan and Pakistan* (New York: Vintage Books, 2001), p. 172.

2. See Roy Gutman, *How We Missed the Story: Osama bin Laden, the Taliban, and the Hijacking of Afghanistan* (Washington: U.S. Institute of Peace, 2008), p. 10.

3. Benazir Bhutto, *Daughter of the East: An Autobiography*, rev. ed. (London: Simon and Schuster, 2007), p. 400.

4. Quoted in Gutman, *How We Missed*, p. 12.

5. Daniel Byman, *Deadly Connections: States That Sponsor Terrorism* (Cambridge University Press, 2005).

6. Kaplan, *Soldiers of God*, pp. 184–88, 223.

7. The massacre is retold by Human Rights Watch, *Afghanistan: The Massacre at Mazar-i Sharif*, Report C1007 (New York: November 1998).

8. Quoted in Douglas Jehl, "Holier than Thou: Behind the Iranian-Afghan Rift," *New York Times*, September 7, 1998.

9. Gutman, *How We Missed the Story*, p. 136.

10. Nick B. Mills, *Karzai: The Failing American Intervention and the Struggle for Afghanistan* (Hoboken, N.J.: John Wiley and Sons, 2007), p. 105.

11. Jason Burke, *Al Qaeda: Casting a Shadow of Terror* (London: I. B. Tauris, 2003), pp. 169–71. Burke interviewed some of the HUM cadre.

12. Jaswant Singh, *A Call to Honour: In Service of Emergent India* (New Delhi: Rupa, 2007) p. 238. Jaswant has also confirmed to me his view that the operation was a stage-setter for 9/11. See also Ahmed Rashid, *Descent into Chaos: The United States and the Failure of Nation Building in Pakistan, Afghanistan and Central Asia* (New York, Viking, 2008), p. 113. Rashid reports Osama ordered the airline hijacking.

13. Gutman, *How We Missed the Story*, p. 192. This book also notes my reaction at the time. The Indians still see the issue as unresolved. The hijackers have never been brought to justice by Pakistan despite India's repeated requests to Islamabad. See "Hijackers Not Returned by Pakistan, Says India," *Dawn* (Karachi), March 20, 2008. The Indians also still feel they got too little help from the United States: see Saikat Datta, "Secrets Choked: India-U.S. Intelligence Sharing," *Outlook* (New Delhi), March 3, 2008.

14. Bill Richardson, *Between Worlds: The Making of an American Life* (New York: G. P. Putnam's Sons, 2005), p. 228.

15. "Taliban Agreed to Hand Over Osama in '98," *Dawn* (Karachi), November 5, 2001.

16. Burke, *Al Qaeda*, p. 171. Burke visited the Kargil front line and saw the HUM fighters there.

17. Strobe Talbott, *Engaging India: Diplomacy, Democracy, and the Bomb* (Brookings, 2004), p. 192.

18. George Tenet, *At the Center of the Storm: My Years in the CIA* (New York: HarperCollins, 2007), pp. 239–40.

19. "Afghan Leader Visits Brussels," *London Daily Telegraph*, November 22, 2001.

20. Gary Schroen, *First In: An Insider's Account of How the CIA Spearheaded the War on Terror in Afghanistan* (New York: Ballantine Books, 2006), p. 89.

21. His widow, Malika al Araud, is still an active supporter of al Qaeda and has published an account of her life: *Les Soldats de Lumière* (Brussels, 2003).

22. Paul Cruickshank, "Suicide Bomber's Widow Soldiers On—Wife of Assassin Professes Undying Affection for bin Laden," CNN.com, August 15, 2006.

23. Osama bin Laden message, "Warns Iraqis against Joining Anti-AQ Councils and Iraqi Government" (Open Source Center, December 29, 2007).

24. Quoted by Associated Press, September 18, 2001.

25. Ahmed Rashid, "Pakistan, the Taliban and the U.S.," *Nation*, October 8, 2001.

26. Gutman, *How We Missed the Story*, p. 99.

27. Pervez Musharraf, *In the Line of Fire: A Memoir* (New York: Free Press, 2006), p. 202.

28. "Mullah Omar in His Own Words," *Guardian* (Manchester), September 26, 2001.

29. "Text of Mullah Omar's Eid Message," *Afghan Islamic Press*, October 21, 2006.

30. Schroen, *First In*, pp. 359–60.

31. David Rhode and David Sanger, "How the Good War in Afghanistan Went Bad," *New York Times*, August 12, 2007, p. 12.

32. Rashid, *Descent into Chaos*, p. 134.

33. Schroen, *First In*, p. 361.

34. Burke, *Al Qaeda*, p. 239.

35. John Warrick, "CIA Chief Links Bhutto Assassination to al Qaeda, Pakistani Fighters," *Washington Post*, January 18, 2008.

## CHAPTER FIVE

1. Gary C. Schroen, *First In: An Insider's Account of How the CIA Spearheaded the War on Terror in Afghanistan* (New York: Ballantine Books, 2005).

2. George Tenet, *At the Center of the Storm: My Years at the CIA* (New York: HarperCollins, 2007), p. 225.

3. Michael Hirsh and Ron Moreau, "Pakistan: America's Dubious Ally in Terror War," *Newsweek*, August 20, 2007.

4. "Al Zawahiri Says bin Laden, Mullah Omar Enjoy Good Health," Al Jazirah TV, October 8, 2002. See also Open Source Center translation, October 8, 2002.

5. Bruce Lawrence, ed., *Messages to the World: The Statements of Osama bin Laden* (London: Verso, 2005), pp. 180–85.

6. The London Arabic newspaper *al-Hayat* did an in-depth story on Zarqa in 2004 after Zarqawi had made it famous. It reports 160,000 Kuwaiti Palestinians of the 250,000 expelled from Kuwait ended up in the city after 1991. See Hazem al-Amin, "The City of Al Zarqaa in Jordan—Breeding Ground of Jordan's Salafi Jihad Movement," *al-Hayat*, December 14 and 15, 2004; and Middle East Media Research Institutes, Special Dispatch 848, January 17, 2005.

7. Benazir Bhutto, *Reconciliation: Islam, Democracy and the West* (New York: HarperCollins, 2008), p. 56.

8. Al-Amin, "The City of Al Zarqaa in Jordan."

9. Yaroslav Trofimov, *The Seige of Mecca: The Forgotten Uprising in Islam's Holiest Shrine and the Birth of al Qaeda* (Auckland: Doubleday, 2007), pp. 248–50.

10. Steve Coll, *The Bin Ladens: An Arabian Famly in the American Century* (New York: Penguin Press, 2008), pp. 226–28.

11. "Zarqawi and Al-Adl's Testament," *Al Sharq al-Awsat,* June 1, 2005.

12. Jaswant Singh, *In Service of Emergent India: A Call to Honor* (Indiana University Press, 2007), p. 204.

13. See Roy Gutman, *How We Missed the Story: Osama bin Laden, the Taliban and the Hijacking of Afghanistan* (Washington: U.S. Institute for Peace, 2008), p. 192.

14. Powell's speech is available at www.whitehouse.gov/new/releases/2003/02.

15. Senate Select Committee on Intelligence, "Report on the U.S. Intelligence Community's Prewar Intelligence Assessments on Iraq," United States Senate, July 7, 2004 (http://web.mit.edu/simsong/www/iraqreport2-textunder.pdf).

16. Michael Isikoff and Mark Hosenball, "Terror Watch: New Doubts on Iraq-Qaeda Links," *Newsweek,* October 26, 2005 (www.msn.com/id/9831216/site/newsekk/page).

17. See Brynjar Lia, "The Ansar al-Islam Group Revisited," Working Paper of the Islamism and European Security Seminar, Department of Political Science, Aarhus University, Denmark, June 15–16, 2006.

18. Mary Ann Weaver, "Inventing al Zarqawi," *Atlantic Monthly,* July 2006, p. 96.

19. Gary Gambill, "Abu Musab al-Zarqawi: A Biographical Sketch," *Jamestown Foundation Terrorism Monitor,* vol. 2, no. 24 (December 16, 2004).

20. Al-Jazeera, October 8, 2002.

21. Al-Jazeera, February 11, 2003.

22. Daniel Benjamin, "Holy Zarqawi: Why the Bush Administration Let Iraq's Top Terrorist Walk," *Slate,* October 29, 2004.

23. See Mohammed M. Hafez, "Martyrdom Mythology in Iraq: How Jihadists Frame Suicide Terrorism in Videos and Biographies," *Terrorism and Political Violence* 19, no. 95 (2007): 115.

24. Nimrod Raphaeli, "The Sheikh of the Slaughterers: Abu Mus'ab al-Zarqawi and the Al Qa'ida Connection," *Inquiry and Analysis Series,* no. 231 (Middle East Media Research Institute, July 1, 2005).

25. Al-Amin, "The City of Al Zarqaa in Jordan." See also Raphaeli, "The Sheikh of the Slaughterers."

26. Stephen Farrell, "Iraq Hangs Insurgent Who Killed Shiite Leader in Bombing of Shrine in 2003," *New York Times,* July 7, 2007.

27. "Mortar Attack Kills 13 in East Baghdad," *Washington Post,* August 6, 2007.

28. Raphaeli, "The Sheikh of the Slaughterers," p. 9.

29. Murad Batal al-Shishani, "Al-Zarqawi's Rise to Power: Analyzing Tactics and Targets," *Jamestown Foundation Terrorism Monitor,* vol. 3, no. 22 (November 17, 2005).

30. Anthony Cordesman, "The Tenuous Case for Strategic Patience in Iraq: A Trip Report," working draft (Washington: Center for Strategic and International

Studies, August 6, 2007). See also Walter Pincus, "Fine Print," *Washington Post*, August 13, 2007.

31. Hafez, "Martyrdom Mythology in Iraq," pp. 97–98.

32. Murad al-Shishani, "Al Zarqawi's Rise to Power."

33. Quoted in ibid., p. 2; and in Hafez, "Martydom Mythology in Iraq," p. 98.

34. Khalid al-Ghannami, "Terrorist Cells in Saudi Arabia Distribute Maqdisi's Books to Their Members," *Al Watan*, July 5, 2005, BBC Monitoring Middle East, July 10, 2005.

35. James Brandon, "Jordan's Jihad Scholar al-Maqdisi Is Freed from Prison," *Jamestown Foundation Terrorism Monitor,* vol. 6, no. 7 (April 3, 2008).

36. Muhammad al Najjar, "The Estrangement between al Zarqawi and al Maqdisi," *Al Sabil*, July 19, 2005, BBC Monitoring International Reports, July 24, 2005.

37. "Letter from al Zawahiri to al Zarqawi," Office of the Director of National Intelligence, New Release 2 (October 11, 2005). According to the CIA, the letter was obtained in Iraq.

38. "Zarqawi's Pledge of Allegiance to al Qaeda: From Mu'askar al Battar, Issue 21," translated by Jeffrey Pool, *Jamestown Foundation Terrorism Monitor*, vol. 2, no. 24 (December 16, 2004).

39. "Abu Abdullah Ahmad al-Imran, Al Siyash al Qitaliyyah li-Qa'idat al Jihad fi bilad al-rafidhayan," August 29, 2005, and reported in Reuven Paz, "Zarqawi's Strategy in Iraq—Is There a 'New Al Qaeda,'" *Project for the Research of Islamic Movements (PRISM) Occasional Papers*, vol. 3, no. 5 (August 2005).

40. Associated Press, June 24, 2006.

41. Tape: "Bin Laden Tells Sunnis to Fight Shiites in Iraq," CNN, July 1, 2006.

42. Thomas Hegghammer, "Terrorist Recruitment and Radicalization in Saudi Arabia," *Middle East Policy* 13, no. 4 (Winter 2006): 41.

43. Raphaeli, "The Sheikh of the Slaughterers."

44. The sermon is entitled "Among a Band of Knights" and is translated in Lawrence, ed., *Messages to the World,* pp. 186–206.

45. Thomas Hegghammer, a Norwegian scholar who has studied the martyrdom biographies of many of the al Qaeda operatives, concludes 90 percent were Saudi nationals and were drawn from all parts of the kingdom and all socioeconomic classes.

46. Christopher Boucek, "Extremist Reeducation and Rehabilitation in Saudi Arabia," *Jamestown Foundation Terrorism Monitor*, vol. 5, no. 16 (August 16, 2007). In March 2007 the author interviewed participants in the program and the Ministry of the Interior managers in the kingdom.

47. Lawrence, *Messages to the World*, pp. 212–32.

48. Ibid., pp. 245–75.

49. Con Coughlin, "Saudi Royal Family Lambasts Michael Moore," *Sunday Telegraph* (London), August 1, 2004.

50. Ned Parker, "The Conflict in Iraq: Saudi Role in Insurgency," *Los Angeles Times,* July 15, 2007.

51. "Many Detainees in Iraq Are Saudis," Associated Press, July 17, 2007.

52. West Point Combating Terrorism Center, "The Sinjar Documents" (West Point, N.Y.: 2008).

53. Thomas Hegghammer has also done a study of Saudis fighting in Iraq, "Saudi Militants in Iraq: Backgrounds and Recruitment Patterns," Norwegian Defence Research Establishment paper, February 5, 2007.

54. Arash Dabestani, "Saudi Fatwa on Shi'i Shrines Angers Iran," BBC News, July 27, 2007.

55. "Saudi Religious Leaders Support Sunni Insurgency in Iraq," *Global Issues Report*, January 24, 2007.

56. Frank Hyland, "Investigation Reveals Ties between Turkish al Qaeda and Iraq," *Jamestown Foundation Terrorism Monitor* vol. 4, no. 26 (August 7, 2007).

57. Bruce Riedel and Bilal Saab, "Al Qaeda's Third Front: Saudi Arabia," *Washington Quarterly,* Spring 2008, p. 41.

58. Octavia Nasr, "Bin Laden Tells Sunnis to Fight Shiites in Iraq," CNN.com, July 1, 2006.

59. Al Libi's arguments have been assessed by Michael Scheur, the first chief of the Bin Laden unit in the CIA in 1996, in "Abu Yahya al Libi: Al Qaeda's Theological Enforcer, Parts One and Two," *Jamestown Foundation Terrorism Monitor*, vol. 4, no. 25 (July 31, 2007), and no. 27 (August 14, 2007).

## CHAPTER SIX

1. See Strobe Talbott, *Engaging India: Diplomacy, Democracy, and the Bomb* (Brookings, 2004), p. 192.

2. William Jefferson Clinton, *My Life* (New York: Alfred A. Knopf, 2004), p. 900.

3. Jonathan Evans, "Intelligence, Counter Terrorism and Trust," November 5, 2007 (www.mi5.gov.uk).

4. Ayman al-Zawahiri, "A Review of Events," interview, released on December 16, 2007.

5. Ibid.

6. Ibid.

7. Benazir Bhutto, "Campaigning in the Face of Terror," *Wall Street Journal*, October 23, 2007.

8. Ayman al-Zawahiri, interview, September 18, 2006, produced by al-Sahab media, trans. Open Source Center (OSC).

9. See the analysis by the Jamestown Foundation, *Global Terrorism Analysis*, vol. 3, no. 37 (September 26, 2006).

10. Zaki Chehab, *Inside Hamas, the Untold Story of the Militant Islamic Movement* (New York: Nation Books, 2007), p. 108.

11. Ibid., pp. 173–97.

12. Al-Jazeera, March 11, 2007.

13. Y net news.com, May 14, 2007.

14. Ayman al-Zawahiri, "The Emancipation of Mankind and Nations under the Banner of the Koran," audio statement and text released January 30, 2005, trans. Foreign Broadcast Information Service (OSC).

15. Ayman al-Zawahiri, interview, al-Sahab media, September 11, 2006, marking the fifth anniversary of 9/11, trans. OSC.

16. "Bin Laden Addresses Message on the 60th Anniversary of 'Israeli Occupation State,'" May 16, 2008, produced by al-Sahab media, trans. OSC.

17. "Bin Laden Urges Egyptians to Help Gaza, Muslims to Regain Palestine," May 18, 2008, produced by al-Sahab media, trans. OSC.

18. Guido Steinberg, "The Return of al Qaeda," Stifung Wissenschaft und Politik Comments 22 (Berlin: German Institute for International and Security Affairs, December 2007).

19. Abdel Bari Atwan, *The Secret History of al Qaeda* (University of California Press, 2006).

20. Brynjar Lia and Thomas Hegghammer, "Jihadi Strategic Studies: The Alleged Al Qaida Policy Study Preceding the Madrid Bombings," *Studies in Conflict and Terrorism* 27 (September 2004).

21. Shlomo Nakdimon, *First Strike: The Exclusive Story of How Israel Foiled Iraq's Attempt to Get the Bomb* (New York: Summit Books, 1987), pp. 18–19.

## CHAPTER SEVEN

1. "Saudi Arrests 28 Linked to Qaeda Plot," *Gulf Times*, December 24, 2007.

2. See, for example, John Esposito and Dalia Mogahed, *Who Speaks for Islam? What a Billion Muslims Really Think* (New York: Gallup Press, 2008).

3. Bruce Riedel, "Camp David: The U.S.-Israeli Bargain," in *The Best of Bitter Lemons: Five Years of Writings from Israel and Palestine*, edited by Yossi Alpher (Jerusalem: Bitter Lemons, 2007), pp. 238–42.

4. George Tenet, *At the Center of the Storm: My Years at the CIA* (New York: HarperCollins, 2007), pp. 139–40.

5. Saad Eddin Ibrahim, "Remarks on Sovereignty and Democracy Promotion," U.S.-Islamic World Forum, February 17, 2008, Doha, Qatar.

6. Lawrence Wright, "The Spymaster," *New Yorker*, January 21, 2008, p. 56.

7. Ronald E. Neuman, "Borderline Insanity: Thinking Big about Afghanistan," *American Interest*, November/December 2007.

8. Nick B. Mills, *Karzai: The Failing American Intervention and the Struggle for Afghanistan* (Hoboken, N.J.: John Wiley and Sons, 2007), p. 220.

9. Ibid.

10. Benazir Bhutto, "I Am What the Terrorists Most Fear," interview with Gail Sheehy, *Washington Post,* January 6, 2008.

11. "Gates of Hell Are Open in Iraq, Warns Arab League Chief," Agence France-Presse, September 14, 2004.

# Bibliography

Abd-Allah, Umar F. 1983. *The Islamic Struggle in Syria*. Berkeley, Calif.: Mizan Press.

Abu Khalil, As'ad. 2004. *The Battle for Saudi Arabia: Royalty, Fundamentalism and Global Power*. New York: Seven Stories Press.

Altman, Israel. 2006. "Democracy, Elections and the Egyptian Muslim Brotherhood." *Current Trends in Islamist Ideology*, vol. 3. New York: Hudson Institute.

Anonymous. 2004. *Imperial Hubris: Why the West Is Losing the War on Terror*. New York: Brassey's.

Atwan, Abdel Bari. 2006. *The Secret History of al Qaeda*. University of California Press.

Bar, Shmuel, and Yair Minzili. 2006. "The Zawahiri Letter and the Strategy of al Qaeda." *Current Trends in Islamist Ideology*, vol. 3. New York: Hudson Institute.

Behera, Navnita Chadha. 2006. *Demystifying Kashmir*. Brookings.

Benjamin, Daniel, and Steven Simon. 2005. *The Next Attack: The Failure of the War on Terror and a Strategy for Getting It Right*. New York: Times Books.

———. 2003. *The Age of Sacred Terror: Radical Islam's War against America*. New York: Random House.

Bergen, Peter. 2007. *The Osama Bin Laden I Know: An Oral History of al Qaeda's Leader*. New York: Free Press.

Bhutto, Benazir. 1988. *Daughter of the East: An Autobiography*. London: Hamish Hamilton; rev. ed. 2007.

———. 2008. *Reconciliation: Islam, Democracy and the West*. New York: HarperCollins.

Brown, Vahid. 2007. *Cracks in the Foundation: Leadership Schisms in Al-Qa'ida 1989–2006*. West Point, N.Y.: West Point Combating Terrorism Center.

Burke, Jason. 2003. *Al Qaeda: Casting a Shadow of Terror*. London: I. B. Tauris.

Byman, Daniel. 2005. *Deadly Connections: States That Sponsor Terrorism*. Cambridge University Press.

———. 2008. *The Five Front War: The Better Way to Fight Global Jihad*. Brookings.

Chehab, Zaki. 2005. *Inside the Resistance: The Iraqi Insurgency and the Future of the Middle East*. New York: Nation Books.

———. 2007. *Inside Hamas: The Untold Story of the Militant Islamic Movement*. New York: Nation Books.

Clarke, Richard A. 2004. *Against All Enemies: Inside America's War on Terror*. New York: Free Press.

Coll, Steve. 2004. *Ghost Wars: The Secret History of the CIA, Afghanistan and Bin Laden, From the Soviet Invasion to September 10, 2001*. New York: Penguin Press.

———. 2008. *The Bin Ladens: An Arabian Family in the American Century*. New York: Penguin Press.

Commission on the Intelligence Capabilities of the United States Regarding Weapons of Mass Destruction. 2005. *Report to the President of the United States*. U.S. Government Printing Office, March 31.

Cronin, Audrey Kurth. 2006. "How Al Qaida Ends: The Decline and Demise of Terrorist Groups." *International Security* 31 (Summer).

Delongbas, Natana. 2007. "Jihad and the Wahhabi Tradition: Continuity or Change?" *Understanding Jihad, Deconstructing Jihadism*. Georgetown University, Edmund Walsh School of Foreign Service.

Durrani, Mahmud Ali. 2000. *India and Pakistan: The Costs of Conflict, The Benefits of Peace*. Brookings.

Eikmeier, Dale. 2007. "Qutbism: An Ideology of Islamic-Fascism." *Parameters* 37 (Spring).

Esposito, John, and Dalia Mogahed. 2008. *Who Speaks for Islam? What a Billion Muslims Really Think*. New York: Gallup Press.

Fair, Christine. 2007. "Militant Recruitment in Pakistan." *Asia Policy*, no. 4, July.

Frantz, Douglas, and Catherine Collins. 2008. *The Nuclear Jihadist: The True Story of the Man Who Sold the World's Most Dangerous Secrets . . . And How We Could Have Stopped Him*. New York: Twelve.

Gregpru, Shaun. 2008. *The ISI and the War on Terrorism*. Brief 28. Bradford: Pakistan Security Research Unit.

Gunaratna, Rohan. 2002. *Inside Al Qaeda*. Columbia University Press.

Gutman, Roy. 2008. *How We Missed the Story: Osama Bin Laden, the Taliban and the Hijacking of Afghanistan*. Washington: U.S. Institute for Peace.

Hamid, Mohsin. 2007. *The Reluctant Fundamentalist*. New York: Harcourt.

Hegghammer, Thomas. 2006. "Terrorist Recruitment and Radicalization in Saudi Arabia." *Middle East Policy* 13 (Winter).

Heikal, Muhammad. 1983. *Autumn of Fury: The Assassination of Sadat*. Bury St. Edmunds: St. Edmundsbury Press.

Hewitt, Vernon. 2001. *Towards the Future? Jammu and Kashmir in the 21st Century*. Cambridge, England: Cromwell Press.

Ibrahim, Saad Eddin. 1982. *The New Arab Social Order: A Study of the Social Impact of Oil Wealth*. London: Croom Helm.

Jebnoun, Noureddine. 2007. *Is the Maghreb the Next Afghanistan? Mapping the Radicalization of the Algerian Salafi Jihadist Movement*. Washington: Center for Contemporary Arab Studies.

John, Wilson. 2003. *Karachi: A Terror Capital in the Making*. New Delhi: Rupa & Co.

Jones, Owen Bennett. 2002. *Pakistan: Eye of the Storm*. Yale University Press.

Kaplan, Robert D. 2001. *Soldiers of God: With Islamic Warriors in Afghanistan and Pakistan*. New York: Vintage Books.

Kepel, Gilles. 1986. *Muslim Extremism in Egypt: The Prophet and Pharaoh*. University of California Press.

Kepel, Gilles, and Jean-Pierre Milelli, eds. 2008. *Al Qaeda in Its Own Words*. Cambridge, Mass.: Belknap Press.

Lamb, Alastair. 1992. *Kashmir: A Disputed Legacy 1846–1990*. Oxford University Press.

Lawrence, Bruce, ed. 2005. *Messages to the World: The Statements of Osama Bin Laden*. London: Verso.

Levitt, Matthew. 2006. *Hamas: Politics, Charity and Terrorism in the Service of Jihad*. Yale University Press.

Levy, Adrian, and Catherine Scott-Clark. 2007. *Deception: Pakistan, the United States, and the Secret Trade in Nuclear Weapons*. New York: Walker.

Lia, Brynjar. 2007. *Architect of Global Jihad: The Life of Al Qaida Strategist Abu Mus'ab al Suri*. London: Hurst.

Lia, Brynjar, and Thomas Hegghammer. 2004. "Jihadi Strategic Studies: The Alleged Al Qaida Policy Study Preceding the Madrid Bombings." *Studies in Conflict and Terrorism* 27 (September).

Markey, Daniel. 2007. "A False Choice in Pakistan." *Foreign Affairs,* July/August.

McDermott, Terry. 2005. *Perfect Soldiers: The 9/11 Hijackers: Who They Were, Why They Did It*. New York: HarperCollins.

Mills, Nick B. 2007. *Karzai: The Failing American Intervention and the Struggle for Afghanistan*. Hoboken, N.J.: John Wiley and Sons.

Mitchell, Richard P. 1969. *The Society of the Muslim Brothers*. Oxford University Press.

Muasher, Marwan. 2008. *The Arab Center: The Promise of Moderation*. Yale University Press.

Nasr, Vali. 2007. *The Shia Revival: How Conflicts within Islam Will Shape the Future*. London: Norton.

National Commission on Terrorist Attacks upon the United States. 2003. *The 9/11 Commission Report*. New York: Norton.

Neumann, Robert. 2007. "Borderline Insanity: Thinking Big about Afghanistan." *American Interest*, November/December.

Post, Jerrold M. 2007. *The Mind of the Terrorist: The Psychology of Terrorism from the IRA to Al Qaeda*. New York: Palgrave.

Rasheed, Madawi al. 2002. *A History of Saudi Arabia*. Cambridge University Press.

Rashid, Ahmed. 2001. *Taliban: Militant Islam, Oil and Fundamentalism in Central Asia*. Yale University Press.

———. 2002. *Jihad: The Rise of Militant Islam in Central Asia*. Yale University Press.

———. 2008. *Descent into Chaos: The United States and the Failure of Nation Building in Pakistan, Afghanistan and Central Asia*. New York: Viking.

Riedel, Bruce. 2007. "Al Qaeda Strikes Back." *Foreign Affairs*, May/June.

———. 2007. "The Return of the Knights: Al Qaeda and the Fruits of Middle East Disorder." *Survival* 49 (Autumn).

Riedel, Bruce, and Bilal Saab. 2008. "Al Qaeda's Third Front: Saudi Arabia." *Washington Quarterly* 31 (Spring).

Romano, David. 2007. "An Outline of Kurdish Islamist Groups in Iraq." Occasional Paper. Jamestown Foundation, September.

Rotberg, Robert I., ed. 2007. *Building a New Afghanistan*. Brookings.

Roy, Olivier. 2007. *Secularism Confronts Islam*. Columbia University Press.

Schanzer, Jonathan. 2005. *Al Qaeda's Armies: Middle East Affiliate Groups and the Next Generation of Terror*. Washington: Washington Institute for Near East Policy.

Schiff, Ze'ev, and Ehud Ya'ari. 1989. *Intifada: The Palestinian Uprising—Israel's Third Front*. London: Simon and Schuster.

Schroen, Gary C. 2005. *First In: An Insider's Account of How the CIA Spearheaded the War on Terror in Afghanistan*. New York: Ballantine Books.

Singh, Jaswant. 2007. *A Call to Honour: In Service of Emergent India*. New Delhi: Rupa.

Sivan, Emmanuel. 1985. *Radical Islam: Medieval Theology and Modern Politics*. Yale University Press.

———. 1987. "The Islamic Republic of Egypt." *Orbis* (Spring).

Talbott, Strobe, and Nayan Chanda, eds. 2001. *The Age of Terror: America and the World after September 11*. New York: Basic Books.

Tenet, George. 2007. *At the Center of the Storm: My Years at the CIA*. New York: HarperCollins.

Trofimov, Yaroslav. 2007. *The Siege of Mecca: The Forgotten Uprising in Islam's Holiest Shrine and the Birth of Al Qaeda*. Auckland: Doubleday.

Vidino, Lorenzo. 2006. *Al Qaeda in Europe*. New York: Prometheus.

Wright, Lawrence. 2006. *The Looming Tower: Al Qaeda and the Road to 9/11*. New York: Alfred A. Knopf.

———. 2008. "The Rebellion Within: An al Qaeda Mastermind Questions Terrorism." *New Yorker*, June 2.

Yamani, Mai. 2000. *Changed Identities: The Challenge of the New Generation in Saudi Arabia*. London: Royal Institute of International Affairs.

Zayyat, Montasser. 2004. *The Road to al Qaeda: The Story of Bin Laden's Right-Hand Man*. London: Pluto Press.

# Index

*Surnames starting with "al" or "al-" are alphabetized by the following part of the name.*